HERMAS AND
CHRISTIAN PROPHECY

A STUDY OF THE ELEVENTH MANDATE

SUPPLEMENTS TO
NOVUM TESTAMENTUM

VOLUME XXXVII

LEIDEN
E. J. BRILL
1973

HERMAS AND CHRISTIAN PROPHECY

A STUDY OF THE ELEVENTH MANDATE

BY

J. REILING

LEIDEN
E. J. BRILL
1973

ISBN 90 04 03771 3

CONTENTS

PREFACE

The subject of this study — originally submitted as a Th. D. dissertation to the Theological Faculty of the University of Utrecht — was suggested to me by Professor W.C. van Unnik, who also promoted its publication in the SUPPLEMENTS TO NOVUM TESTAMENTUM. I wish to express my deep gratitude for the inspiration, encouragement, criticism and friendship with which he has followed my work through the various stages of its development.

This book is written in a Dutchman's English, but Dr. Peter Staples, of the Institute of Ecumenical Studies in Utrecht, has seen to it that it is not too Dutch but acceptable to those readers whose mother tongue is one of the various branches of the English language. I wish to express to him my sincere appreciation for his invaluable help.

Bilthoven, Netherlands   J. REILING
September 1973.

BIBLIOGRAPHY AND ABBREVIATIONS

I. EDITIONS, TRANSLATIONS AND COMMENTARIES OF HERMAS CITED BY THE NAME OF THE AUTHOR

M. DIBELIUS, *Der Hirt des Hermas*, H. N. T. *Ergänzungsband* (Tübingen, 1923), p. 415-644.

A. VON HARNACK, *Hermae Pastor, Patrum Apostolicorum Opera*, Fasciculus III (Leipzig, 1877).

R. JOLY, *Hermas Le Pasteur, Sources Chrétiennes 53* (Paris, 1958).

K. LAKE, *The Apostolic Fathers, Loeb Classical Library*, vol. II, p. 1-305 (London, 1930).

G. F. SNYDER, *The Shepherd of Hermas, The Apostolic Fathers, A New Translation and Commentary*, vol. 6 (London, 1968).

H. WEINEL, *Der Hirt des Hermas, Neutestamentliche Apokryphen herausgeg. von E. Hennecke*, zweite Auflage (Tübingen, 1924), p. 327-384.

id., *Handbuch zu den Neutestamentlichen Apokryphen* (Tübingen, 1904), p. 290-322.

M. WHITTAKER, *Der Hirt des Hermas, Die apostolischen Väter I*, zweite Auflage (Berlin, 1967).

II. WORKS OF REFERENCE CITED BY THE NAME OF THE AUTHOR(S)

W. BAUER, *Griechisch-Deutsches Wörterbuch zu den Schriften des Neuen Testaments und der übrigen urchristlichen Literatur*, fünfte Auflage (Berlin, 1958).

F. BLASS and A. DEBRUNNER, *A Greek Grammar of the New Testament and Other Early Christian Literature*; A Translation and Revision of the ninth-tenth German edition, incorporating supplementary notes of A. Debrunner, by Robert W. Funk (Chicago, 1961).

G. H. W. LAMPE, *A Patristic Greek Lexicon* (Oxford, 1968).

H. G. LIDDELL and R. SCOTT, *A Greek-English Lexicon*, New Edition by H. St. Jones (Oxford, 1940).

H. L. STRACK und P. BILLERBECK, *Kommentar zum Neuen Testament aus Talmud und Midrasch* (München, 1922-'28).

J. J. WETTSTEIN, *Novum Testamentum Graecum* (Amsterdam, 1751-'52, repr. Graz, 1962).

III. ABBREVIATIONS

A. H.	Irenaeus, *Adversus Haereses* (book I-II ed. Harvey (Cambridge 1857), book III-V ed. Sagnard *et. al.*, *Sources Chrétiennes* (Paris, 1952-'69)).
G. G. A.	Göttinger Gelehrte Anzeigen
H. E.	Eusebius, *Historia Ecclesiastica*, ed. Schwartz, kleine Ausgabe (Leipzig, 1922)
H. N. T.	Handbuch zum Neuen Testament
H. Th. K. N. T.	Herders Theologischer Kommentar zum Neuen Testament
H. Th. R.	Harvard Theological Review
J. B. L.	Journal of Biblical Literature

J. E. H.	Journal of Ecclesiastical History
J.T. S.	Journal of Theological Studies
K. A. T.	Kommentar zum Alten Testament
N. T.	Novum Testamentum
N. T. S.	New Testament Studies
P. G.	Migne, Patrologiae cursus completus, Series Graeca
P. L.	Migne, Patrologiae cursus completus, Series Latina
P. W. R. E.	Pauly-Wissowa, Real-Encyclopädie der classischen Altertumswissenschaften
R. A. C.	Reallexikon für Antike und Christentum
R. B.	Revue Biblique
R. G. G.	Die Religion in Geschichte und Gegenwart
Stud. Patr.	Studia Patristica
Th. L. Z.	Theologische Literaturzeitung
Th. W. N. T.	Theologisches Wörterbuch zum Neuen Testament
Vig. Chr.	Vigiliae Christianae
Z. N. W.	Zeitschrift für die Neutestamentliche Wissenschaft und die Kunde der älteren Kirche

INTRODUCTION

The Christian church of our age is often called upon to speak prophetically to the great issues of the day but nobody has as yet raised the idea of restoring prophecy as an official ministry in the church. Nor is it very likely that this will ever happen. From time to time some outstanding preacher or teacher of the church is, unofficially, called a prophet but no Christian minister would dare to claim that title.

The modern call for prophecy is not so much a call for prophets as a call for prophetic speaking. It is significant that the adjective 'prophetic' is heard very often, but not the substantives 'prophecy' and 'prophet', let alone the verb 'to prophesy'. It is also significant that the modern call for prophetic speaking never refers to the early Christian prophets but always to Jesus and the prophets of the Old Testament.

There is, however, a growing movement in present day Christianity in which the situation is reversed, namely the Pentecostal movement. In its idiom the substantives and the verb are more in vogue than the adjective. Its orientation is almost completely on New Testament prophecy, and the Pentecostal Christians zealously practice that gift in their congregations.[1] The spread and impetus of this movement have also reached the traditional churches and, within those churches, have aroused a new interest in the gift of prophecy as an instrument which serves for the upbuilding of the church. The renewal of this gift within the church may well be an indispensable condition for the restoring of the prophetic ministry of the church in the world.

All this has resulted in a renewed interest in early Christian prophecy. Understandably, this renewed interest concentrates upon the New Testament texts dealing with Christian prophecy, especially 1 Cor. 12 and 14 where it is so graphically described in its congregational functioning.

Yet even these direct sources leave many questions unanswered,

---

[1] Cf. N. Block-Hoell, *The Pentecostal Movement; its Origin, Development, and Distinctive Character* (Oslo, 1964), p. 147; W. J. Hollenweger, *Enthusiastisches Christentum; die Pfingstbewegung in Geschichte und Gegenwart* (Wuppertal-Zürich, 1969), p. 393ff., and references there.

because they came into being, not as introductions to, or explanations of, the phenomenon of Christian prophecy, but in order to further its proper functioning.

The unanswered questions not only concern those who seek in the New Testament guidance for the life and well being of the church of today, but also the historian of the Christian church; the more so when the latter is anxious to serve the former. But the historian cannot be content only with the New Testament texts. He sees them as evidence of something which existed not only in the apostolic age but also in later generations till the end of the second century A.D. He can understand and clarify the New Testament stage of Christian prophecy only when he also takes into account its later stages. Hence he gathers and studies all relevant evidence of this period and even of later times, if it can throw light on his object of study. He is prepared to listen to voices from outside Christianity if they can help him to understand the nature and functioning of Christian prophecy. Much brilliant work has already been done in these fields of research; and in the course of the present study we shall have ample occasion to mention the names of many scholars with distinction.

There is, however, one document, which has received remarkable scant attention, even though it is more detailed than most other sources. This document is the 11th Mandate of the Shepherd of Hermas. It is the aim of the present study to explore this document, expressly in the context of the total history of early Christian prophecy, and also with a hope that the functioning of prophecy in the church of Christ of our own age may be served.

The 11th Mandate dates back to the middle of the first half of the second century A.D. This means that it is post-apostolic and also prior to the rise of Montanism. It presents a picture of early second century prophecy. The reason why so far no student of Christian prophecy has dealt with it in some depth, may be that it is part of the Shepherd of Hermas, a text which did not rate very high in the estimation of scholars until recently. On the other hand, it has also received little attention from the students of Hermas, probably because its subject matter stands somewhat apart in the work of Hermas and is not directly relevant to Hermas' main concern, the second repentance, nor to other important themes, such as the ecclesiology of *Vis.* III and *Sim.* VIII and IX, or the christology of *Sim.* V.

Be that as it may, for several reasons the 11th Mandate deserves a thorough investigation. In the first place, its lively description of the activities of the prophet and his counterpart, the false prophet, in the life of the church complements that of other sources and explicitly reveals a number of points which are not clear, or only hinted at, in them; this applies also to our main New Testament source, 1 Cor. 14.

Secondly, the 11th Mandate pictures prophecy as it functioned in the church before the rise of Montanism which so gravely jeopardized prophecy and so unfavourably affected its appreciation. A study of this document may help to overcome ingrained prejudices against the gift of prophecy which have been prominent in the Christian church ever since.

In the third place, the 11th Mandate portrays the church in conflict with pagan divination, and, at the same time, freely uses hellenistic materials to spell out its own message about prophetic inspiration. This leads us to give fresh thought to the problem of the relationships between Christianity and its environment.

Finally, a study of the 11th Mandate has a contribution to make to the understanding of its author. It has more and deeper connections with the rest of his work than is commonly assumed. It throws light on his faith and on the important place which the Holy Spirit plays in it. It has a bearing on Hermas' understanding of his own ministry. Here emerges the picture of a man with a message, a man who is beyond the depreciation in which so many older scholars used to hold him; a man who is more than an assembler of various and sometimes contradicting traditions put together clumsily and without skill.

The diverging perspectives in which the 11th Mandate must be studied in order to do justice to the foregoing aspects, cause some problems with regard to the structure of the present study and to the presentation of the evidence. This study is not a history of early Christian prophecy as a whole, but a contribution towards such a history. It concentrates on the 11th Mandate and is fundamentally an exegesis of its text. This exegesis is found spread over all chapters. But on many points detailed investigations have to be inserted in order to bring out finer points which remain hidden unless studied in a microscopic way. Also the connections with other early Christian developments have to be established, and the relationship with analogous phenomena in the hellenistic environment. Finally, on many points parallel materials from elsewhere in Hermas must be adduced in order to place the ideas of the 11th Mandate in the perspective of Hermas' own thinking and experience as a Christian.

The course of our investigation is as follows :

Chapter I: *Christian Prophecy*, is a brief sketch of the main problems concerning Christian prophecy which are relevant to a study of the 11th Mandate.

Chapter II: *Hermas*, is devoted to the author of the 11th Mandate and outlines the main areas of problems with which the student of this text is confronted.

Chapter III: *The Eleventh Mandate*, presents a paraphrase and a running commentary on the text.

Chapter IV: *Prophecy and Divination*, deals with the false prophet, the criteria by which he is judged and his activities as a Christian diviner.

Chapter V: *Prophecy and the Spirit*, describes the Christian prophet and gives an interpretation of the account of his inspiration.

Chapter VI: *Prophecy and the Church*, treats the relationship between the prophet and the church and attempts to determine the place of Hermas' view of that relationship within the developments of early Christian history.

Chapter VII: *Hermas and the Prophet*, compares the portrait of the prophet with Hermas' description of his own experience and ministry.

Chapter VIII: *Conclusions*, brings together the conclusions and formulates points which are relevant for future research.[1]

---

[1] A few remarks of a technical nature are to be made. (a) The text printed in the Appendix and used in this book is that of Whittaker's second edition but occasionally other editions are used or referred to. They are listed in the Abbreviations; (b) All editions, translations and commentaries of Hermas are referred to by the name of the author. They are also listed in the Abbreviations; (c) The present writer is very much indebted to the English translations of the Shepherd which were at his disposal and were very helpful. They have regularly been quoted, but in a number of places other renderings appeared preferable. For those renderings, indicated by single quotation marks, the author is responsible.

CHAPTER ONE

CHRISTIAN PROPHECY

The discovery of the Didache in 1883 marked the beginning of a new era in the history of research into Christian prophecy.[1] It had been preceded some thirty years before by the discovery of the Greek text of the Shepherd of Hermas, of which the first reliable edition appeared in 1888.[2] As early as 1884 the first comprehensive treatment of prophecy in the apostolic and the post-apostolic age by N. Bonwetsch appeared.[3] Ever since the subject has continued to command the interest of scholars. Although a history of this research is not intended here there is reason to mention two special studies which have not, perhaps, greatly influenced the course of the research, but have been, and are still, invaluable stores of source material on which every student of the subject has drawn with profit. The first is Heinrich Weinel, *Die Wirkungen des Geistes und der Geister im nachapostolischen Zeitalter bis auf Irenaeus.*[4] Weinel followed the trail which Hermann Gunkel had blazed eleven years earlier.[5] Gunkel's starting point was the question: "An welchen Symptomen hat man im Urchristentum festgestellt, dass eine Erscheinung Wirkung des Heiligen Geistes sei ?".[6] This leads Weinel to make the following statement of principle: "Wer die Absicht hat, die Pneumatologie der ältesten Christenheit darzustellen, muss ... zuerst die Erlebnisse beschreiben auf denen sich eine Lehre vom Geist aufgebaut hat".[7] Underlying this statement is the often forgotten fact that for the early Christians the Spirit was not a concept but a matter of experience. Weinel succeeded in describing the various experiences of the Spirit with great sympathy

---

[1] Cf. O. Linton, *Das Problem der Urkirche in der neueren Forschung* (Uppsala, 1932), p. 39ff.

[2] Cf. Whittaker, p. IXf.

[3] N. Bonwetsch, Die Prophetie im apostolischen und nachapostolischen Zeitalter, *Zeitschrift für kirchliche Wissenschaft und kirchliches Leben* 5 (1884), p. 408-424; 460-477.

[4] Freiburg, 1899, henceforth referred to as *Wirkungen.*

[5] In *Die Wirkungen des Heiligen Geistes nach den populären Anschauungen der apostolischen Zeit und der Lehre des Apostels Paulus* (Göttingen, 1888, 1909³).

[6] *Op. cit.*, p. 5

[7] *Wirkungen*, p. VII.

and understanding. The phenomena of Christian prophecy are not treated as a separate entity, but as a part of the manifold manifestations of the Spirit. As far as the Christian sources are concerned, Weinel's work may be considered exhaustive; this makes it an indispensable tool even today.[1]

A second book to be mentioned with distinction is Erich Fascher, *ΠΡΟΦΗΤΗΣ, Eine sprach- und religionsgeschichtliche Untersuchung*.[2] It collects and discusses briefly all the texts from Greek, Egyptian, Jewish and Christian sources, that are related to the word προφήτης, its synonyms and its opposites. It was not Fascher's intention to draw from his materials an overall picture of the various types of prophets which the ancient world brought forth. In the preface he writes: "Die Geschichte des Prophetismus kann erst geschrieben werden wenn noch zahlreiche Begriffe dieser Art untersucht sind".[3] This sentence brings out one of Fascher's hidden presuppositions, namely, that all the prophets he reviews can be brought under the one heading "Prophetismus". Conceivably, we do owe the book to this tacit assumption, but this assumption is, in itself, too general. Yet the wealth of materials which Fascher has collected makes all students of the subject his debtors.

Of the comprehensive treatments of the past quarter of a century the following may be mentioned: that by H. A. Guy,[4] by G. Friedrich,[5] and, most recently, by E. Cothénet.[6] These provide useful surveys of the materials and of their interpretations.[7] They give, however, only limited attention to post-apostolic developments and to the relationship with analogous forms of contemporary non-Christian prophecy. The former have been dealt with by H. von Campenhausen who placed them in the context of ecclesiastical ministry and spiritual

---

[1] Cf. the recension by W. Bousset, *G. G. A.* 163 (1901), p. 753-776. The main point to which he takes exception, namely that for the early Christians the experience of regeneration is decisive with regard to their own certainty and with a view to winning outsiders (p. 758f., *Wirkungen*, p. 60ff.) is also the point on which Weinel is distinctly different from Gunkel, cf. *infra*, p. 136.

[2] Giessen, 1927, henceforth referred to by the name of the author.

[3] P. III.

[4] H. A. Guy, *New Testament Prophecy; its Origin and Significance* (London, 1947).

[5] G. Friedrich, Art. προφήτης, *Th. W. N. T.* VI, p. 829-863.

[6] E. Cothénet, Le Prophétisme dans le Nouveau Testament, *Suppl. au Dictionnaire de la Bible*, t. VIII, c. 1221-1337 (Paris, 1971).

[7] This applies specifically to Cothénet's article.

authority.[1] The latter has been expounded especially by R. Reitzenstein in his various works.[2] In this sketch of Christian prophecy the following issues will be discussed briefly: (a) the position of the prophets in the church; (b) the function of prophecy; (c) the authentication of the prophetic message; (d) the nature of the prophet's inspiration.

THE POSITION OF THE PROPHETS

Among the subjects which have attracted the attention of scholarship, the position of the prophets in the church holds pride of place. In the same year in which Bonwetsch' article appeared, Harnack published his thesis of itinerant apostles, prophets and teachers whose ministry was not confined to a local congregation but embraced the whole church.[3] This thesis was repeated very briefly in his *Dogmengeschichte*,[4] and more extensively, in *Die Mission und Ausbreitung des christentums in den ersten Jahrhunderten*.[5] Apostles, prophets and teacher are an "enthusiastische Trias",[6] which is already present in the earliest period of church history.[7] They were not elected by the churches, but appointed by a divine calling of which Acts 13 offers a good example.[8] Harnack finds this tripartite ministry to the whole church also in the Shepherd. He thinks that in the "hierarchy" of Hermas the omission of the prophet is intentional, because Hermas considered himself a prophet.[9]

Harnack's thesis did not remain unchallenged from the part of the adherents of the so called *Consensus*.[10] As far as the prophets are con-

---

[1] H. Freiherr von Campenhausen, *Kirchliches Amt und geistliche Vollmacht in den ersten drei Jahrhunderten* (Tübingen, 1953).

[2] R. Reitzenstein, *Poimandres; Studien zur griechisch-ägyptischen und frühchristlichen Literatur* (Leipzig, 1904; repr. Darmstadt, 1966); *Die Hellenistischen Mysterienreligionen nach ihren Grundgedanken und Wirkungen* (Leipzig, 1927³; repr. Darmstadt, 1956). Though outdated as far as their theories are concerned, both works are treasures of source materials.

[3] *Die Lehre der zwölf Apostel nebst Untersuchungen zur ältesten Geschichte der Kirchenverfassung und des Kirchenrechts, Texte und Untersuchungen* II, 1-2 (Leipzig, 1884).

[4] I⁴ (Tübingen, 1909), p. 236f.

[5] I⁴ (Leipzig, 1924), p. 340-379. The following quotations refer to this work.

[6] P. 357.

[7] P. 348f.

[8] P. 347.

[9] P. 351f. Cf. *Vis.* III 5, 1; *Sim.* IX 15, 4; 16, 5; 17, 1; 25, 2.

[10] Cf. O. Linton, *Das Problem der Urkirche*, p. 46ff.

cerned, his idea of an itinerant supra-local prophetic order[1] was attacked by Greeven[2] and by von Campenhausen.[3] They both pointed out that in the earliest times there is no mention of an itinerant prophetic ministry. The prophets belonged essentially to the local churches; but, within those churches, they were distinguished from the rest because they were permanently endowed with the Spirit.[4]

Harnack and Greeven present two different "trajectories"[5] of Christian prophecy. According to the former, the prophets were from the beginning supralocal, itinerant ministers who spoke the word under direct inspiration; later, they became more or less settled in local churches and, in the end, disappeared. In the view of the latter, prophecy was in the beginning the possession of all believers but gradually became the permanent gift of individuals who, by virtue of this *charisma*, acquired a special position in the (local) church, and, in the end, disappeared. The point where the trajectories converge is to be found in the Didache which does indeed mention prophets who wished to settle in a local church.[6]

The evidence, however, points to a more complex development. The wording of the warning against false prophets in Matthew 7:15, suggests the picture of wandering prophets who visit the congregations.[7] The same is true of Matthew 10:41.[8] Luke mentions prophets who went from Jerusalem to Antioch.[9] The mission of Jude and Silas to Antioch is another case of prophets who go from one church to another.[10] All this means that in the area of Palestine and Syria itinerant prophets were known. This is implicitly confirmed by the evidence of the Didache and the Gospel of Thomas; the former states in 13,1: πᾶς δὲ

---

[1] "Prophetenstand" (*Mission* I, p. 363, a rendering of προφητικὴ τάξις (*ib.* n. 1). To this idea we will return *infra*, p. 125.

[2] H. Greeven, Propheten, Lehrer, Vorsteher bei Paulus, *Z. N. W.* 44 (1952-53), p. 1-43, esp. p. 3-15.

[3] *Op. cit.*, p. 65ff.

[4] Greeven, *art. cit.*, p. 7f.

[5] The term is introduced by James M. Robinson and Helmut Köster in their *Trajectories through Early Christianity* (Philadelphia, 1971).

[6] Cf. *infra*, p. 9.

[7] Προσέχετε ἀπὸ τῶν ψευδοπροφητῶν, οἵτινες ἔρχονται πρὸς ὑμᾶς. Cf. also *infra*, p. 58f.

[8] Ὁ δεχόμενος προφήτην εἰς ὄνομα προφήτου. Cf. also *infra*, p. 11.

[9] Cf. Acts 11:27: ἐν ταύταις δὲ ταῖς ἡμέραις κατῆλθον ἀπὸ Ἱεροσολύμων προφῆται εἰς Ἀντιόχειαν.

[10] Cf. Acts 15:32: καὶ αὐτοὶ προφῆται ὄντες ; this takes up vs. 27: Ἰούδαν καὶ Σιλᾶν, καὶ αὐτοὺς διὰ λόγου ἀπαγγέλλοντας τὰ αὐτά.

προφήτης ἀληθινός, θέλων καθῆσθαι πρὸς ὑμᾶς ἄξιός ἐστι τῆς τροφῆς αὐτοῦ. Whether this refers to a permanent settlement or to a somewhat prolonged stay,[1] it is clear that the prophet is still an itinerant minister. The 42th *logion* of the Gospel of Thomas: "become those who pass by", probably must be understood as: "become wanderers", i.e. wandering prophets.[2] And if Celsus' vicious picture of Christian prophets in Phoenicia and Palestine is correct on this point, even at that late date there were still itinerant prophets.[3]

There is, however, also another side to the picture. In 1 Corinthians 12 and 14 there is nothing which suggests the picture of wandering prophets. Von Campenhausen rightly remarks that, if the prophets in the pauline churches were itinerant ministers, this would have been mentioned in 1 Corinthians 9:5.[4] The same picture is presupposed in Paul's other letters. Also the false prophets mentioned in 1 John 4:1 appear to be teachers of the local church.[5] All this points to a picture of prophecy as a local ministry which existed alongside that of the itinerant prophets.

There is, however, yet another distinction to be made. Besides the official prophets, itinerant or resident, prophecy also functioned as a congregational *charisma*. According to Greeven, this form of prophecy is even to be considered as the oldest. Of 1 Corinthians 14 he writes: "Wir tun einen Blick in einen Prozess, an dessen Abschluss das Charisma der Prophetie beschränkt erscheint auf einzelne, dadurch herausgehobene Gemeindeglieder. Aber dieser Abschluss ist noch nicht erreicht: die Anfänge, in denen die Prophetie ein Besitz der ganzen Gemeinde war, scheinen noch durch".[6] This, then, would be the first

---

[1] The former is advocated by R. Knopf, *H. N. T. Ergänzungsband* (Tübingen, 1920), p. 34, *ad loc.*; the latter by J. P. Audet, *La Didachè, Instruction des Apôtres* (Paris, 1958), p. 455f., *ad loc.*

[2] The Coptic text uses the Greek word παράγειν which may mean 'to pass by', 'to pass on one's way', cf. Liddell-Scott. s.v. B. For this interpretation of the *logion*, cf. G. Quispel, *Makarius, das Thomasevangelium und das Lied von der Perle* (Leiden, 1967), p. 20f.

[3] Cf. Origen, *c. Cels.* VII 9: οἱ δὲ καὶ ἀγείραντες καὶ ἐπιφοιτῶντες πόλεσιν ἢ στρατοπέδοις, κτλ. Cf. also H. Chadwick, *Origen: Contra Celsum* (Cambridge, 1953), p. 402f. *ad loc.*

[4] *Op. cit.*, p. 65f.

[5] Cf. 1 Jn 2:19: ἐξ ἡμῶν ἐξῆλθαν. Cf. also *infra*, p. 59.

[6] *Art. cit.*, p. 8.

stage of Greeven's "trajectory" of Christian prophecy. Yet even here the evidence suggests that the developments of history have been more complex. Congregational prophecy is presupposed in Acts 2:4ff. It is present in the Ephesian church, as is shown by Acts 19:6. In 1 Corinthians there is more evidence which points to congregational prophecy than that which suggests the presence of a prophetic order. Probably, this form of prophecy has also left traces in the Apocalypse.[1] Though the evidence is scant, there is reason to assume that even in the second century congregational prophecy still existed. When in his *Dialogue with Tryphon*, Justin wants to show ὅτι τὰ πάλαι ἐν τῷ γένει ὑμῶν ὄντα εἰς ἡμᾶς μετετέθη, his evidence is: παρὰ γὰρ ἡμῖν καὶ μέχρι νῦν προφητικὰ χαρίσματά ἐστιν.[2] This would hardly be a forceful argument if prophecy were in decline. Yet he does not mention these contemporary prophets by name, and this suggests that it was congregational prophecy which he had in mind. This is confirmed by Irenaeus who also does not name contemporary prophets but points to the presence of prophetic gifts in the church.[3]

All this leads to the conclusion that there existed three forms of the prophetic ministry in early Christianity: the itinerant prophet, the local prophet and congregational prophecy. It is with regard to this last form of prophecy that the 11th Mandate has a significant contribution to make. It evokes the picture of a prophetic ministry, open to all believers and subject to testing by believers. This picture confirms and, on several points, clarifies that of 1 Corinthians 14.

The question of the position which the prophets held in the church has yet another aspect, that of their relationship with the leadership of the church. Harnack's idea of the itinerant apostles, prophets and teachers implied an opposition between them and the local ministry; the latter was a non-charismatic, administrative and liturgical ministry and consisted of bishops and deacons.[4] Even though this idea has been severely criticised, it is, in one form or another, still found. Bornkamm regards the 3rd letter of John as evidence of a

---

[1] Cf. *infra*, p. 143f.

[2] *Dial.* 82, 1.

[3] Cf. *A. H.* II 32, 2: *alii autem et praescientiam habent futurorum et visiones et dictiones propheticas*; V 6, 1: *quemadmodum et multos audimus fratres in ecclesia prophetica habentes charismata*. For later evidence cf. Pseudoclem., *De Virginitate* I, XI 10; *Constit. Apost.* VIII 1, 12.

[4] *Die Lehre der zwölf Apostel*, p. 140ff.

conflict between a local church officer and the representative of a free, non-local authority.[1] Kragerud interpreted the Fourth Gospel as the manifesto of a Johannine circle, representing "den Wanderprophetismus", against the institutional ministry of bishops and presbyters.[2] The conflict in Corinth which caused 1 Clement to be written is interpreted along the same lines by Meinhold.[3]

When, however, prophecy is considered to be originally a local ministry, the prophet's position is usually seen as that of a leader. or the leader, of a local church. This is Greeven's interpretation of the προιστάμενοι which are mentioned in several letters of Paul.[4] Käsemann thinks that Matthew 10:41 reflects the situation of local congregations in Palestine, consisting of members who are called δίκαιοι under the leadership of a prophet.[5] Bornkamm and Satake think that the Apocalypse, far from reflecting the situation in the churches of Asia Minor, recalls the situation found in the churches of Palestine.[6]

The divergences between the positions described above are functional, situational and geographical. Methodically, they have in common that they rest on inferences and not on direct evidence, and hence they cannot be regarded as final. There is no direct evidence which assigns to prophets a position of local leadership, and it is to be doubted whether they ever held such a position. Nor is it necessary that there is a conflict between the prophets and the local ministry. When the Didache states concerning the local bishops and deacons: ὑμῖν ... λειτουργοῦσι καὶ αὐτοὶ τὴν λειτουργίαν τῶν προφητῶν καὶ διδασκάλων. μὴ οὖν ὑπερίδητε αὐτούς· αὐτοὶ γάρ εἰσιν οἱ τετιμημένοι ὑμῶν μετὰ τῶν προφητῶν καὶ διδασκάλων (15, 1f.), it is clear that there exists no conflict between them and the prophets and teachers. The latter may have enjoyed a somewhat greater prestige but this will hardly

---

[1] G. Bornkamm, art. πρέσβυς κτλ., *Th. W. N. T.* VI, p. 670ff.

[2] A. Kragerud, *Der Lieblingsjünger im Johannesevangelium* (Oslo, 1959). Cf. Cothénet, *art. cit.,* c. 1317.

[3] P. Meinhold, Geschehen und Deutung im Ersten Clemensbrief, *Zeitschrift für Kirchengeschichte* 1939, p. 82-129.

[4] Cf. *art. cit.,* p. 31ff.

[5] E. Käsemann, Die Anfänge christlicher Theologie, *Exegetische Versuche und Besinnungen* (Göttingen, 1964), II, p. 89ff.

[6] Bornkamm, *art. cit.,* p. 663ff.; A. Satake, *Die Gemeindeordnung in der Johannesapokalypse* (Neukirchen, 1966).

have exceeded the appreciation which visiting ministers usually enjoy over against their local colleagues.

In the case of congregational prophecy, the situation could conceivably be different. Logically, it would have its place in a church without an established leadership. This appears to have been the situation in Corinth where only κυβερνήσεις are found and no leaders or ministers are mentioned.[1] The same situation seems to be presupposed in Romans 12.[2] But the church of Thessalonica had as its leaders τοὺς κοπιῶντας ἐν ὑμῖν καὶ προϊσταμένους ὑμῶν ἐν κυρίῳ καὶ νουθετοῦντας ὑμᾶς.[3] This is an indication that congregational prophecy does not necessarily require a church without fixed leadership. The Shepherd of Hermas presents the picture of a church in which the congregational prophets appear to cooperate with the leaders of the church. We will take this up in chapter VI.

THE FUNCTION OF PROPHECY

It is not easy to define Christian prophecy exactly and to draw clear lines of distinction between the prophet, the apostle and the teacher. The order in which they appear in 1 Corinthians 12:28 could indicate a difference in rank. Such a difference whould be natural as far as the apostles are concerned but would hardly be correct with regard to prophets and teachers. Yet it is remarkable that, for instance, Barnabas is named among the prophets and teachers of the church in Antioch (Acts 13:1), and appears, together with Paul, as an apostle in the next chapter (14:14). In Ephesians 2:20 apostles and prophets appear together as the foundation of the church, and in 4:11 apostles, prophets, evangelists, pastors and teachers are mentioned as God's gifts to the church for the equipment of the saints. But in the Didache the prophets and the teachers are mentioned together as if forming one group.

All this goes to show that the title prophet does not include a definition of prophecy. But when we turn to the few indications in our sources which concern the function of prophecy, the picture does not become much clearer. According to Paul, the prophet λαλεῖ οἰκοδομὴν καὶ παράκλησιν καὶ παραμυθίαν (1 Cor. 14:3), but Chevallier rightly

---

[1] 1 Cor. 12:28.
[2] Rom. 12:8.
[3] 1 Thess. 5:12.

concludes that these words cannot serve as a good definition of prophecy because they are not even specific characteristics of prophecy.[1]

We can, however, outline tentatively the function of prophecy by
comparing it in a general way with those functions in the church
with which it is usually mentioned together. The apostles preach the
Gospel to unbelievers, the prophetic ministry is primarily church
centered. This is what prophecy has in common with the teaching
ministry. But the difference between these two is that prophecy has
no fixed content. The teacher has to transmit and expound the tradition
of the Gospel and the Scriptures. On this point, the teacher is in a
similar position to the apostle. But this difference between prophecy
on the one side, and apostleship and teaching on the other may lead
us to the crucial point. All three are ministries of the Spirit, all three
are ministries of the spoken word. But the apostle and the teacher
can, as it were, perform their ministry at any time. The prophet can
only speak when the Spirit inspires and commissions him. The classic
formula for this is found in Irenaeus, in a context which will concern
us later in this study: οἷς ἂν ὁ θεὸς ἄνωθεν ἐπιπέμψῃ τὴν χάριν
αὐτοῦ, οὗτοι θεόσδοτον ἔχουσι τὴν προφητείαν, καὶ τότε λαλοῦσιν
ἔνθα καὶ ὁπότε θεὸς βούλεται.[2]

If this is the way in which prophecy comes to pass, it follows that
prophecy cannot be a regular ministry in the sense that its performance
can be predicted in advance. It is dependent on the will of the Lord.

To sum up, prophecy is a church-centered ministry through which
the Lord speaks to the church what He has to say when He wants
it said. By virtue of this nature, prophecy has the function "d'éclairer
par la révélation de Dieu l'existence des chrétiens, soit comme com-
munauté, soit comme individu", to quote Chevallier once more.[3] It
is a pastoral ministry.

The fact that prophecy, by definition, does not have a fixed content
raises the question whether Christian apocalyptic prophecy is legitimate, because apocalyptic does have fixed traditions which are passed
on. There is but one example of an apocalypse which claims to be
a prophetic message, and that is the Apocalypse of John. Its prophetic
nature does not, however, appear from the strictly apocalyptic parts
of the book, but from the messages to the churches in chs. 2 and 3,

---

1 M. A. Chevallier, *Esprit de Dieu, paroles d'hommes* (Neuchatel, 1966), p. 196f.
2 *A. H.* I 13, 3; cf. *infra.*, p. 64.
3 *Op. cit.*, p. 198.

and from the emphatic message that the *parousia* is near, with which it closes (22:6-19).[1]

Furthermore, apocalyptic is not a ministry of the spoken word but a form of literature. It is understandable that later Christian apocalyptic writers have returned to the form of their older Jewish counterparts: their writings are anonymous.

These observations lead to the conclusion that Christian prophecy is not apocalyptic, though it may use apocalyptic forms and patterns. Even then it remains what it is: a pastoral ministry which passes on the direct messages of the Lord.

From the point of view of its functioning, prophecy is always in danger of losing its specific function and of becoming more like the teaching and the preaching ministry. This can be illustrated from the development of the concept of false prophecy in late first and early second century sources. As this brings us to the time of Hermas we will deal with it in chapter IV in which we investigate the false prophet of the 11th Mandate.

The Authentication of Prophecy

The mention of false prophets in the preceding paragraph leads us to the problem of authentication, which is intrinsically connected with prophecy. How is the truth of the prophetic message to be established? Is it self-authenticating? Or does it need external authentication? As long as it is only the message which is at issue, there is no need for the term 'false prophet'. This is the situation in the Old Testament, where the term 'false prophet' does not appear. It is also true of the Christian prophets. Von Campenhausen's statement: "Paulus rechnet noch nicht mit 'falschen Profeten' ",[2] is true; but the necessity of the διάκρισις πνευμάτων shows that the problem of authentication did exist. When the authentication begins to involve not only the spirit or the Spirit which speaks through the prophet, but also the prophet himself, then the false prophet appears on the scene. The word ψευδο-προφήτης was there; it was probably coined because of an association between false prophecy and pagan divination in the mind of the

---

[1] In a comparable way the message of the false prophets mentioned in the synoptic apocalypse (Mk 13:5f.; 21f.) concerns the appearance and the identification of the coming Christ, and not the transmission of apocalyptic traditions.

[2] *Op. cit.*, p. 200.

Septuagint translators of Jeremiah and Zechariah.[1] Its basic meaning
is, 'a prophet who tells ψευδῆ, rather than, 'a man who ψευδῶς claims
to be a prophet', a verbal rather than a nominal meaning. But further
usage has blurred this distinction to such an extent that the exact
meaning of ψευδοπροφήτης cannot be determined in terms of verbal
or nominal meaning. To understand the role of the prophet in a certain
situation we must carefully search the evidence of his activities and
compare it to the evidence concerning other false prophets. To give
one example, the ψευδοπροφήτης Bar Jesus of Acts 13:5ff. is vastly
different from the ψευδοπροφῆται who deny that Jesus Christ has
come in the flesh (1 John 4:1ff.). Part of the difference is that in the
case of Bar Jesus, the word indicates that he is not what he purports
to be, a prophet; and, in 1 John, the prophets teach falsehood: nominal
meaning vs. verbal meaning. But it is far more important to note
that Bar Jesus is a μάγος who operates in the pagan world at the
court of the Roman proconsul; whereas the false prophets in 1 John
are teachers who originate from, and probably operate within, the
church.[2]

The Christian use of ψευδοπροφήτης will have our attention in
chapter IV because of its direct relevance to the 11th Mandate. Here
it may suffice to indicate briefly the lines along which the process
of authentication may come to pass in the Christian church. From the
Old Testament, two criteria are taken over. The first is based on the
eventual outcome of what the prophet has said (ex eventu). The second
is based on the moral conduct of the prophet (ex vita). Both are also
found outside the Jewish-Christian world, as naturally might be expected. The criterion ex eventu, however, is only applicable when prophecy
contains an element of prediction. This is not necessarily the case
with Christian prophecy, and the application of this criterion in the
Christian realm may well point to a change in the concept of prophecy.
To these criteria we find added a doctrinal standard, and this has a
definite bearing on the concept of prophecy. All this will receive due
attention in chapter IV. But the διάκρισις πνευμάτων which we

---

[1] Cf. present writer, The Use of ΨΕΥΔΟΠΡΟΦΗΤΗΣ in the Septuagint, Philo
and Josephus, N. T. 13 (1971), p. 147-156, esp. p. 151f.

[2] For Acts 13:6ff. cf. H. Conzelmann, Die Apostelgeschichte, H. N. T. 7 (Tübingen,
1963), p. 73f. ad loc. To the relationship between prophecy, divination and magic we
shall return infra, p. 82f. For 1 Jn 4:1-3 cf. M. de Jonge, De Brieven van Johannes
(Nijkerk, 1968), p. 178-187. ad. loc.

find in the 11th Mandate is performed by the Spirit itself through the gathered congregation! This reveals the deepest dimension of the problem of authentication; it is the foundation and the presupposition of all other criteria, because it rests on the principle that only the Spirit knows the true man of the Spirit.

INSPIRATION

Prophecy rests, by definition, on revelation. Inspiration is one of the many forms of revelation which are found in the world of religion. It supposes the picture of a breath or spirit entering a man. This picture is found in many religions, including Hebrew and Christian religion. More than anything else the question of prophetic inspiration has been at the heart of the discussion on the relationship between Christian and hellenistic forms of prophecy. We have seen that Fascher saw a "Geschichte des Prophetismus" as the ultimate goal of his own study and of the many more which were yet to follow, which implies that there is to be found one "Prophetismus" in Antiquity. This leaves questions about origin and borrowing open. Others, however, have taken a more radical view. In the same year in which Fascher's book appeared, Reitzenstein wrote in the third edition of his famous book on the hellenistic mystery religions: "Kein Mensch behauptet dass der Inhalt des frühchristlichen ἐνθουσιασμός dem Heidentum entlehnt sei; aber bestreiten soll man nicht länger, dass seine Form und Auffassung tatsächlich übernommen ist, so gut wie die Wundererzählungen".[1] A few years earlier H. Leisegang had attempted to prove that the Christian idea of the Spirit was derived from hellenistic mysticism, and that the Christian prophet was the interpreter of the glossolalian in the same way as Plato wanted the ecstatic and frenzied utterances of the seers to be interpreted by conscious and sober prophets.[2] However much they may diverge from one another, Reitzenstein's and Leisegang's views remain within the context of the question of whether or not there has been Christian borrowing. So does H. Bacht's criticism of Reitzenstein's position.[3] According to him, the hellenistic prophet

---

[1] *Hellen. Mysterienreligionen*, p. 240.

[2] H. Leisegang, *Pneuma Hagion, Der Ursprung des Geistbegriffs der synoptischen Evangelien aus der griechischen Mystik* (Leipzig, 1922; repr. Hildesheim, 1970), p. 119ff.

[3] H. Bacht, Die Prophetische Inspiration in der kirchlichen Reflexion der vor-montanistischen Zeit, *Theol. Quartalschrift* 125 (1944), p. 1-18. He refers mainly to

has a split consciousness which prevents him from remembering afterwards what he saw or heard. This state of mind is accompanied by loud cries, passionate impulsive motions or a state of cataleptic trance, apathy to bodily pains, etc.[1] With this is contrasted the picture of prophetic inspiration as presented by Christian writers, and then the obvious conclusion follows: there are no points of resemblance between Christian and hellenistic prophets.[2] This conclusion is possible only when ecstasy — in the sense of a total loss of consciousness — is held to be characteristic of hellenistic divination. But this is an oversimplification, behind which we may suspect apologetic tendencies.[3]

There is, however, another position possible, which, in a general sense, comes closer to Fascher's idea of a "Prophetismus". Conceivably, the Christians did share with their environment certain ideas and pictures which relate to prophetic inspiration. For the prophet his inspiration by the Spirit is a personal experience with all the marks of uniqueness. This individual experience, however, is at the same time transpersonal. This appears from the reports of experiences of prophetic inspiration; the reports come all dressed up in the language of the environment and the traditions and pictures prevailing there. In the view of Reitzenstein, the pictures in which the inspiration is reported are form-elements which may be detached in order to set free the specific content. Here, a study of the 11th Mandate has a significant contribution to make; because it will show that the inspiration of the true prophet is reported in terms and pictures which are undoubtedly hellenistic. Yet the strong denunciation of the hellenistic divination which the false prophet practices, found in the same document, rules out the possibility of conscious borrowing and leaves us with a clear case of the sharing of certain ideas and pictures pertaining to prophetic inspiration. When we want to understand and appreciate this we must move beyond the question of Christian borrowing or not.

The use of the terms ecstasy and enthusiasm referring to prophetic

---

Hopfner, art. Mantike, *P. W. R. E.* XIV 1, c. 1262 who in his turn refers to J. Tambornino, *De Antiquorum Daemonismo* (Giessen, 1909), *passim*. But the majority of Tambornino's quotations refer to possession in general, rather than to divination.

[1] *Art. cit.*, p. 10f., 8.

[2] *Ib.*, p. 18.

[3] The same tendency is found in K. Prümm, *Religionsgeschichtliches Handbuch für den Raum der altchristlichen Umwelt* (Rome, 1954), esp. p. 427-434.

inspiration calls for some further considerations. Especially the adjectives 'ecstatic' and 'enthusiastic' are in vogue to characterise primitive Christian experience of the Spirit. We will deal with their use and abuse in due course. When, however, they pertain to prophetic inspiration, it is a different matter which sometimes causes considerable confusion. Inspiration is usually viewed as an ecstatic experience. But what exactly does 'ecstatic' mean? There is a psychological concept of ecstasy as "einen völligen Mono-Ideismus",[1] i.e. "an abnormal state of consciousness in which one is so intensely absorbed by one single idea or one single feeling, or by a group of ideas or feelings, that the normal stream of psychological life is more or less arrested".[2] Transposed into the sphere of religion, this means that "consciousress is entirely filled with the presence of God, with ideas and feelings belonging to the divine sphere".[3] But Lindblom himself replaces the concept of ecstasy by another, namely that of "the revelatory state of mind" because it is a more general term.[4] This state of mind "includes all degrees of mental exaltation, from ecstasy in the strict sense to states of mind which approximate to the normal consciousness".[5]

Two observations are in order. In the first place, this concept of ecstasy, or the "revelatory state of mind", is also applicable to experiences which eventually lead to mystic union.[6] But, phenomenologically speaking, the prophet and the mystic are not in the same class. The prophet is fundamentally a proclaimer, a man with a message. The mystic is a solitary. His experience of union is relevant and meaningful to himself in the first place, if not exclusively. His ecstasy is inner-directed while the prophet's experience is outward-directed.[7] The latter is a means to an end while the mystic's experience is part of the end itself.

Secondly, this concept of ecstasy is described in terms of a state of mind and not in terms of a relationship. For those who experience

---

[1] Cf. A. Schimmel, art. Ekstase, R. G. G. II³, c. 410.

[2] J. Lindblom, *Prophecy in Israel* (Oxford, 1963), p. 4f.

[3] *Ib.*

[4] *Ib.*, p. 173f.

[5] *Ib.*

[6] Cf. e.g. J. B. Pratt, *The Religious Consciousness* (New York, 1924), p. 394ff.

[7] "Mysticism is calm, aesthetic contemplation, but prophecy is stormy in emotion and urgent in ethical demands" (Paul E. Johnson, *Psychology of Religion* (New York, no date), p. 119. Cf. also Fr. Heiler's expositions about mystical and prophetic religion in *Das Gebet* (München, 1920), p. 248-283.

ecstasy to any degree and in any form, it is the relationship with God that matters. Between the prophet and his god, something is happening which affects profoundly their mutual relationship. Any concept of prophetic inspiration must deal with this change in the relationship. When this change is called 'ecstasy' it is best to take that word in its classic sense; thus ἔκστασις means that the νοῦς is no longer in command.[1] Its complement is ἐνθουσιασμός i.e. being full of God, *plenus deo*, in Christian terms, πλήρης τοῦ πνεύματος.[2] In this particular sense, any prophet, i.e. any inspired bearer of a divine message, is an ecstatic and an enthusiast. Consequently, when taken in their technical sense, these terms are inadequate to characterise certain forms of prophetic inspiration over against others. When such a characterisation is needed, we have to start from another angle and see what part human consciousness and human will play in the inspirational experience.

(1) Will and consciousness may both be eliminated and the prophet becomes a passive instrument in the hands of the inspiring deity. There is no recollection afterwards of what happened.

(2) The will may be eliminated; consciousness is not lost but behaves passively. The prophet observes that the deity speaks through him and there is a clear recollection afterwards.

(3) Both will and consciousness remain intact and the prophet speaks what is revealed to him as a divine message.

Varying degrees of mental exaltation go with each of these types. In the case of type (1) the prophet may be seized by uncontrolled convulsions, gesticulations, shouting, crying, etc., to an abnormal degree, but in the case of (3) there may be little more than an elated feeling.

This provisional classification will have to be implemented in future research. It may, however, be a useful tool in discerning the inspiration accounts of the 11th Mandate.

This concludes the tentative picture of Christian prophecy in the first and second century A.D. It is drawn for the purpose of bringing out the specific features of the 11th Mandate, and, in its turn, it will be clarified and brought to life by it. To this document and its author we now turn.

---

[1] Cf. F. Pfister, art. Ekstase, *R. A. C.* IV, c. 945ff.
[2] Cf. *infra*, p. 111ff.

CHAPTER TWO

HERMAS

The Shepherd of Hermas has the reputation of being "one of the most enigmatic writings to have come down to us from Christian antiquity".[1] It is said that it "bristles with problems, both literary and theological".[2] The present state of research and opinion is well described in Professor Barnard's article and in the introductions of Joly's edition and of Snyder's translation.[3] In the framework of the present study it is, however, desirable to outline the main areas of problems with which a student of the 11th Mandate finds himself confronted.

The appearance of the commentary on Hermas by Martin Dibelius in the *Handbuch zum Neuen Testament* was a landmark in scholarship.[4] Before him students of Hermas had mainly occupied themselves with questions of literary unity and literary sources.[5] Dibelius, however, maintained that the many discrepancies which are found in Hermas are not to be explained in terms of literary criticism but along the lines of "eine traditionskritische Erklärung"[6] which distinguishes and traces the various and often conflicting traditions absorbed by Hermas. In some respects Dibelius had remarkable success as e.g. in the case of the pneumatology of the Mandates,[7] the allegory of the tower,[8] and the epiphany of the Shepherd.[9] But to carry through a thorough

---

[1] L. W. Barnard, The Shepherd of Hermas in recent study, *Heythrop Theological Journal* IX (1968), p. 29.

[2] W. Coleborne, A linguistic Approach to the Problem of Structure and Composition of the Shepherd of Hermas, *Colloquium* 3 (1969), p. 133.

[3] Joly, p. 11-57; Snyder, p. 1-24.

[4] *Der Hirt des Hermas*, H. N. T. *Ergänzungsband* (Tübingen, 1923), p. 415-644.

[5] For a survey cf. O. Bardenhewer, *Geschichte der altkirchlichen Literatur* I, (Freiburg, 1913², repr. Darmstadt, 1962), p. 481ff.

[6] P. 420.

[7] P. 517ff.

[8] P. 459f.

[8] P. 459f.

[9] P. 492; cf. also his Der Offenbarungsträger im Hirten des Hermas, *Harnack-Ehrung* (Leipzig, 1921), p. 105ff., reprinted in *Botschaft und Geschichte* II (Tübingen, 1956), p. 80-93.

tradition criticism was not feasible within the compass of a commentary of that size, and Dibelius has not gone back to it afterwards. Perhaps there was also a lack of affinity between Hermas and his learned commentator in whose eyes Hermas was little more than representing "das Alltagschristentum der kleinen Leute" who does not master his materials and speaks "eine ungeschickte und umständliche Sprache".[1]

To what results an in-depth study of the work of Hermas may lead was shown clearly and convincingly by Erik Peterson. In 1947 he published an article entitled: "Beiträge zur Interpretation der Visionen im Pastor Hermae".[2] This article showed in great detail that the 'revelatory apparatus' of the first three Visions closely resembled hellenistic divination, specifically that of the magical papyri, even though the revelatory situation was opposite. In 1958 a critical analysis of the fifth Vision appeared which also confirmed this conclusion for the introduction to the book of the Mandates and the Similitudes.[3]

Methodically, Peterson's contributions are more than important. They are one by one models of the way in which Hermas is to be studied. Every tradition and every picture has to be viewed in the widest possible context, and only when they have come to life against their own background, their meaning and function in the work of Hermas become visible. The present study is, in its own modest way, an attempt to do for the 11th Mandate what Peterson did for the Visions.

Despite the fact that Peterson's articles appear in every bibliography on Hermas, he has found few imitators. This may be due to the sudden rise of interest in the Qumran texts which lessened the interest of many scholars in possible relationships between Hermas and the hellenistic world.[4] But part of the reason is also that Peterson himself disparaged his own discoveries because he considered the work of Hermas to be a schoolproduct in which elements from hellenistic

---

[1] P. 425.

[2] The article appeared originally in *Miscellanea Jerphanion, Orientalia Christ. Periodica* XIII (1947), p. 642ff.

[3] Kritische Analyse der fünften Vision des Hermas, *Festschrift für B. Altaner*; *Historisches Jahrbuch der Görresgesellschaft* Band 77 (München, 1958), p. 362ff. The two articles, together with two other articles on Hermas by Peterson (Die Begegnung mit dem Ungeheuer, and die "Taufe" im Acherusischen See) were reprinted in *Frühkirche, Judentum und Gnosis* (Freiburg, 1959; henceforth referred to as *Frühkirche*), p. 254-332.

[4] Cf. *infra*, p. 25f.

divination literature appear only as "Einkleidung";[1] and he also
saw its value predominantly in its information about "die Ent-
wicklung der Askese innerhalb des Judenchristentums".[2] This makes
it easy for other writers to ignore the work of Peterson, or to note
that the hellenistic elements concern only the wording and not the
doctrine.[3]

AUTHORSHIP AND HOME

On one other point it appears necessary to take exception to Peterson's position, namely his case for a collective authorship. The evidence
which he presents is only circumstantial: since Jewish apocalypses
are not "Volksbücher", but products of a school in which eschatological
traditions were transmitted "unter gewissen Gesichtspunkten", and
since in Hermas the school-situation is presupposed, it follows that the
Shepherd of Hermas is to be seen as the product of a school.[4] But the
references to the school situation of the synagogue which Peterson
finds in Hermas are, at best, only very vague. He points to the $\kappa a\theta\acute{\epsilon}\delta\rho a$
on which the false prophet is sitting and interprets it as the seat of
Moses.[5] But our analysis of the text will show that this interpretation
is far from convincing.[6] Hence, it is advisable not to build such a
far reaching conclusion on such weak evidence. The book itself purports
to be written by one author and carries a personal note throughout,
even if this personal element is not necessarily autobiographical.

The cases for a multiple authorship, as made by St. Giet,[7] and, more
recently, by W. Coleborne[8] are quite a different matter. Giet's conclusions which rest on a very detailed exegetical study are as follows:

---

[1] Cf. *Frühkirche*, p. 284.

[2] Cf. *Frühkirche*, p. 282.

[3] Cf. Joly, p. 54: "L'élément hellénique ... concerne l'affabulation, non la doctrine";
he refers to Peterson specifically. L. Pernveden, *The Concept of the Church in the Shepherd
of Hermas* (Lund, 1966), dismisses Peterson as having "worked with comparisons from
the phenomenology of religion" (p. 291, cf. also p. 26 and p. 34), and pays no further
attention to his work.

[4] Cf. *Frühkirche*, 283f.

[5] *Mand.* XI 1: $\H{\epsilon}\tau\epsilon\rho o\nu$ $\H{a}\nu\theta\rho\omega\pi o\nu$ $\kappa a\theta\acute{\eta}\mu\epsilon\nu o\nu$ $\grave{\epsilon}\pi\grave{\iota}$ $\kappa a\theta\acute{\epsilon}\delta\rho a\nu$. On the seat of Moses cf.
E. L. Sukenik, *Ancient Synagogues in Palestine and Greece* (London, 1934), p. 57ff.

[6] Cf. *infra* p. 30f.

[7] *Hermas et les Pasteurs* (Paris, 1963).

[8] Cf. *art. cit.* (*supra* p. 20, n. 2) and his The Shepherd of Hermas, A case for Multiple
Authorship and some Implications, *Stud. Patr.*, Vol. X Part I (Berlin, 1970), p. 65-70.

there are three different authors: the first author wrote Visions I, II, III and IV sometime between 100 and 140 A.D.[1] The second added to this the 9th Similitude; he is the author to whom the *Canon Muratori* refers; this implies a date around the middle of the second century A.D.[2] The third author wrote the 5th Vision, the Mandates and Similitudes I-VII. After inserting his writings between those of his predecessors, he added the 10th Similitude. Thus he brought the work to its completion.[3] This "ingenious attempt to grapple with the literary problems of the *Shepherd*" is modified by L. W. Barnard in this sense that, in his opinion, there is a greater probability that there were originally two works, namely (i) *Vis.* I-IV and (ii) *Vis.* V-end. He places the composition of the former late in the first century and that of the latter around 135.[4] This divides the book in its present form according to the revealers which occur in each part.

Giet's interpretation was subjected to a severe and detailed criticism by Joly,[5] who rejected it completely. This is not the place to enter into this discussion here but with a view to the subsequent investigation it must be said that, in the present writer's opinion, there is but one author who wrote the various parts of the book at different times; there is no conclusive evidence that the various parts ever had a separate existence. This is also relevant with regard to Coleborne's very complex picture of the authors of the Shepherd. He proved, at least to his own satisfaction, "that the Shepherd is to be fragmented into the following portions: V 1 - 4, R. M, E (R and E the work of the same hand), S 1-7, S 8 and S 9".[6] In this nomenclature R stands for *Vis.* V, M for *Mand.* I - XII 3, 3, and E for the rest of *Mand.* XII. The absence of *Sim.* X is due to the fact that it is only extant in Latin and cannot be subjected to the linguistic analysis of the Greek text which underlies Coleborne's conclusions. This analysis rests on what Coleborne calls an *"Apparatus Discernendi"* which is as yet unpublished.[7] But a careful examination of the "Apparatus" has shown that it

---

[1] *Op. cit.*, p. 294ff.

[2] *Ib.*, p. 288f.

[3] *Ib.*, p. 302f.

[4] *Art. cit.*, p. 32.

[5] Hermas et le Pasteur, *Vig. Chr.* 21 (1967), p. 201-218.

[6] *Art.* cit., p. 136f.

[7] Cf. *Studia Patr.* X, p. 65, n. 3 and 6.

is far from convincing;[1] it is, therefore, preferable to maintain the position of single authorship.

As to the author's home there is no serious reason to doubt the tradition which connects the Shepherd with Rome. The opening line of the book points to it.[2] Our only other source, the Muratorian fragment, is clear on this point.[3] That the Shepherd was written *in toto* during the episcopacy of Pius, appears improbable; but this may well be the time of the final stage of the work. The first part is very probably earlier, and may be dated in the first quarter of the second century A.D.[4]

PERSONAL ELEMENTS

The acceptance of single authorship raises another question: to what extent do the writings contribute to the life story of their author? This is a thorny problem for which contradictory solutions have been suggested. In 1927 W. J. Wilson published a lengthy article in which he freely used the data of the Shepherd to reconstruct Hermas' career as a Christian and as a prophet[5]. In the same year Professor J. de Zwaan wrote a portrait of Hermas the Christian; he also used the materials of the Shepherd as evidence of its author's life story.[6] Four years earlier, however, Dibelius had argued for an opposite opinion and maintained that all the autobiographical elements must be explained allegorically. The members of Hermas' family and their experiences are to be considered as examples of the experience of common Christians who need and receive a renewed repentance.

---

[1] This is the conclusion to which Mr. A. Hilhorst has come after a detailed examination of the "Apparatus"; Mr. Hilhorst is preparing a study on the latinisms and semitisms in the Shepherd in which he will substantiate this conclusion.

[2] *Vis.* I 1, 1: ὁ θρέψας με πέπρακέν με ... εἰς 'Ρώμην.

[3] Cf. Preuschen, *Analecta* II (Tübingen, 1910², repr. Frankfurt 1968), p. 32: *Pastorem vero nuperrime temporibus nostris in urbe roma herma conscripsit sedente cathedra urbis romae aeclesiae pio eps fratre eius.*

[4] This is suggested by the reference to Clement in *Vis.* II 4,3 (cf. Dibelius, p. 453; Joly, p. 97 n. 5 is less sure), and by the absence of references to Gnostics and other heretics who came to Rome in 135 A.D. and after.

[5] The Career of the Prophet Hermas, *H. Th. R.* 20 (1927), p. 21-62.

[6] Hermas, de Romeinsche Christen, *Jezus, Paulus en Rome* (Amsterdam, 1927), p. 149-164. De Zwaan's portrait of Hermas is more sympathetic than Wilson's, and his psychological observations show more appreciation and discernment than Wilson's rather depreciative judgments.

What remains when all personal elements are detached is a man for whom the personal experience of renewed repentance meant some sort of a prophetic revelation. This revelation, and not the visions which he purported to have had, inspired him to write his book.[1]

On the whole Dibelius' opinion has carried the day,[2] even though dissident voices were heard from time to time.[3] But the evidence is not easy to grasp and is far from being unequivocal. A definite solution seems to be impossible. The 11th Mandate has little to contribute to the study of these problems. Yet it may suggest another perspective; if not for the biography of Hermas, at least for the question of his self-understanding. Hermas is, whatever his life story may have been, a man with a message. Hence the question arises: is the picture of the prophet in the 11th Mandate a self-portrait of Hermas? Or, if not that, what does it tell us, by way of contrast or analogy, about his ministry? To this personal aspect of the 11th Mandate we will return at the end of this study.

BACKGROUNDS

The presence of Jewish elements in the work of Hermas has long been recognised, but — in the words of Snyder — "the most important consensus of recent research on the Shepherd is to place the writing squarely in the milieu of Jewish Christianity".[4] Yet, "there remains much which appears alien to any form of Jewish or Christian literature The author lived in a segment of society that was deeply immersed in Roman culture and he utilizes this environment as a means of communicating his message of repentance".[5] These statements clearly reveal present day opinion about Hermas' backgrounds: he belongs to Jewish-Christianity, but lives in a non-Christian environment from which he borrows what materials he can use.

Within the context of this opinion, the attempt of J. P. Audet to define exactly the author's time, place and descent, appears to be the most extreme. In 1953 he published a long article on the literary

---

[1] Dib., p. 419f.

[2] Cf. Joly, p. 15-21.

[3] E.g. R. van Deemter, *Der Hirt des Hermas, Apokalypse oder Allegorie?* (Delft, 1929); A. von Ström, *Allegorie und Wirklichkeit im Hirten des Hermas* (Lund, 1935).

[4] Snyder, p. 16.

[5] *Ib.*, p. 17.

and doctrinal affinities of the *Manual of Discipline*.[1] In this article he concluded that Hermas was born in Italy of Jewish parents who had previously belonged to the Qumran community and after the war of 70 A.D. had been sold into slavery. In Rome, Hermas may himself have joined a Jewish group which, within the fold of the Roman church, continued to follow its own traditions of thought and discipline.[2] This conclusion is also adopted by Daniélou[3] and Lluis-Font.[4]

This opinion would place Hermas on the fringe of second century Christianity and, as pointed out by Joly,[5] deny any proper Christian value to his theology and degrade it to "un reflux du judaïsme". But, more important than that, it fails to offer an explanation for the many elements in Hermas which cannot be explained from the background of Qumran. If Hermas were born and educated in such a specific religious environment he would have to be more consistent with the views of that environment and not show so many other influences.

There is, however, reason to question also the general opinion about Hermas as a Jewish Christian living in, and utilizing, a non-Christian environment. Is this a satisfactory way to explain the presence and the function of hellenistic elements? Our study of the 11th Mandate will show that at least here the hellenistic elements are more than literary devices to communicate a message. Rather, they are part of the content and this suggests that the milieu of Hermas was too complex to admit of one qualification only. A complete understanding of this milieu cannot be found on the basis of the study of the 11th Mandate only. Much more work has yet to be done. But this study may help to arrive at a more adequate stating of the problem. It is not the presence of hellenistic materials in a Jewish-Christian book that is to be explained, nor, conceivably, the opposite, but the blending of genuine Jewish-Christian elements with these unmistakable hellenistic elements which constitutes the milieu of Hermas.

---

[1] *Affinités litéraires et doctrinales du Manuel de Discipline*, R. B. 60 (1953), p. 41-82.

[2] *Ib.*, p. 82.

[3] *Théologie du Judéo-Christianisme* (Paris, 1958), p. 49, where Daniélou expresses himself with less confidence than in his *Les manuscripts de la Mer Morte et les origines du Christianisme* (Paris, 1957), p. 120ff. Peterson (*Frühkirche*, p. 308) does not commit himself.

[4] Sources de la doctrine d'Hermas sur les deux esprits, *Revue d'Ascétique et de Mystique* 39 (1963), p. 83-98, esp. p. 96f. For the doctrine of the two spirits cf. *infra*, p. 134f.

[5] Judaïsme, Christianisme et Hellénisme dans le Pasteur d'Hermas, *La Nouvelle Clio* V (1953), p. 394-406.

CHAPTER THREE

THE ELEVENTH MANDATE

Among the writings of Hermas the 11th Mandate stands apart with regard to both its subject matter and its form. As far as the former is concerned, it is the only text which pertains to Christian prophecy. There are two other places where prophets are mentioned but these prophets belong to the past, not to the present.[1] The absence of any other reference to Christian prophecy in the book of Hermas has led Snyder to take an opposite view of the 11th Mandate. Far from accepting it as evidence of Christian prophecy, he maintains that "the form of Didache 11-13 on true and false prophets is used by the author to attack false teachers who cater to the desires of the falsely pious". This assumption rests on the opinion that "even though the false prophet was a concern of the early church (Did. 11-13; Origen, *Contra Celsum* 6:24, 41; 7, 11), neither the prophet as an office nor the false prophet as a threat concerns him" (i.e. Hermas).[2]

Snyder's statements, however, are untenable. The 11th Mandate itself shows beyond doubt that the prophet and the false prophet are a concern of Hermas. Furthermore, it is to be doubted whether in the 11th Mandate the "form" of *Didache* 11-13 is used at all. The literary form of the two documents is entirely different and there is no reason to assume that Hermas knew the teaching of the Didache. Also the viewpoint of the two texts is definitely not the same. The Didache gives straightforward criteria by which the itinerant ministers of the church are to be judged and refers to apostles, prophets, teachers and to everyone who comes in the name of the Lord. Hermas, however, is concerned with an entirely different situation, namely the conflict between Christian prophecy and pagan divination. Hence the idiom of the two documents is not the same, apart from a few general words like προφήτης, δοκιμάζειν, πνεῦμα. Finally, the Didache does not distinguish sharply between the various itinerant ministers,[3] whereas the 11th Mandate refers to prophets specifically.

---

[1] *Vis.* II 3, 4 quotes the book 'Ελδὰδ καὶ Μωδάτ, τοῖς προφητεύσασιν ἐν τῇ ἐρήμῳ τῷ λαῷ. *Sim.* IX 15,4 refers to προφῆται τοῦ θεοῦ καὶ διάκονοι αὐτοῦ who belong to a generation preceding that of the apostles, cf. *infra*, p. 151, n. 2.

[2] Snyder, p. 86f.

[3] Cf. *infra*, p. 60.

Even if the 11th Mandate pertains to Christian prophecy and its opposite, there is still the question what reason the author could have to insert it in his work, the more so since it is only remotely related to Hermas' primary concern, namely that of the second repentance. Conceivably, Hermas included the 11th Mandate to give guidance to the church with regard to prophets and false prophets because he thought that the church needed it. This would be a very natural and satisfactory explanation why we find this Mandate in the book of Hermas. But when we realize that Hermas himself is a man who has to speak to the church, the question becomes all the more intriguing. What connection is there between Hermas and the picture of the Christian prophet in the 11th Mandate?

This question cannot be answered at this stage of our investigation. We will return to it at the end, after we have examined the picture of the Christian prophet in full detail.[1]

STRUCTURE

The formal peculiarity of the 11th Mandate is that it begins with a similitude; but this does not determine the structure. The Mandate may be divided into three different parts, each of which has its own contribution to make to the whole:
(a) paragraphs 1-6; (b) paragraphs 7-17; and (c) paragraphs 17-21.

(a) The first part initially takes the form of a similitude, as is shown by its opening line ἔδειξέ μοι κτλ.[2] and the Shepherd's question, βλέπεις ...; followed by Hermas' answer: βλέπω, φημί, κύριε.[3] But, since the opening line does not contain a picture which has to be interpreted allegorically but describes a real human situation, the rest of this first part is an exposition by the Shepherd on the false prophet, his activities, and his followers, including a few remarks on the Spirit from above and on the believers who are not ensnared by

---

[1] Cf. ch. VII.

[2] This opening is common in apocalyptic and prophetic literature, cf. Jer. 24:1; Zech. 1:9; 2:3; 3:1; Apoc. 4:1; 17:1; 21:9f.; Enoch 22, 1; 24, 1; 66, 1. *Test. Lev.* 9, 6; *Test. Jud.* 15, 5; Slav. Enoch 6, 1; 7, 1; 10, 1, etc. Gk Baruch 2, 2; 3, 1; 6, 1. The normal form is that something is shown and subsequently explained allegorically or symbolically but often the explanation is absent when the vision is self-explaining as in Apoc. 21:10. The verb δείκνυμι is a key word in Hermas' revelatory idiom, occurring 26 times, but in an opening scene only here and *Sim.* III, IV and VI.

[3] Cf. e. g. *Sim.* IV 1; VI 2, 1; VIII 6, 1; IX 7, 4.

the false prophet. The main characteristic of the false prophet appears to be that he practices divination on request.

(b) The second part has a different structure. It begins with a somewhat unexpected question of Hermas how a man can tell a prophet from a false prophet, unexpected because in the preceding paragraphs an unambiguous criterion had been established: the false prophet divines on request! This might create suspicion that Hermas unites two separate documents which represent different traditions on the false prophet. But this is not the case because the same criterion reappears in 8, and the important theme of emptiness is dominant in both the first and the second part of the Mandate. Hermas' question at the beginning of the second part merely has the function of making possible a further exposition on the *diakrisis* between the true and the false prophet.

This exposition is well balanced. After naming the criterion by which the prophet and the false prophet are to be judged, namely ἀπὸ τῆς ζωῆς, the exposition on the prophet follows in two sections; the first, introduced by πρῶτον μέν (8), describes his behaviour as a Christian and as a prophet; the second, introduced by οὖν (9), relates his appearance in the gathered congregation and what happens there. Paragraph 10 contains the transition to the next part of the exposition.

The exposition on the false prophet, intruodced by ἄκουε νῦν (11, taking up ἄκουε in 8), consists of two sections which parallel those on the prophet; the first is introduced by πρῶτον μέν (12) and describes the false prophet's behaviour as a Christian and as a prophet; the second, introduced by εἶτα (13), relates the way in which he communicates with his own adherents, and his *demasqué* when he happens to appear in the meeting of the gathered congregation. Both his communication with his followers, and his exposure in the congregation are each illustrated by a parable on the theme of emptiness (13b, 15). The last paragraph, 16, takes up the words of the opening words of the second part and thus brings this part of the Mandate to its logical conclusion.

(c) The third part of the Mandate is the mandate proper as is shown by its opening words: σὺ δὲ πίστευε, κτλ. The repeated injunctions to trust the Spirit from above and to stay away from the earthly spirit are illustrated by two pairs of parables; the first pertains to the lack of power of the earthly spirit, the second to the power of the spirit from above.

In all three parts of the Mandate the dialogue is only minimal. In

the first part it is limited to Hermas' confirmation βλέπω, φημί, κύριε
(1); in the second part to the question how to tell the prophet from the
false prophet (7); and in the third part to a question which prepares
the way for the Shepherd's conclusions on the earthly spirit (19). But
such minimal dialogue is not unusual in Hermas.[1] Yet it is indispensable because it is part of the revelation event, and hence essential
for the authentication of Hermas' message.

CONTENT

After examining the structure of the 11th Mandate we turn to its
content. Our exposition cannot always follow the course of the text; on
the most fundamental issues it is necessary to bring together materials
from different parts of the Mandate and discuss them thematically.

The second part of the Mandate relates the issues which constitute
the picture of the prophet and the false prophet. These issues raise
numerous questions which go beyond the context of the 11th Mandate
and hence cannot be treated in the framework of this exposition of
the text. To them the three following chapters are devoted. Consequently, the second part receives less attention here.

As in the examination of the form of the Mandate, our exposition
follows the division into three parts.

(a)   *The False Prophet and his Followers* (1-6)

The opening of the 11th Mandate presents the picture of a real
human situation: people are sitting on a bench and listen to a man
sitting on a chair. Elsewhere in Hermas the bench and the chair appear
when the Elderly Lady sits down on them, about to give her revelations
to Hermas.[2] In that context Peterson has identified both the bench
and the chair as belonging to the apparatus of hellenistic magical
divination; on them the deity will sit down to give his revelation
to the μάγοι.[3]

Here, however, the situation is different: not the deity, but the
(false) prophet sits on the chair. It is not the moment of revelation[4] but

---

[1] Cf. *infra*, p. 161.
[2] The bench in *Vis.* III 1, 4: συμψέλιον ... ἐλεφάντινον, the chair in *Vis.* I 2, 2:
καθέδραν λευκὴν ἐξ ἐρίων χιονίων γεγονυῖαν.
[3] Cf. *Frühkirche*, p. 254ff.
[4] In ancient divination the seer is usually alone at the moment of revelation, cf.
Th. Hopfner, *Griechisch-Aegyptischer Offenbarungszauber* II (Leipzig, 1924), p. 17.
and references there.

that of its transmission to the questioners. Now the ways in which oracles are made known vary considerably in oracular and private divination, but, as far as our knowledge goes, there is no evidence that the opening scene of the 11th Mandate reflects divinatory usage.[1] To explain this scene, Peterson has pointed to a school situation, probably that of a synagogue school.[2] There is, however, no reason to refer to the synagogue specifically.[3] Chairs and benches belong to the class rooms of all ancient schools, and the situation is always as described by Isidorus: *subsellia vero ceterorum, cathedra doctorum.*[4] The school scene is, however, in no way decisive. There is no allusion to a teacher or to teaching in the rest of the Mandate. The school scene merely has an introductory function, namely to introduce the *dramatis personae.*[5] Their identification follows forthwith.

The people on the bench are identified as πιστοί and the man on the chair as a false prophet, who attempts to destroy the διάνοια of the δοῦλοι τοῦ θεοῦ.[6] But he is successful only with the δίψυχοι, not with the πιστοί. The first time πιστοί refers to Christian believers

---

[1] Our knowledge on the subject is limited. In Coropae the γραμματεὺς τοῦ θεοῦ handed out τὰ πινάκια which contain the answers, cf. Dittenberger, *Sylloge* III³ (Leipzig, 1920), Nr. 1157 (p. 300ff.), M. P. Nilsson, *Geschichte der griechischen Religion* II² (München, 1961), p. 103ff. In Abonuteichos, the answers were written on the scrolls on which the inquirers had written their questions, cf. Lucian, *Alex.* 19. A remote resemblance to the scene in *Mand.* XI is found in Lebadea: the inquirer who had descended in order to receive the oracles from Trophonios is, upon his return, placed ἐπὶ θρόνον Μνημοσύνης· καθεσθέντα δὲ ἐνταῦθα ἀνερωτῶσιν (οἱ ἱερεῖς) ὁπόσα εἶδέ τε καὶ ἐπύθετο (Paus. IX 39, 13). In private divination the Chaldaean diviner Diophanes gives his predictions *frequentis populi circulo conseptus* (Apuleius, *Metam.* II 13, 3). The scene of question and answer in the Berlin Magical Papyrus (Preisendanz, *Papyri Graecae Magicae* I (Leipzig, 1928), I 175f., p. 10f.) is simply: ἐὰν δὲ τίς σε ἐρωτήσῃ ... σὺ δὲ ... λέγε τῷ ἐπερωτῶντί σε.

[2] *Frühkirche*, p. 283f.

[3] Συναγωγή in 9 and 13f. refers, not to the building, but to the meeting, cf. *infra*, p. 122.

[4] *Etym.* XX 11, 9; καθέδρα as the teachers' chair also Juvenal, *Sat.* VII 203; Seneca, *De Brevitate Vitae* X 1; θρόνος in the same meaning Plato, *Protag.* 315c; Philostr., *Vita Sophist.* I 23, 1 (526), on the chair of rhetoric at Athens; Dittenb., *Syll.* II³, Nr. 845, 2f.: ὁ... ἐπὶ τῆς καθέδρας σοφιστής. Cf. L. Hug. art. Subsellium, *P. W. R. E.* IV A, c. 502ff.

[5] D. E. Aune, *The Cultic Setting of Realized Eschatology* (Leiden, 1972), p. 180f., thinks that *Mand.* XI 1 shows "that the prophet is normally seated on a chair before a group on benches", but he overlooks the introductory function of the opening scene. In 9 there is no trace of the prophet sitting before the congregation.

[6] The participle ἀπολλύων is conative.

32   THE ELEVENTH MANDATE

in general;[1] but it is replaced by δοῦλοι τοῦ θεοῦ,[2] and this gives
the author an opportunity to use πιστοί a second time, but now
in a more specific sense which is dearer to him, namely that of faithful
Christians[3] with whom the double-minded believers are contrasted.
This contrast is elaborated in 4, where πιστοί is taken up by ἰσχυροὶ
ἐν τῇ πίστει τοῦ κυρίου, ἐνδεδυμένοι τὴν ἀλήθειαν. These words
must be understood in terms of the Spirit.[4] They denote people who
have the power of the Holy Spirit, and in that power they are able to
resist the false prophet's attempts to destroy their διάνοια and to break
them.[5]

Their opposites are the δίψυχοι. The concept of διψυχία plays a
great part in the writings of Hermas. Together with the cognate verb
and adjective, it occurs some fifty times.[6] Its meaning is, basically,
the opposite of ἐξ ὅλης καρδίας:[7] a divided allegiance; they have
the Lord on their lips, not in their heart.[8] Hence it is also the opposite

---

[1] This is normal Christian usage, cf. e. g. 1 Tim. 4:3; Ign., *Eph.* 21, 2; *Magn.* 5, 2.
In this general meaning in Hermas only here, *Sim.* IX 22, 1 quoted *infra*, p. 66, and
Sim. VIII 9, 1: πιστοὶ μὲν γεγονότες, πλουτήσαντες δέ, κτλ.

[2] This term for the believers is very frequent in Hermas (about 50 times). Its origin
is still unexplained. Pernveden, *op. cit.* p. 177ff. rightly rejects Rengstorf's explanation
(art. δοῦλος, *Th. W. N. T.* II, p. 277) that the church came to be regarded as the real
Israel and that Jesus was not regarded as δοῦλος because both arguments do not apply
to Hermas, but his own explanation that the believers are called δοῦλοι θεοῦ and not
δοῦλοι Χριστοῦ because for Hermas the church has been created before anything else,
is also unconvincing. In the light of Hermas' vision of the church as consisting of potential
prophets (cf. *infra*, p. 124f.) it is tempting to interpret the term δοῦλοι θεοῦ as an extension
to all believers of the O. T. phrase 'My/Thy/His servants, the prophets' (cf. 2 Kings
9:7; 17:13, 23; 21:10: 24:2; Jer. 7:25; Ezek. 38:17; Amos 3:7; Zech. 1:6; Dan. 9:6, 10;
Ezra 9:11 which have δοῦλοι; Jer. 26 (33):5; 35 (42):15; 44 (51):4; Dan. 9: 6, 10 LXX
have παῖδες). Cf. also Apoc. 10:7; 11:18.

[3] In this meaning also *Vis.* III 5, 4; *Mand.* IX 9; *Sim.* VIII 7, 4; 10, 1.

[4] Faith is understood as a πνεῦμα in *Mand.* IX, cf. *infra*, p. 123f. The idea of clothing
is in Hermas also closely connected with the Spirit, cf. *infra*, p. 133f.

[5] Cf. *infra*, p. 45f.

[6] Against ten times in other early Christian literature (Jas 1:8; 4:8; *Did.* 4, 4; Barn.
19, 5; 1 Clem. 11, 2; 23, 2f.; 2 Clem. 11, 2. 5; 19, 2). In Hermas it is only marginally
connected with the Two Ways doctrine (it does not occur in *Mand.* VI), and in the Two
Spirit system it does not stand for the condition of man caught between the spirits
(Snyder, p. 83) but is itself an earthly spirit (cf. *infra*, p. 102, n. 4).

[7] This phrase occurs 16 times in Hermas, often in connection with the second repentance, cf. e.g. *Vis.* I 3, 2; II 2, 4: IV 2, 5; *Mand.* V 1, 7; XII 6, 1.

[8] *Sim.* IX 21, 1. The δίψυχοι are half dead and half alive, because they are involved
in their own affairs (*Sim.* VIII 8, 1-3, cf. 7, 1f.).

of πίστις: doubt, uncertainty with regard to God and salvation,[1] and with regard to their own affairs.[2] Appropriately, the 11th Mandate says that they πυκνῶς μετανοοῦσι (4). This is interpreted as meaning that they often repent,[3] or that they often change their minds.[4] Since a frequently repeated repentance is contrary to Hermas' concept of the second μετάνοια, the latter meaning is more appropriate here.[5] The double-minded are the weaklings in the faith who do not know how to make up their minds, and are always unsure about themselves and the future. This uncertainty drives them out to the false prophet in order to ask him what the future has in store for them.

There is yet another aspect of διψυχία which must be taken into account in order to understand its full meaning in the 11th Mandate. This comes to light when the teaching of the 9th Mandate is compared. In that context the δίψυχοι are those who doubt whether their prayers will be heard and their requests granted. In contrast to faith which is from above and has great power, διψυχία ἐπίγειον πνεῦμά ἐστι παρὰ τοῦ διαβόλου, δύναμιν μὴ ἔχουσα (11). This is exactly what is said in the 11th Mandate about the spirit which is in the false prophet: it is earthly, empty, it has no power and comes from the devil.[6] The same spirit is in the false prophet and in his double-minded audience. There exists an affinity between them, not so much a psychological as a pneumatological affinity. This affinity draws the double-minded to the false prophet and makes him successful with them.

With the double-minded the false prophet succeeds in what he failed to accomplish with the strong in the faith, namely to destroy their διάνοια. This must be understood, in the same sense. Not the man succeeds but the spirit which is in him. In the graphic description

---

[1] *Mand.* IX 5; *Vis.* III 2, 2; *Sim.* VIII 9, 4.

[2] *Mand.* X 2, 2. It is a pastoral, rather than a theological concept, and is primarily to be understood from its usage in Hermas, and not from other sources or traditions, as maintained by O. F. J. Seitz in his various articles on the subject (The Relationship of the Shepherd of Hermas to the Epistle of James, *J. B. L.* 63 (1944), p. 131-140; Antecedents and Significance of the term δίψυχος, *J. B. L.* 66 (1947), p. 211-219; After-thoughts on the term 'Dipsychos', *N. T. S.* 4 (1958), p. 327-334).

[3] Thus Harnack, Taylor, Lake and Snyder.

[4] Thus Weinel, Dibelius and Joly.

[5] Cf. *Vis.* III 7, 3: people who heard the word and wish to be baptized in the name of the Lord, change their mind (μετανοοῦσιν) when they remember the purity of truth.

[6] 17: τῷ δὲ πνεύματι τῷ ἐπιγείῳ καὶ κενῷ μηδὲν πίστευε, ὅτι ἐν αὐτῷ δύναμις οὐκ ἔστιν : ἀπὸ τοῦ διαβόλου γὰρ ἔρχεται.

of the gentle Spirit which is driven out by the evil spirit which is ὀξυχολία, the man in whom the spirit lives is κενὸς ἀπὸ τοῦ πνεύματος τοῦ δικαίου, and τὸ λοιπὸν πεπληρωμένος τοῖς πνεύμασι τοῖς πονηροῖς ... καὶ ὅλος ἀποτυφλοῦται ἀπὸ τῆς διανοίας τῆς ἀγαθῆς.[1] When the διάνοια of the believers is destroyed, they have lost the faculty of spiritual discernment;[2] including that of distinguishing the spirits; and they take a soothsayer for a prophet.

They go to him ὡς ἐπὶ μάντιν[3] i.e. as the heathen go to a soothsayer. A little further, however, the author modifies his statement and writes that the double-minded μαντεύονται ὡς καὶ τὰ ἔθνη. Like μάντις[4] this verb has a strong pagan connotation, and hence consulting the false prophet is tantamount to the sin of idolatry.[5]

This judgment on divination is important because on this point Hermas is in accordance with very old traditions. In the Old Testament

---

[1] Mand. V 2, 7. For this use of κενός and πεπληρωμένος, cf. infra, p. 38ff.

[2] Cf. Mand. X 1, 5: men who came to believe but got caught in worldly business ἀποπλανῶνται ἀπὸ τῆς διανοίας αὐτῶν καὶ οὐδὲν ὅλως νοοῦσι περὶ δικαιοσύνης, but their νοῦς is busy with their own affairs. A similar thought in Sim. IV 7.

[3] The only witness of the Greek text, A, has μαν ..., which is supplied as μάντιν by Harnack, Lake, Whittaker and Joly. This is supported by L¹ and L² (divinum) and E (eorum instar qui divinationem exercent). Divinus is a well known equivalent of vates, but sometimes "there is at least a shade of contempt in the word" (A. S. Pease, M. Tulli Ciceronis De Divinatione, repr. 1963, p. 360, on II 3, 10). Some older editors supply μάγον which is followed by Dibelius (though pointing to L²!), perhaps because of its contemptuous note. Snyder, though rendering 'soothsayer', comments: "The magos is not technical here ..., but a denunciation of the teacher's method of saying that which he pleased in public" (p. 86f.). For this amazing explanation cf. supra, p. 27.

[4] With regard to divination μάντις and προφήτης are closely connected in Greek literature. The Delphian Pythia is πρόμαντις and προφῆτις at the same time. The former denotes her as the one who can see into the future, the latter as the one who speaks what the 'god made her say' (cf. H. Krämer. art. προφήτης A II, Th. W. N. T. VI, p. 786f., cf. also p. 789; there is no article on μάντις in Th. W. N. T.). Aeschylus, Septem 609ff., Agam. 1098f. (following Wecklein and Groeneboom), Eum. 17-19; Euripides, Orest. 360ff; Fascher 13ff. Plato's use of προφήτης is ambiguous: Charm. 173c: τοὺς δὲ ὡς ἀληθῶς μάντεις καθιστάναι ἡμῖν προφήτας τῶν μελλόντων, is in line with the above picture, but Tim. 72 a b distinguishes between them: the prophets who are appointed judges ἐπὶ ταῖς ἐνθέοις μαντείαις are by some called μάντεις but these people do not know that they are τῆς δι'αἰνιγμῶν ... φήμης καὶ φαντάσεως ὑποκριταί and should be called προφῆται μαντευομένων. This, however, looks more like an ideal construction than a description of actual fact at known Greek oracles, cf. P. Amandry, La Mantique appollinienne à Delphes (Paris, 1950), p. 120ff.

[5] Μείζονα ἁμαρτίαν means greater sin than they had already, namely the διψυχία. ἐπιφέρω in the meaning 'to bring upon (oneself)', only here and Vis. I 2, 4; 1 Clem. 47, 4 v. 1. in biblical and early Christian literature.

pagan divination in its various forms is forbidden[1] ; but there are forms of divination within Jahwism which were considered quite legitimate.[2] The Septuagint brings out this contrast semantically by choosing the rather colourless προφήτης to render נביא and by reserving μάντις and its cognates for those explicitly forbidden forms of divination.[3] This tradition is continued. Only in Acts 16:16 and here in the 11th Mandate the word group μάντις is represented and both times it is pagan divination which is envisaged. The same is true of the Apologists.[4]

At the same time, however, this branding of divination within the church as pagan shows that the emphatic rejection of divination was not able to prevent its intrusion into the church. When we want to understand this phenomenon of divination within the church, we must compare it with pagan divination, and this is what will be attempted in some detail in the next chapter.[5]

The double-minded come to the false prophet and ask τί ἄρα ἔσται αὐτοῖς.[6] This is normal divinatory procedure and accordingly the

---

[1] Cf. e.g. Deut. 18:9-14; Lev. 19:26, 31; 20:6, 27; 2 Kings 17:17; 21:6; Lindblom, *Prophecy*, p. 87f.

[2] Cf. e.g. Gen. 25:22; 1 Sam. 9:9; 1 Kings 14:5; 22:5; 2 Kings 3:11; 8 : 8; Jer. 21:2 (דרש) ; Judges 1:1; 18:5; 20:18-28; 1 Sam 10:22; 14:37; 22:10, 13; 23:2, 4; 28:6; 30:8; 2 Sam. 2:1; 5:19, 23 (שאל) ; 2 Sam. 21:1 (בקש). None of these verbs are technical terms and as a rule the way in which an oracle was sought is noti ndicated, but cf. 1 Sam. 28:6: The Lord did not answer him (i.e. Saul), *either by dreams, or by Urim, or by prophets*. Cf. Y. Kaufmann, *The Religion of Israel* (London, 1960), p. 87-93, who uses 'divination' only with reference to pagan forms. H. M. Orlinsky, *The seer in Ancient Israel, Oriens Antiquus* IV (1965), p. 153-174, distinguishes sharply between divination (though he avoids the word because of its connotation of pagan practices, p. 154, n. 3) and prophecy; the former is a common Near Eastern phenomenon. This distinction, however, is not borne out by the Old Testament which uses נביא also for the prophets whom Orlinsky calls seers, cf. Rendtorff, art. προφήτης etc. B III, *Th. W. N. T.* VI, p. 799-809.

[3] Cf. e.g. Deut. 18:14: τὰ γὰρ ἔθνη ταῦτα ... οὗτοι κληδόνων καὶ μαντείων ἀκούσονται. The same is true of Philo (cf. *De Spec. Leg.* IV 8 (51): people who practice divination can be called rightly false prophets; I 9 (60): Moses did not permit the use of any sort of μαντική), but Josephus calls the Essene prophets μάντις (cf. present writer, *art. cit.*, p. 155f.).

[4] Cf. e.g. Tatian, *Orat.* 1, 1; 8, 4; 19, 2f; Athenag. *Suppl.* 21, 5; Arist., *Apol.* 11, 1. This remains so in later Christian literature.

[5] Cf. *infra*, p. 79ff.

[6] For this and similar questions in divination, cf. *infra*, p. 83f.

writer uses the verb ἐπερωτάω.[1] But he also stresses the fact that the false prophet ὅλως οὐ λαλεῖ ἐὰν μὴ ἐπερωτηθῇ (6). Though this is in itself also normal divinatory procedure, it is for Hermas an outstanding point of contrast between the false and the true prophet. The latter does not answer when questions are put to him.[2]

The answers to the questions which people ask about their own future are given κατὰ τὰ ἐπερωτήματα αὐτῶν,[3] and κατὰ τὰς ἐπιθυμίας τῆς πονηρίας αὐτῶν.[4] In short: καθὼς αὐτοὶ βούλονται (2).

This criticism is only seldom made explicitly. The false prophets of the Old Testament are accused of speaking after their own heart and it is implied that this is also after the heart of those who consult them.[5] This is also true in the story of Micaiah ben Jimlah: when he is called upon to speak like the other prophets, it is clearly implied that they had said what the king wanted to hear.[6] Sometimes, however, the accusation is made overtly. In Ezek. 12:21-28 it is intimated that the prophecies of the false prophets do not come to fulfilment because their visions are false and their divination is flattering; in the future there will be no more divination of this kind.[7] In Is. 30:10 people are said to call upon the prophets and the seers to tell them "smooth words".[8] Josephus tells that Jeroboam was deceived by the old false prophet because he told him what was pleasing him.[9] Finally, Eusebius

---

[1] For Hermas' use of ἐπερωτᾶν cf. infra p. 99f. In the LXX it is a very common word for consulting Jahwe, cf. e.g. Num. 23:4; Josh. 9:14, etc. From early times it is a common word in oracular terminology, cf. Herod. I 53; 55; 67; 91; VI 35; 86 γ; 135; VII 169; VIII 122; Thucyd. I 25, 1; 118, 3; II 54, 4; Dittenb., Sylloge III³, Nr. 977, 24f.; 1160; 1168, 16; I³, Nr. 204, 45; Amandry, op. cit., p. 153 (2); 155 (6); 161 (10, XLIII); H. W. Parker, The Oracles of Zeus (Oxford, 1967), p. 259; 261f.; 265f.; 272. But it is not exclusive; Lucian always uses the simplex, cf. e.g. Alex. 32 (ἤροντο); 20, 26, 37 (ἐρωτήσεις), and Plutarch has only once ἐπερωτάω in this sense, cf. Apophth. Laconica 10, 209A. In P. G. M. I 175f., quoted on p. 31, n. 1 both ἐρωτάω and ἐπερωτάω occur in the same sentence.

[2] 8. Cf. infra, p. 98f.

[3] This phrase (only here in the Apostolic Fathers) is explained by the following.

[4] Repeated without the qualifying genitive in 6 and 13. Ἐπιθυμία is very frequent in Hermas and almost always used in malam partem.

[5] Cf. e.g. Jer. 14:13f.; 23:16, 26; Ezek. 13:3.

[6] 1 Kings 22:6, 8, 13.

[7] LXX: οὐκ ἔσται ἔτι ... μαντευόμενος τὰ πρὸς χάριν.

[8] M uses the same word as in Ezek. 12:14 (חזק) but it is not rendered in LXX.

[9] Ant. VIII 236: ... ἀπατώμενος ὑπ'αὐτοῦ τὰ πρὸς ἡδονὴν λέγοντος.

points out that the pagan sorcerers are unreliable because they some-times promise people pleasant things.[1]

When we turn to hellenistic divination, we find that the objection that oracles tell people only what they like to hear is not found often. In the most vicious criticism of oracular practices, Lucian's *Alexander*, we find that people are easily deceived by the various tricks of the divinatory trade; but the author does not say explicitly that Alexander tells them what they like to hear.[2] Hermas' remark that the false prophet speaks καθὼς αὐτοὶ βούλονται is more in line with the Hebrew-Christian judgment on divination.

It is, however, worth noting that in this context the author first writes: (the false prophet) λαλεῖ μετ'αὐτῶν: and then changes the idiom into πληροῖ τὰς ψυχὰς αὐτῶν, he fills their souls. This is a much more meaningful expression. The same verb is used elsewhere in the 11th Mandate; in the next paragraph it is stated that the devil fills the false prophet with his spirit; and in 9 the angel of the prophetic Spirit fills the prophet with the Holy Spirit. This is the idiom of inspira-tion.[3] Hence the phrase πληροῖ τὰς ψυχὰς αὐτῶν carries certain over-tones: not only does the false prophet speak according to their wishes but he fills their souls with the spirit which is in him. Such filling, how-ever, is only possible when there is an affinity between him who fills and those that are filled. We have already seen that such an affinity exists.[4]

This brings us to the false prophet. As we have noted, he attempts to destroy the spiritual discernment of the believers and succeeds in doing so with the double-minded. This gives him a chance to fill their souls when he answers their questions. Remarkably enough, his soul-filling answers are called κενά in the next clause! The repeated and pointed use of the word 'empty' here and elsewhere in the 11th Mandate shows that it is a key word. To this we will turn presently.

But the false prophet does more than speak according to the wishes of his followers. He also speaks some words which are true (τινα ...

---

[1] *Praep. Evang.* IV 1, 10 (132 c): τῶν γοήτων ... τότε μὲν τὰ πρὸς ἡδονὴν ἑκάστῳ προυπισχνουμένων.

[2] Cf. e.g. 20: Alexander opened the scrolls in which the questions came to him, read the questions, rolled up again the scrolls and τὰ δοκοῦντα πρὸς αὐτὰς (i.e. the questions) ἀπεκρίνετο. Cf. also for the political and social influence of the oracles, Nilsson, *Greek Popular Religion* (New York, 1940), p. 125-138.

[3] Cf. *infra*, p. 111ff.

[4] Cf. *supra*, p. 33.

ῥήματα ἀληθῆ), because the devil fills him with his spirit to see if he will be able to break some of the righteous. This is a remarkable statement. We would grossly misunderstand it if we would think that only when he speaks the truth, the false prophet is filled by the devil. He is always full of the devil's spirit, and this is emphasized here only because it explains why some of his words are true: the devil has access to the truth.[1] This is a weapon which he uses when he attempts to break some of the believers.[2]

So much for the false prophet's and the devil's joint attempts to destroy the faith and the allegiance of the believers. We now turn to what is behind those attempts. What possesses the false prophet to act like this ? The answer to this question is twofold: (a) he is from the outset identified as μηδεμίαν ἔχων ἐν ἑαυτῷ δύναμιν πνεύματος θείου (2). There is nothing of the divine Spirit in him. He is κενός, empty; (b) this does not, however, mean that there is no spirit in him, but this πνεῦμα is ἐπίγειον ... καὶ ἐλαφρόν, δύναμιν μὴ ἔχον (6). In one word: this spirit is empty too (17).

These two answers are each other's complement and are vitally important to grasp Hermas' understanding of the spirits. They deserve to be examined at some length.

THE EMPTY PROPHET

In a biting and pointed statement Hermas passes his judgment on the false prophet and his activities: αὐτὸς γὰρ κενὸς ὢν κενὰ καὶ ἀποκρίνεται κενοῖς. His answers are πρὸς τὸ κένωμα τοῦ ἀνθρώπου (3).[3] He himself is empty, the people who come to him are empty,

---

[1] Cf. Origen, *In Num. Hom.* 16, 7: ... *potest interdum etiam a parte diaboli ad hominum notitiam futurorum venire praescientia.* For the devil's knowledge of the future, cf. *infra*, p. 69f.

[2] For δίκαιοι in this meaning, cf. *infra*, p. 123. ῥῆξαι is the reading in the quotation of this passage in Clement, *Strom.* I xvii 85, 4. A reads ῥάξαι, from ῥάσσω, 'to beat', 'to dash to the ground', cf. Bauer s.v. ῥήσσω. This is supported by the Latin versions (L¹: *deiciat;* L²: *adlidat*, cf. also E: *prosternat*) but (1) ῥῆξαι is the *lectio difficilior* and supported by an old witness, and (2) perhaps the two verbs converged in Koine, cf. Blass-Debrunner § 101.

[3] The phrase πρὸς τὸ κένωμα is peculiar, but to be understood in the context of Hermas' idea of full and empty. Κένωμα means 'state of emptiness' in a literal sense in Clement, *Paed.* II 10, 88, 2: τὸ κένωμα τῆς ὑστέρας, followed by the general statement τὸ γὰρ κενὸν πᾶν ἐπιθυμεῖ πληρώσεως, and in a spiritual sense in Clement, *Exc. Theodot.* 31, 3f.: The Aeon who fell in ἀγνωσία and ἀμορφία ... ὅθεν καὶ κένωμα Γνώσεως εἰργά-

and the answers are empty too.[1] This is another way of expressing the affinity between the false prophet and his adherents. It is taken up in the second part of the Mandate: the false prophet κολλᾶται τοῖς διψύχοις καὶ κενοῖς and speaks with them κατὰ τὰς ἐπιθυμίας αὐτῶν κενῶς· κενοῖς γὰρ καὶ ἀποκρίνεται (13). This correspondence in emptiness between the false prophet and his following is illustrated by a parable: the empty vessel which is placed with other vessels is not broken (when knocking against them, presumably) but all empty vessels harmonize with one another.[2]

In the paragraph which deals with the exposure of the false prophet in the congregation (14), κενός is, again, the key word, but this time it is used in a more pointed sense than previously because it is set off against its counterpart: the congregation into which he happens to come is identified as a συναγωγὴ πλήρης ἀνδρῶν δικαίων ἐχόντων πνεῦμα θεότητος (14) and again, as πνεύματα δικαίων (15): the congregation is full of the Spirit over against the emptiness of the false prophet and his followers. When the former happens to appear in the congregation, he is emptied (κενοῦται) and the earthly spirit flees from him. Yet the parable which follows to illustrate this emptying strikes a somewhat different note: if you stack wine or oil in a storeroom and one of the vessels placed there is empty, you will find it still to be empty when you unstack the room.[3] In the same way, the false prophet is exposed as what he was all the time. Logically, an empty prophet cannot be

---

σατο, cf. also Iren. A. H. I 4, 1. Τοῦ ἀνθρώπου refers to the man who puts his questions to the false prophet.

[1] The use of κενός is, of course, ambiguous: 'empty' and 'vain', cf. the proverb κενὰ κενοὶ βουλεύονται (Corpus Paroemiographorum Graecorum, ed. Leutsch-Schneidewin (Göttingen, 1839, repr. Hildesheim, 1965), I 270; II 119; 475). A similar use of κενός is found Soph., Antigone 707ff: ὅστις γὰρ αὐτὸς ἢ φρονεῖν μόνος δοκεῖ ἢ γλῶσσαν ἣν οὐκ ἄλλος ἢ ψυχὴν ἔχειν, οὗτοι διαπτυχθέντες ὤφθησαν κενοί.

[2] The exact rendering of the illustration is less easy than the grasping of its general meaning. συντιθέμενον usually means 'being put together', but pots are not broken by placing them together. Hence it is rendered 'placed together in such a way that it knocks against them' (cf. Bauer s.v.), as required by the context. συμφωνοῦσιν (plural, referring to τὰ κενὰ σκεύη as if personal beings, cf. Blass-Debrunner § 133) is best understood literally: they produce the same sound.

[3] Στιβάζω is used here in the same meaning as στοιβάζω 'to pack', 'to stack', cf. Liddell-Scott s.v. στοιβάζω and W. Crönert, G. G. A. 171 (1909), p. 656. ἀποστιβάζω is found only here and its meaning is clear from the context. The illustration is related to that in Mand. XII 5, 3 and may be Hermas' version of a proverb like the Dutch: "Er komt niet meer uit de kruik dan er in zit".

emptied, and for the moment the author, carried away by his own preoccupation with the idea of κενός, seems to forget that there was a spirit in the false prophet. But this preoccupation stems from the conviction that to be a Christian is, for Hermas, to have the Spirit.[1] The 11th Mandate is not the only place where κενός and its counterpart are used in such a pointed way. In the 5th Mandate the 'full in the faith' (τοὺς πλήρεις ὄντας ἐν τῇ πίστει) are contrasted with the 'empty and double-minded' (τοὺς ἀποκένους καὶ διψύχους ὄντας). The former are protected from the attempts of the evil spirit ὀξυχολία, because the δύναμις of the Shepherd is with them.[2] When this spirit succeeds to penetrate, the gentle Spirit which is in man is driven out and the man is henceforth empty of the Spirit and filled with evil spirits.[3] The same idea is found in the 12th Mandate. The empty fear the devil as though he had power, but those who are full in the faith strongly resist him.[4] In the same way, certain Christians who do not have the fruit of justice, are identified as empty of the Spirit and without the fruit of truth.[5]

All this goes to show that Hermas uses the word κενός in a personal sense to denote the absence of faith, or truth, or, especially, the Spirit. This usage is without precedent in early Christian literature. In another context we will see that, together with its counterpart, it must be understood as a creation of Hermas in order to make the two Spirits doctrine fit the conviction that a Christian is full of the Spirit.[6]

Yet these conclusions do not explain the emphatic use of κενός in the 11th Mandate. In this text it appears as many times as elsewhere,[7] and this suggests that Hermas may have had more compelling

---

[1] Cf. infra, p. 134f. It is, however, to be noted that it is not the prophet but the false prophet who claims to be πνευματοφόρος. This word is used in Hos. 9:7 LXX and Zeph. 3:4 LXX in a pejorative sense (irrespective of reading πνευματόφοροι or πνευματοφόροι in the latter place). It is not found in Philo and Josephus, nor in early Christian literature apart from this place. Obviously Hermas understood it to be characteristic of an alleged prophet to call himself πνευματοφόρος.. For later usage in bonam partem cf. Lampe s.v.

[2] Mand. V 2, 1.

[3] Ib. 2, 7, quoted supra, p. 34.

[4] Mand. XII 5, 2: ὅσοι δέ, φησίν, ἀπόκενοί εἰσιν, φοβοῦνται τὸν διάβολον ὡς δύναμιν ἔχοντα. Ib. 5,4: ὅσοι οὖν πλήρεις εἰσὶν ἐν τῇ πίστει, ἀνθεστήκασιν αὐτῷ ἰσχυρῶς.

[5] Sim. IX 19, 2: ἀπὸ δὲ τῆς πίστεως κενοί εἰσι καὶ οὐδεὶς ἐν αὐτοῖς καρπὸς ἀληθείας. Cf. also Sim. VI 2, 1: the angel of luxury and deception ἐκτρίβει τὰς ψυχὰς τῶν δούλων τοῦ θεοῦ τῶν κενῶν.

[6] Cf. infra, p. 134f.

[7] Including ἀπόκενος which does not occur in the 11th Mandate.

reasons to use it here than he had in other connections. This suspicion grows stronger when we see that he even ventures to transfer κενός from the empty man to the spirit which is in him and to forge the phrase κενὸν πνεῦμα which is logically impossible! But it is precisely this paradoxical phrase which, when viewed in its proper perspective, reveals the bitter conflict between Christian prophecy and hellenistic divination within the Christian community.

THE EMPTY SPIRIT

The phrase τὸ κενὸν πνεῦμα is not only illogical, but also very uncommon. It is found once in Irenaeus' *Adversus Haereses* and a few times in the Greek Magical Papyri. These occurrences provide some clues as to its provenance and its implications.

The one passage in Irenaeus in which the phrase τὸ κενὸν πνεῦμα occurs is *A.H.* I 13, 2. This is part of the account of the prophetic activities of the Gnostic teacher Marcus; between this account and the 11th Mandate there exist many similarities, to such an extent that we may safely assume that Irenaeus used materials of the 11th Mandate for his picture of Marcus. We will deal with this in more detail in the next chapter.[1] In the present context it is sufficient to state that Irenaeus will have borrowed the idea of the empty spirit from Hermas. Yet the context in which he uses it is very significant; he describes how, under the spell of Marcus, some woman starts to prophesy. She speaks ληρώδη καὶ τὰ τυχόντα πάντα κενῶς καὶ τολμηρῶς, ἅτε ὑπὸ κενοῦ τεθερμαμμένη πνεύματος. Like Hermas, Irenaeus ascribes this false inspiration also to an empty spirit through which the woman's soul is heated. As we shall see in the next chapter the idea of a soul becoming hot is not uncommon in hellenistic divination.[2] As a matter of course, Christian writers understood this idea in a vituperative sense. Irenaeus used it in order to identify Marcus and his women followers as pagan 'enthusiasts' in the popular sense of the word.

The idea of the empty spirit serves a related purpose because it identifies the spirit-agent of this 'enthusiasm. Irenaeus is at pains to make clear that this is not some *ad hoc* explanation of his own: it is corroborated by a quotation from someone called ὁ κρείσσων ἡμῶν, apparently indicating some person with authority for Irenaeus and

---

[1] Cf. *infra*, p. 64; 85; 103.
[2] Cf. *infra*, p. 93.

his readers.¹ This quotation is very remarkable : τολμηρὸν καὶ ἀναιδὲς ψυχὴ κενῷ ἀέρι θερμαινομένη. It is a corroboration of Irenaeus' statement, provided that ἀήρ and πνεῦμα are synonymous.² It shows that the idea of being heated or inspired by a spirit which is called κενός was not the invention of Hermas, but common property of second century Christianity, and served to identify the spirit at work in pagan divination.

So much for the function of the phrase τὸ κενὸν πνεῦμα. Yet this does not explain its origin nor the process by which it became suitable to this function. The origin cannot be found in the Hebrew-Christian realm because the phrase does not occur in the Septuagint or in the New Testament. Nor does κενός appear in texts relating to pagan gods or evil spirits.³

The occurrences of τὸ κενὸν πνεῦμα in the Magical Papyri are a different matter. Here the phrase does indeed appear but in a sense which is divergent from its use in Hermas and Irenaeus. In a London papyrus of the 4th century A.D. we find the invocation: ἐπικαλοῦμαι σέ, τὸν ἐν τῷ κενῷ πνεύματι δεινὸν καὶ ἀόρατον θεόν.⁴ The same invocation is found in a Greek passage in a demotic magical papyrus of the second or third century, and the μάγος adds the significant words: τὰς σὰς μαντείας ἐπιτέλλω.⁵ In this context the phrase ἐν τῷ κενῷ πνεύματι indicates the place where the invoked god is,⁶ and denotes a cosmological concept. In Hermas, however, it is a pneumatological concept. Why would Hermas borrow this phrase and reinterpret

---

¹ The identity of ὁ κρείσσων ἡμῶν is hard to ascertain. Harvey thinks of Polycarp or Pothinus (ad loc., p. 119). G. Fichter, Sprüche und Auslegungen der Presbyter des Irenäus, in Hennecke, Neutestamentliche Apokryphen (Tübingen, 1924²), p. 540-551, mentions also Melito from Sardes as a possibility, and thinks that, at least in I Prooem. 2; 13, 3; 15, 6; III 17, 4; 23, 3; IV 4, 2; 41, 2; V 17, 4, the sayings came to Irenaeus in a written form.

² This is explicitly stated in Plut., Placita Philos. 876 B: λέγεται δὲ συνονύμως ἀὴρ καὶ πνεῦμα but this is in a cosmological context. Conceivably, the phrase κενὸς ἀήρ has its roots in a popular philosophical idiom.

³ Significantly, Hebrew שׁוא 'vain', "nichtig" when referring to idols, is rendered by means of an adverbial phrase qualifying not the pagan idols but the main verb of the clause, cf. Jer. 18:15 where εἰς κενὸν ἐθυμίασαν renders לשׁוא יקטרו, and Ps. 31 (30):7 where ἐμίσησας τοὺς διαφυλάσσοντας ματαιότητας διὰ κενῆς renders (thou hatest) השׁתמרים הברי־שׁוא (διὰ κενῆς goes with φυλάσσοντας).

⁴ P. G. M. V 121 f. (Preis. I 184ff.).

⁵ Ib. XIVc 17 (Preis. II 132f.) Cf. also XII 367 (Preis. II 82, 4th century).

⁶ Cf. the parallel phrase ἐν τῷ στερεῷ πνεύματι in P. G. M. VII 961f. (Preis. II 42).

it to refer to the πνεῦμα of the devil who fills the false prophet with it ? The reason for such a transformation would have to be that for Hermas this phrase carried enough association with pagan divination to brand the man who had such a spirit, and his practices, as utterly pagan.

Such an explanation of the provenance of the idea of an empty spirit rests on the assumption that Hermas was familiar with the milieu and the language of magical divination. This assumption finds confirmation in a closer examination of the other terms relating to the spirit of the false prophet. This spirit is ἐπίγειον ... καὶ ἐλαφρόν, δύναμιν μὴ ἔχον (6). In the closing appeal of the Mandate, this is repeated in a slightly different and expanded form: τῷ δὲ πνεύματι τῷ ἐπιγείῳ καὶ κενῷ μηδὲν πίστευε, ὅτι ἐν αὐτῷ δύναμις οὐκ ἔστιν· ἀπὸ τοῦ διαβόλου γὰρ ἔρχεται (17).[1] When these statements are contrasted to those on the Spirit of the true prophet we get the following picture:

Spirit of the true prophet	Spirit of the false prophet
(a) ἀπὸ θεοῦ δοθέν	ἀπὸ τοῦ διαβόλου ἔρχεται
(b) ἄνωθεν	ἐπίγειον
(c) ἔχον ... δύναμιν	δύναμιν μὴ ἔχον

In this table there is no place for ἐλαφρόν and κενόν because they have no counterpart.[2] As for the contrasting phrases of the table, they appear nowhere else in Hermas except Mand. IX 11 where they refer to faith and double-mindedness.[3] They would be appropriate

---

[1] An interesting parallel of the correlation empty/powerless - full/effective is found in Corp. Herm. XVI 2 where it is said that the Greeks have λόγους ... κενούς, ἀποδείξεων ἐνεργητικούς, which is Greek philosophy; the text continues: ἡμεῖς δε οὐ λόγοις χρώμεθα, ἀλλὰ φωναῖς μεσταῖς τῶν ἔργων. As Festugière, in A. D. Nock - A.-J. Festugière, Corpus Hermeticum II (Paris, 1945), p. 232ff., n. 7, points out, it is the magical power of the Egyptian words that is envisaged. The same idea, but not in the context of magical power, is found in Did. 2, 5: ...ἔσται ὁ λόγος σου ... οὐ κενὸς ἀλλὰ μεμεστωμένος πράξει.

[2] The fact that these adjectives are placed between ἐπίγειον and the phrase which states that the earthly spirit is powerless suggests that ἐλαφρόν and κενόν are very close to one another in meaning. It is worth noting that Hermas is the only early Christian author to use ἐλαφρός in connection with a spirit (cf. also Mand. V 2, 4: ὀξυχολία -which is a πονηρότατον πνεῦμα - πρῶτον μὲν μωρά ἐστιν, ἐλαφρά τε καὶ ἄφρων.) It is not sure whether the word carried similar overtones as κενός. Mand. XII 4, 5: ὑμεῖς, οἱ κενοὶ καὶ ἐλαφροὶ ὄντες ἐν τῇ πίστει, suggests that in the 11th Mandate ἐλαφρός is, like κενός transferred from the man to the spirit in him.

[3] Only Mand. X 2, 6: τὸ πνεῦμα τὸ δοθὲν εἰς τὴν σάρκα ταύτην resembles ἀπὸ θεοῦ δοθέν but the underlying concept is different.

in the 2nd Mandate (where καταλαλιά and σεμνότης are contrasted), in the 5th Mandate (ὀξυχολία and μακροθυμία), and in the 10th Mandate (λύπη and ἱλαρότης). The fact that they appear only in connection with faith and double-mindedness, and with the issue of true and false prophecy is an indication that within the framework of the Two Spirits doctrine these two issues are distinct from the rest and belong closely together. This close connection is also apparent in the fact that the strong in the faith resists the false prophet and that the prophet is inspired in the assembly of righteous men who have faith in the divine Spirit.[1] To characterise this complex: faith/divine Spirit-double-mindedness/spirit from the devil, the author uses a traditional form from wisdom literature. This transpires when James 3:15-17 is compared. Here are contrasted a wisdom coming from above (ἄνωθεν κατερχομένη) and an earthly wisdom (ἐπίγειος, ψυχική, δαιμονιώδης).[2] Despite this close resemblance between Hermas and James, there is no reason to assume literary dependence.[3] It is rather a question of a common tradition. The idea that wisdom is a gift from God, or the gods, and comes from above is widespread in Antiquity.[4] It is also well known in Israel, especially in wisdom literature.[5] The connection between wisdom and Spirit is found as early as Exodus 31:3 and 35:31, where רוח and חכמה appear in juxtaposition.[6] It is elaborated in the Wisdom of Solomon. Wisdom is a φιλάνθρωπον πνεῦμα (1,6); in it is a πνεῦμα νοερόν (7, 22); wisdom and τὸ ἅγιον πνεῦμά σου are parallel (9, 17). From these traditions the sayings about a wisdom and a spirit coming from above will probably stem. That they are contrasted to an earthly counterpart is due to the dualistic mode of

---

[1] For this phrase cf. infra, p. 123f.

[2] It is worth noting that Hermas uses ἐπίγειος in the 11th Mandate only in connection with the spirit from the devil which is in the false prophet. In Mand. IX 11 it is used with reference to διψυχία which is an ἐπίγειον πνεῦμα.. This use suggests that it does not have moral connotations.

[3] Cf. Dibelius, Der Brief des Jakobus (Göttingen, 1959¹⁰), p. 194-197. ad loc.

[4] Cf. H. Gcse, art. Weisheit, R. G. G. VI³, c. 1574ff.

[5] G. von Rad, Weisheit in Israel (Neukirchen, 1970), p. 77ff., points out that the evidence which describes wisdom expressis verbis as a gift from Jahwe is found in later sources; he refers to Job, Proverbs, Qohelet and Daniel.

[6] The LXX develops this to a πνεῦμα θεῖον σοφίας.

thought which both James and Hermas betray.[1] For the latter, the saying is a means to bring out very sharply the fundamental and irreconcilable contrast between the Spirit of God and the spirit of the devil; between faith and its opposite, double-mindedness; between the prophet, the man of the Spirit, and the man of the spirit, the false prophet. What distinguishes them here is δύναμις. The Spirit has it, the spirit not. Now the connection between the Spirit and δύναμις is common enough in early Christian literature,[2] but not the contrast between the powerful Spirit and a spirit without power. Hermas' use of the concept of δύναμις elsewhere offers no clue.[3] In the context of the 9th and the 11th Mandate there is no definite indication how this presence or absence of power is experienced.[4] There is no reason to think of ἐνεργήματα δυνάμεων (1 Cor. 12:10) or similar events. The δύναμις remains unspecified. All this makes the contrast between the Spirit and the spirit the more emphatic. Does it, perhaps, contain a deeper note of conflict which is not obvious to the modern reader?

Two pointers present themselves. In the first place, the 11th Mandate states emphatically that consulting the false prophet is tantamount to idolatry.[5] This suggests that the contrast between Spirit and spirit is actually an integral part of the frontier conflicts between Christianity and paganism, or, more correctly since the false prophet operates

---

[1] But the contrast between the earthly wisdom (σοφία ... χαμαὶ ἐρχομένη) and the wisdom which ἄνω πρὸς τὰ οὐράνια βλέπει, θεῶν συνόμιλος, in Heliodorus, *Aethiop.* III 16 (quoted by Windisch, *Die kathol. Briefe, H. N. T.,* (Tübingen, 1951), p. 25 on Jas 3:13-18) shows that such a contrast may also appear where no such dualism exists. Cf. also the remarkable ἀρχή-formula in the Leyden Magical Papyrus J 384 (*P. G. M.* XII, 327ff., Preis. II 80): ἠκούσθη μου τὸ πνεῦμα ὑπὸ πάντων θεῶν καὶ δαιμόνων, ἠκούσθη μου τὸ πνευμα ὑπὸ πνεύματος οὐρανοῦ, ἠκούσθη μου τὸ πνεῦμα ὑπὸ πνεύματος ἐπιγείου, κτλ.

[2] They are more or less synonymous in Lk. 1:17, 35; Acts 1:8; 10:38; 1 Cor. 2:4; Eph. 3:16; 1 Thess. 1:5. Elsewhere δύναμις characterizes πνεῦμα, cf. e.g. Lk. 4:14.

[3] This use is varying; relevant to our investigation are the following areas: (1) Often δύναμις is connected with the Spirit but in an indirect way, cf. e.g. *Mand.* V 2, 1: ἡ δύναμις τοῦ κυρίου μετ'αὐτῶν ἐστιν, referring to τοὺς πλήρεις ὄντας ἐν τῇ πίστει where the idea of the presence of the Spirit is underlying; the same applies to μακροθυμία (V 2, 3: ἰσχυρὰν δύναμιν ἔχουσα) and πίστις (IX 11: ἔχει δύναμιν μεγάλην); also the power of prayer (X 3, 2; *Sim.* II 5) rests on the same idea (2) The maidens, who are ἄγια πνεύματα, δυνάμεις εἰσὶ τοῦ υἱοῦ τοῦ θεοῦ (*Sim.* IX 13,2). As their names betray (15, 2) they are moral powers, effective in good works (14, 1), cf *infra,* p. 133.

[4] *Mand.* XI 14 describes the clash of the Spirit and the spirit, but does not deal with the question of δύναμις.

[5] Cf. *Mand.* XI 4. and *supra,* p. 34f.

within the church, pagan intrusion in the Christian community. Secondly, the reason why the earthly spirit has no power is important; ἀπὸ τοῦ διαβόλου γὰρ ἔρχεται,[1] and in the devil is no power either.[2] The context in which the latter statement is made reveals perfectly what kind of power is meant. The devil, says Hermas, σκληρός ἐστι καὶ καταδυναστεύει αὐτῶν, but the Shepherd assures him that the devil cannot do that to those servants of the Lord who hope in him with all their heart: δύναται ὁ διάβολος ἀντιπαλαῖσαι, καταπαλαῖσαι δὲ οὐ δύναται.[3] When they believe in the Lord they will have δύναμιν τοῦ κατακυριεῦσαι τῶν ἔργων τοῦ διαβόλου.[4] These phrases are significant because they belong to the language of demonology.[5] The concept of power is to be understood in terms of possession. This throws a new light on the powerless spirit of divination. Power is a key word in magical texts generally, and in those relating to divination in particular.[6] It is an attribute of the gods and demons who are involved.[7] The magicians and diviners boast of its possession.[8] And finally the magic or divinatory act displays δύναμις,, or is itself called δύναμις[9].

---

[1] Ib., 17.

[2] Cf. Mand. VII 2; XII 4, 6.

[3] Mand. XII 5, 1f.

[4] Ib., 6.

[5] For κατακυριεύω (also Mand. VII 2) cf. Acts 19:16; for καταδυναστεύω cf. Acts 10:38 and Plut., Isid. et Osir. 367 D: the Egyptians always call Typhon Seth, ὅπερ ἐστὶν καταδυναστεῦον ἢ καταβιαζόμενον; for καταπαλαίω cf. Lucian, Cont. 8: καταπαλαισθεὶς [ὑπὸ] τοῦ θανάτου. With ἐν αὐτῷ δύναμις οὐκ ἔστι καθ' ὑμῶν (Mand. XII 4, 6) cf. P. G. M. XII 303 (Preis. II 78): δύνασθαι καὶ ἰσχύειν κατὰ πάντων and the δύναμις κατὰ σκορπίων of the scorpion stone (J. Röhr, Der okkulte Kraftbegriff im Altertum (Leipzig, 1923), p. 9).

[6] Cf. Röhr, op. cit., passim; F. Preisigke, Vom göttlichen Fluidum nach ägyptischer Anschauung (Berlin, 1920); id., Die Gotteskraft in frühchristlicher Zeit (Berlin, 1922).

[7] Cf. e.g. P. G. M. I 192 (Preis. I 12): ταῦτα (i.e. various divinatory practices) εὖ ἀνύει ὁ κραταιὸς πάρεδρος. Ib. XIII 130f. (II 66): μέγα δυναμένῳ δαίμονι. Ib. XIII 714 (II 119): (after an enumeration of what the invoked god will do) δύναται γὰρ πάντα ὁ θεὸς οὗτος. Ib. XXXVIII 5 (II 176): (invocation of an unnamed goddess) δεῦρό μοι, τὴν δύναμιν ἔχουσα.

[8] Cf. e.g. ib. XII 258ff. (II 75f.): τέλεσόν μοι τήνδε τὴν πρᾶξειν ἐπὶ τῷ φοροῦντί μοι τήνδε τὴν δύναμιν ἐν παντὶ τόπῳ, ἐν παντὶ χρόνῳ ... φοροῦντί μοι ταύτην δύναμιν.

[9] Of magic acts, cf. e.g. ib. III 282 (I 44): προγνωστικὴ πρᾶξις πᾶσαν ἐνεργίαν ἔχουσα Ib. IV 1719 (I 126): πρᾶξις ἡ καλουμένη ξίφος, ἧς οὐδέν ἐστιν ἴσον διὰ τὴν ἐνέργειαν. Ib. 2565 (152): a certain prayer-formula δύναται πάντα ἐπιτελεῖν. δύναμις as a magic act. e.g. IV 1333 (I 116): ἀρκτικὴ δύναμις πάντα ποιοῦσα. Ib. VII 918 (II 40): ἔστιν δὲ ἰσχυρὰ ἡ δύναμις. Magic objects also have δύναμις, cf. e.g. XIII 742 (II 121): ἐπιγνοὺς

All this goes to show that the emphatic denial of the earthly spirit's power serves the same purpose as the branding of this spirit as being empty, namely to denounce divination on request as idolatry; at the same time it confirms the assumption that Hermas was familiar with the milieu and the language of magical divination, and it is a preliminary indication of his *Sitz im Leben*: he is to be placed somewhere near the borderline between Christianity and the world of hellenistic divination and magic.

So much for the false prophet and the spirit that inspires him. It remains to deal briefly with the Spirit which is the counterpart of that spirit. To the characteristics of the Spirit mentioned above[1] must be added a feature which is very important to Hermas: every Spirit which comes from God, οὐκ ἐπερωτᾶται ἀλλὰ ... ἀφ' ἑαυτοῦ λαλεῖ πάντα (5). This is transferred from the Spirit to the prophet in the next part of the Mandate (8). This feature serves also to bring out the fundamental antithesis between prophecy and divination. We will give due attention to it when we examine the picture of the prophet.[2]

So far, the 11th Mandate has yielded the picture of a bitter conflict between Christian prophecy and hellenistic magic divination, between the man through whom the Spirit speaks ἀφ' ἑαυτοῦ and the man who gives his oracles on request. But, in the last analysis, it is a conflict between the divine Spirit and the spirit of the devil, as is brought out so poignantly by the use of κενός: the διάκρισις πνευμάτων in the next part of the Mandate ends with the emptying of the false prophet: κενοῦται ὁ ἄνθρωπος ἐκεῖνος, καὶ τὸ πνεῦμα τὸ ἐπίγειον ἀπὸ τοῦ φόβου φεύγει ἀπ' αὐτοῦ (14).

(b) Distinguishing the Spirits (6-16)

The second part begins with a question from Hermas: How will one[3] know which is the prophet and which is the false prophet? The function of this question has already been examined in our analysis of the literary structure of the Mandate, as has also the specific structure of this part.[4] It is worth noting that ὁ προφήτης means

---

... τῆς βίβλου τὴν δύναμιν. *Ib.* 359 (105): of cinnamon: αὐτῷ γὰρ ὁ θεὸς τὴν δύναμιν περιέθηκε, also 101 (92) and 656 (117).

[1] Cf. *supra*, p. 43.

[2] Cf. *infra*, pp. 98f.

[3] Ἄνθρωπος is here equivalent to the indefinite pronoun, cf. Bauer, s.v. 3aβ.

[4] Cf. *supra*, p. 29.

'the true prophet' without additional qualifying adjective. This shows that, different from Hebrew where נביא refers to true and to false prophets, the noun προφήτης is not a *vox media*. This is common Christian usage, and it is clear that from the outset Hermas' account of the distinguishing of the prophets moves along the lines of early Christian traditions.[1]

The Shepherd urges Hermas to test the prophet and the false prophets by the standards which he is about to set forth (ὥς σοι μέλλω λέγειν); he uses δοκιμάζειν, the technical term for the testing of prophets,[2] teachers,[3] or other ministers of the church.[4] These standards, however, are brought together under the heading ζωή: ἀπὸ τῆς ζωῆς δοκίμαζε τὸν ἄνθρωπον τὸν ἔχοντα τὸ πνεῦμα τὸ θεῖον. This statement is balanced by that concerning the false prophet at the end of this part: δοκίμαζε οὖν ἀπὸ τῶν ἔργων καὶ τῆς ζωῆς τὸν ἄνθρωπον τὸν λέγοντα ἑαυτὸν πνευματοφόρον εἶναι (16). The addition ἀπὸ τῶν ἔργων shows that ζωή has here the meaning 'way of life'. This meaning is not common in Hermas, nor in early Christian literature in general.[5] Since it is used in a comprehensive sense and refers not only to moral conduct but also to the behaviour as a prophet or false prophet its meaning must not be defined too narrow.

THE 'LIFE' OF THE PROPHET

After this introduction follows the description of the standards by which Hermas can recognize the man who has the Spirit from above. It consists of two parts. The first, introduced by πρῶτον μέν, describes his behaviour as a Christian and as a prophet; the second, introduced by οὖν, relates his prophetic ministry in the congregation. At this juncture we will restrict ourselves to his behaviour as a Christian since the other aspects will be examined at length in chapters V and VI.

---

[1] For Greek usage cf. *supra*, p. 34, n. 4.

[2] Cf. *Did.* 12, 1: δοκιμάσαντες αὐτὸν γνώσεσθε, referring to itinerant prophets.

[3] Cf. 1 Jn 4:1: δοκιμάζετε τὰ πνεύματα, referring to teachers who are found to be false prophets, cf. *infra*, p. 59; 67f.

[4] 1 Tim. 3:10 (of deacons); 1 Clem. 42, 4; 44, 2 (of bishops and deacons appointed by the apostles, and of their successors). Cf. also *Const. Apost*, II 1, 3; 2, 3; 3, 1; III 16, 1; VII 31, 1.

[5] In Hermas only in the 11th Mandate; elsewhere it denotes "Heilsgut", cf. Dib., p. 498f. Bauer, s.v. ζωή, does not mention the meaning 'way of life'. The verb ζάω sometimes refers to conduct, cf. e.g. Lk. 15:13, Bauer s.v. 3a.

The man who has the Spirit from above is gentle and quiet and humble and abstains from all wickedness and futile desire of this world. Also, he makes himself more needy than all men. The adjectives πραΰς, ἡσύχιος and ταπεινόφρων or related words often occur together in early Christian paraenetic.[1] Some passages suggest that the qualities which they express are the fruit of the Spirit,[2] but these qualities are expected of all Christians, and not of the prophets or other πνευματικοί in particular.[3] To abstain from all wickedness and from all futile desire of this world is, again, something which all Christians should do and which they are called upon to do throughout all the work of Hermas.[4] There remains the clause ἑαυτὸν ἐνδεέστερον ποιεῖ πάντων τῶν ἀνθρώπων. The same expression occurs in Mand. VIII 10 in an enumeration of what Christians should do by all means and on which they are not to be restrained.[5] Again, it is normal Christian conduct that is expected of the prophet. This has a bearing on Hermas' concept of prophecy: the first requirements of a prophet is that he is a believer of good Christian behaviour.[6] It follows that

---

[1] Cf. Mt. 11:29 (πραΰς καὶ ταπεινός); 1 Pet. 3:4 (πραέος καὶ ἡσυχίου πνεύματος); Eph. 4:2 (ταπεινοφροσύνης καὶ πραΰτητος); Barn. 19:4 (πραΰς ... ἡσύχιος); Ign., Eph. 10:2 (πραεῖς ... ταπεινόφρονες). For the specific biblical connotation of ταπεινός and related words, cf. Kwa Joe Liang, Het begrip deemoed in I Clemens (Utrecht, 1951), p. 69-127.

[2] Cf. 1 Pet. 3:4; Gal. 5:22f.; 6:1.

[3] For certain overtones of πραΰς and ἡσύχιος cf. infra, p. 121. In Pseudoclement., Epistula de Virginitate I 11 (ed. Funk-Diekamp II, p. 21f.) those who have received a χάρισμα πνευματικόν are called upon to serve the church ἐν πάσῃ ταπεινοφροσύνῃ καὶ πραότητι.

[4] 'Απέχομαι is a common term in early Christian paraenetic, cf. Acts 15:20, 29; 1 Thess. 4:3; 5:22; 1 Pet. 2:11; Did. 1, 4; 1 Clem. 17, 3; Ign., Philad. 3, 1. It is very frequent in Hermas, a sign that the contact with the outside world was more of a problem for him than for the other Christian authors.

[5] The exact meaning of ἐνδεής in this connection must be the same in Mand VIII 10 and XI 8. The literal rendering (cf. Lake, "makes himself poorer than al men") which is suggested by what follows in VIII 10 (χρεώστας μὴ θλίβειν καὶ ἐνδεεῖς) implies the idea of voluntary poverty which is not found elsewhere in Hermas. Vis. III 1, 2 (ἐνδεὴς ... εἰς τὸ γνῶναι πάντα) is not relevant because the meaning 'more eager than all other people to receive revelations' makes no sense in Mand. VIII 10. When interpreted in a figurative way (cf. Liddell-Scott s.v. 3), as suggested by L²: hominibus omnibus se humiliorem praestat (cf. L¹ and L² in Mand. VIII 10: humilior), it comes close to ταπεινόφρων, rendered as humilis in L¹. Probably, the latter refers to the inner disposition and the phrase ἑαυτὸν ἐνδεέστερον ποιεῖ πάντων τῶν ἀνθρώπων to the corresponding behaviour.

[6] Cf. infra, p. 97.

Dibelius' judgment, "Das entscheidende Kriterium ist das sittliche", is correct in this sense only that the moral criterion serves to distinguish the false prophet from the true Christians. So much for the prophet as a Christian. Since his prophetic behaviour and ministry will be dealt with in later chapters, we may leave him for the moment and turn to the description of the false prophet.[1]

THE 'LIFE' OF THE FALSE PROPHET

The opening line of this description does not refer to the false prophet personally but to the spirit which is in him. The definition of this spirit here differs from that given in 6 on two points: instead of ἐλαφρόν it is called κενόν and the qualification μωρόν is added. The former has already been dealt with above.[2] The addition of μωρόν is another example of how adjectives referring to persons or their dealings may be transferred to the evil πνεῦμα which is active in them.[3]

With characteristic ease the writer turns from the spirit to the man. The following points are raised: (a) his aspirations: he elevates himself

---

[1] The clause οὕτως οὖν φανερὸν ἔσται τὸ πνεῦμα τῆς θεότητος is the proper close of the section 8-10; the omission of οὖν in P^ox is due to the fact that the quotation there is yet to be followed by an explanatory clause. The second clause: ὅση οὖν περὶ τοῦ πνεύματος τῆς θεότητος τοῦ κυρίου ἡ δύναμις αὕτη, is probably a corrected corruption. To mark the change of the subject from περὶ τοῦ πνεύματος τῆς θεότητος to περὶ τοῦ πνεύματος τοῦ ἐπιγείου, a clause like ὅσα οὖν περὶ τοῦ πνεύματος τῆς θεότητος ταῦτα would have been appropriate. Somehow, the words τοῦ κυρίου ἡ δύναμις were inserted, perhaps as a correction of κενοῦ καὶ δύναμιν appearing in the next line and possibly written twice inadvertently, and subsequently corrected into τοῦ κυρίου ἡ δύναμις. Finally, ὅσα and ταῦτα may have been adjusted and changed into ὅση and αὕτη. The ancient versions vary considerably: talis est vis Spiritus Domini (E) is a simplification of the Greek text of A; quae autem ad agnoscendam virtutem illius spiritus sancti pertinent, haec sunt (L²), appears to be a reinterpretation of A, omitting κύριος and introducing the idea of recognition. L¹ connects it with the preceding clause: sic ergo dinoscitur spiritus divinitatis quia quicumque (v. 1. quaecumque) spiritu divinitatis loquitur, loquitur sicut dominus vult. This is a comment on the closing words of 9: καθὼς ὁ κύριος βούλεται, and probably an attempt to deal with the inappropriate τοῦ κυρίου in the Greek. Most translators render the Greek text, 'such is the power of the Lord concerning the Spirit of the deity', but in the text as it stands τοῦ κυρίου before ἡ δύναμις is emphatic. This is brought out by Snyder: "So whatever power pertains to the spirit of the deity is of the Lord", but in the context this emphasis is pointless.

[2] Cf. supra, p. 41ff.

[3] Referring to persons μωρός is used in Sim. VIII 7, 4: πάντες οὗτοι μωροί εἰσιν, and IX 22, 4: μωροὶ καὶ ἀσύνετοι if this reading is correct. In Mand. V 2, 4 ὀξυχολία, which is a πονηρότατον πνεῦμα, is called μωρά, ἐλαφρά τε καὶ ἄφρων.

and wants to have a seat of honour; (b) his conduct: he is bold and shameless and talkative; he lives in great luxury and in many other pleasures; and, worst of all, he accepts money for his prophecies; and (c) his attitude in the church: he avoids meeting with righteous men, but clings to the double-minded, and is finally exposed in the congregation. Several of these points are discussed in the next chapter and may be passed over here.

(a) The false prophet is introduced as the man who thinks he has the Spirit.[1] A little below he is called 'the man who says that he is a Spirit-bearer'. This introduction is typical of his aspirations: because he is a πνευματικός he elevates himself and claims the πρωτοκαθεδρία. This is the contrasting counterpart of the prophet's behaviour whose humility and gentleness were emphasised (8). Warnings against self-elevation and striving after the seat of honour are sometimes found together in early Christian paraenetic. In Matthew 23:1-12 Jesus' complaint about the scribes and the Pharisees who love the πρωτο-κλισία at feasts and the πρωτοκαθεδρία in the synagogues is followed by the well-known saying "whoever exalts himself will be humbled and whoever humbles himself will be exalted".[2] This saying is also reflected in apostolic and post-apostolic warnings.[3]

As Dibelius points out, self-recommendation is an essential characteristic of what he calls "synkretistischen Prophetentums".[4] It is noteworthy that the only people in the book of Hermas who are said to be ὑψοῦντες ἑαυτούς are the ἐθελοδιδάσκαλοι of Sim. IX 22, 1-3, probably an allusion to Gnostic teachers.[5] Whether πρωτοκαθεδρία refers to an official position of leadership in the church[6] is to be doubted

---

[1] Ὁ δοκῶν may be deliberately ambiguous; he thinks he has the Spirit, and, understood in a conative sense, he tries to give the impression that he has the Spirit.

[2] Cf. also Lk. 14: 11 in a comparable context (πρωτοκλισία); 18:14.

[3] Cf. Jas 4:10; 1 Pet. 5:6; Did. 3, 9; Barn. 19:3.

[4] P. 540. He refers to Acts 8:9; Origen, c. Celsum VII 8; Mart. Petri et Pauli 15; Pseudoclem., Recogn. III 47; Iren. A. H. I 13, 1; Lucian, Alex. 24; Peregr. 12. Apollonius of Tyana appears to have been different, cf. G. Petzke, Die Traditionen über Apollonius von Tyana und das Neue Testament (Leiden, 1970), p. 187ff, who shows that Apollonius preferred "Titel aus der geistigen Sphäre wie σοφός und φιλόσοφος". Cf. also H. D. Betz, Der Apostel Paulus und die sokratische Tradition (Tübingen, 1972), p. 73ff.

[5] This does not make the false prophet a Gnostic teacher, cf. infra, p. 65f.

[6] Elsewhere πρωτοκαθεδρία appears to refer to such a position, cf. Mt. 23:6; Mk 12:39; Lk. 20:46, referring to the lawyers and the Pharisees; Vis. III 9,7: τοῖς προηγουμένοις τῆς ἐκκλησίας καὶ τοῖς πρωτοκαθεδρίταις, explicitly referring to church leaders.

52   THE ELEVENTH MANDATE

in view of the fact that he prophesies only κατὰ γωνίαν and avoids
the meetings of the congregation. Dibelius thinks that it refers to
striving after "alter prophetischer Autorität gegenüber den προη-
γούμενοι",[1] conceivably a position as reflected in *Didache* 13.[2] In
the present context, however, it is best understood as a claim to that
authority which the prophet naturally has when he speaks καθὼς ὁ
κύριος βούλεται. Since the false prophet has nothing to say because
he is not inspired by the Spirit, he must claim this authority explicitly.[3]

(b)   The conduct of the false prophet concerns his attitude in public
(he is ἰταμὸς καὶ ἀναιδὴς καὶ πολύλαλος), and his way of life. The
former will be dealt with in the next chapter since it has a bearing
on his behaviour as a prophet.[4] As to his way of life he lives ἐν τρυφαῖς
πολλαῖς καὶ ἐν ἑτέραις πολλαῖς ἀπάταις. This is typically the idiom
of Hermas and it denotes a life in sinful luxury.[5] It is one of the common
features in the description of false teachers and prophets, sometimes
in rather general, sometimes in more specific terms. The false teachers
of the 2nd letter of Peter are characterised as ἐντρυφῶντες ἐν ταῖς
ἀπάταις αὐτῶν.[6] The Gnostic μάγος Marcus and his disciples are reported
to have seduced many women.[7] The false prophets which the *Ascension
of Isaiah* mentions are inspired by the spirit of error and fornication
and conceit and the love of gold.[8] The same features are found outside
Christianity. Alexander of Abonuteichos is criticised for his sexual
wantonness.[9] Peregrinus is reported to have lived in great luxury
on funds of the Christians.[10]

---

[1] P. 541.

[2] Αὐτοὶ (i.e. the prophets) γάρ εἰσιν οἱ ἀρχιερεῖς ὑμῶν.

[3] Conceivably, the opening scene (cf. *supra*, p. 30f) may reflect the πρωτοκαθεδρία
of the false prophet.

[4] Cf. *infra*, p. 91ff.

[5] Apart from a few exceptions all occurrences of τρυφή and ἀπάτη and related words
in early Christian literature are found in Hermas. Here they occur often together. Cf.
Sim. VI *passim.* For the atmosphere which they evoke, cf. *Mand.* XII 2, 1: ἐπιθυμία
γυναικὸς ἀλλοτρίας ἢ ἀνδρὸς καὶ πολυτελείας πλούτου καὶ ἐδεσμάτων πολλῶν ματαίων καὶ
μεθυσμάτων καὶ ἑτέρων τρυφῶν πολλῶν καὶ μωρῶν.

[6] 2 Pet. 2:13; cf. also vv. 2f., and Jude 12ff.

[7] Cf. Iren., *A. H.* I 13, 4: some women confessed καὶ κατὰ τὸ σῶμα ἠχρειῶσθαι ὑπ'
αὐτοῦ (i.e. Marcus), καὶ ἐρωτικῶς πάνυ αὐτὸν πεφιληκέναι. 5: καὶ μαθηταὶ δὲ αὐτοῦ τινες ...
ἐξαπατῶντες γυναικάρια πολλὰ διέφθειραν.

[8] *Asc. Is.* III 28.

[9] Cf. Lucian, *Alex.* 39. 41f., and H. D. Betz, *Lukian von Samosata und das Neue
Testament* (Berlin, 1961), p. 114ff.

[10] Cf. Lucian, *Peregr.* 16.

The most astonishing thing in his behaviour, however, is that he accepts money for his prophecies; if he is not paid he does not prophesy. The length and emphasis with which the author dwells on this subject betrays how important this question is to him, and this is surprising. In the Christian church the rule is that the labourer deserves his wages.[1] This rule is applied to the prophets explicitly in the Didache,[2] but when a prophet ἐν πνεύματι says: δός μοι ἀργύρια ἢ ἕτερά τινα, οὐκ ἀκούσεσθε αὐτοῦ (11, 12). Even if the prophet is entitled to be supported by the believers, it is improper for him to ask for any remuneration. This is a common Jewish-Christian conviction as appears from comments on 1 Sam. 9:8 ('I have with me the fourth part of a shekel, and I will give it to the man of God to tell us our way') by writers as far apart as Josephus[3] and Theodoret.[4] Hence Apollonius, the ecclesiastical writer, rebukes the Montanist prophetess Priscilla for having accepted gold and silver and expensive clothes.[5] But it is to pagan divination that the accusation of accepting payment is usually directed.[6] Nor does it come from the Christian side only. It is much older than that. Creon's complaint: τὸ μαντικὸν γὰρ πᾶν φιλάργυρον γένος,[7] echoes widespread sentiment.[8] Cicero mentions and rejects: eos qui quaestus causa hariolentur.[9] Alexander of Abonuteichos charged one drachme and two obols for each oracle which

---

[1] Cf. Lk. 10:7; 1 Cor. 9:13f; 1 Tim. 5:17f.

[2] 13, 1: πᾶς δὲ προφήτης ἀληθινός, θέλων καθῆσθαι πρὸς ὑμᾶς, ἄξιός ἐστι τῆς τροφῆς αὐτοῦ. The prophets must receive the first fruit of the wine press and the threshing floor and of cattle and sheep: αὐτοὶ γάρ εἰσιν οἱ ἀρχιερεῖς ὑμῶν (13, 3).

[3] Josephus, Ant. VI 48: Saul and his servant ὑπὸ ἀγνοίας τοῦ μὴ λαμβάνειν τὸν προφήτην μισθὸν ἐπλανῶντο.

[4] Theodoret, Quaest. in I Reg. 368f. (Migne 80, 549): τοῦτο τῆς Σαοὺλ ὑποψίας οὐ τῆς τοῦ προφήτου δωροδοκίας τεκμήριον. The story shows τοῦ προφήτου τὸ ἀδωροδόκητον.

[5] Euseb., H. E. V 18, 4: δοκεῖ σοι πᾶσα γραφὴ κωλύειν προφήτην λαμβάνειν δῶρα καὶ χρήματα; ὅταν οὖν ἴδων τὴν προφῆτιν εἰληφυῖαν καὶ χρυσὸν καὶ ἄργυρον καὶ πολυτελεῖς ἐσθῆτας, πῶς αὐτὴν μὴ παραιτήσωμαι;

[6] Cf. e.g. Euseb., Praep. Evang. IV 2, 5 (134b): the seers often promise recovery and salvation to the sick, κἄπειτα πιστευθέντες ὡς δὴ θεοὶ καὶ τῆς ἐνθέου ταύτης ἐμπορίας μεγάλους τοὺς μισθοὺς εἰσπραξάμενοι.

[7] Sophocles, Antigone 1055. Whether Eurip., Helena 755f. and Iphig. Aul. 520, to which Jebb ad loc. refers, are also relevant is doubtful.

[8] Cf. Aristophanes, Aves 960ff; Pax 1052-1127. Plato, Politeia II 364 B: ἀγύρται δὲ καὶ μάντεις ἐπὶ πλουσίων θύρας ἰόντες πείθουσιν ὡς ἔστι παρὰ σφίσι δύναμις ἐκ θεῶν. Isocrates Aegin. 5ff (385): Thrasyllus who inherited books on divination from a μάντις and as an itinerant diviner (πλανὴς γενόμενος) ... οὐσίαν πολλὴν ἐκτήσατο.

[9] De Divinatione I 58.

amounted to seventy or eighty thousand drachmas a year.[1] The Chaldaean diviner Diophanes, *non parvas stipes, immo vero mercedes opimas iam consecutus*, charged a hundred denarii for each oracle.[2] All this explains the emphatic rejection of accepting payment for prophecies in the 11th Mandate: it is part of the conflict between prophecy and divination. He who accepts money once more gives himself away as a pagan diviner within the Christian church.[3]

(c) The following paragraph describes the relationship of the false prophet to the church. He stays away from the meeting of righteous men, because if he happens to appear there he will be unmasked as having only the earthly spirit and that spirit will flee from him.[4] The company with which he surrounds himself are double-minded and empty. This takes up the description of his adherents in 2-4 and adds to it one important detail: κατὰ γωνίαν αὐτοῖς προφητεύει, in contrast to the prophet who does not speak καταμόνας. This is not the usual practice of pagan diviners who give their oracles in public.[5] The meetings of the false prophet and his followers are secret because what they practice is forbidden in the church.[6] At the same time their secrecy discredits them; not only in the eyes of their fellow Christians,[7] but also of their pagan environment.[8] In this paragraph κενός is, as we

---

[1] Lucian, *Alex.* 23: ἐτέτακτο δὲ καὶ ὁ μισθὸς ἐφ᾽ ἑκάστῳ χρησμῷ δραχμὴ καὶ δυ᾽ ὀβολώ.

[2] Apuleius, *Metam.* II 13, 2. Cf.Val. Max I 3, 3: the Chaldaei were expelled from Rome by C. Corn. Hispalus in 139 B.C., *levibus et ineptis ingeniis ... quaestuosam mendaciis suis caliginem injicientes*; Gellius XIV 1, 1: *Chaldaei ... aeruscatores et cibum quaestumque ex mendaciis captantes*. Others were prepared to prophesy at lower prices, cf. Max. Γυρ. 13, 3 (Hobein): τῶν ἐν τοῖς κύκλοις ἀγειρόντων ... οἳ δυοῖν ὀβολοῖν τῷ προστυχόντι ἀποθεσπίζουσιν. Juven. VI 546f.: *aere minuto qualiacumque voles Judaei somnia vendunt.*

[3] The subject deserves a more thorough treatment; Professor W. C. van Unnik is preparing a study on the subject under the title, "Evangelium gratis dandum".

[4] Cf. *infra*, p. 72f.

[5] Cf. *supra* p. 31, n. 1, and the so called χρησμοὶ αὐτόφωνοι which Alexander issued through the statue of Asclepius (Lucian, *Alex.* 26).

[6] Cf. *infra*, p. 80.

[7] Cf. Acts 26:26: οὐκ ἔστιν ἐν γωνίᾳ πεπραγμένον τοῦτο, and Haenchen *ad. loc.* This refers to the facts of the Gospel and its preaching. Against Celsus' criticism why God sent the Spirit into one corner (εἰς μίαν γωνίαν) if it was his purpose to deliver the human race from evil (Orig., *c. Cels.* VI 78, cf. also IV 23; 36) Origen replies: ἔμελλεν ἐκχεῖσθαι ἀπὸ μιᾶς γωνίας ὁ λόγος ἐπὶ πᾶσαν τὴν οἰκουμένην (cf. also V 50). Tatian, *Oratio ad Graecos* 26, 3: τοὺς λόγους ἐπὶ τὰς γωνίας ἀποκρύπτετε referring to pagan philosophers.

[8] To do something ἐν γωνίᾳ is discrediting, Cf. Plato, *Gorgias* 485D: to the man who devotes himself to philosophy ὑπάρχει ... ἀνάνδρῳ γενέσθαι φεύγοντι τὰ μέσα τῆς πόλεως καὶ τὰς ἀγορὰς ... καταδεδυκότι δὲ τὸν λοιπὸν βίον βιῶναι μετὰ μειρακίων ἐν

have seen, the key word.[1] After our detailed examination of the rest of this part of the 11th Mandate we may conclude that for Hermas this word was more than just an important word, but in a certain sense a code-word, and capable of carrying all the associations and overtones which expose him to whom the word is applied as false, comparable, in its own way, to ψευδο- in the word ψευδοπροφήτης. It brings out, not that the false prophet does not speak the truth, nor that he falsely claims the title 'prophet', but that it is not the Spirit from God which is in him but the spirit of the devil which is the spirit of pagan divination.

(c) *"Trust the Spirit" (17-21)*

The last part of the Mandate contains the commandment proper: trust the Spirit which comes from God, do not trust the earthly and empty spirit. This injunction is found at the beginning and, in a slightly different and shortened form, at the end. Between them a parable is placed which consists of two pairs of illustrations.[2] The two illustrations

---

γωνίᾳ τριῶν ἢ τεττάρων ψιθυρίζοντα. Themistius, *Orat.* XXII (265b), mentions would-be philosophers, οἳ σφίσιν ἀποχρῆν ὑπειλήφασιν ἐν γωνίᾳ μόνῃ πρὸς τὰ μειράκια ψιθυρίζειν, φεύγειν δὲ τὰ μέσα τῆς πόλεως cf. also *Orat.* XXIII (284b): (the adversaries) εἰς τοὐμφα-νὲς προελθεῖν οὐκ ἐθέλουσιν ... ἀλλ' ἐν γωνίαις που καταδεδύκασιν ἢ χηραμοῖς. In XXVIII (341d): οἱ δὲ ἀπὸ Σωκράτους γενεᾶς ... φρίττουσί τε καὶ εὐλαβοῦνται τὰς ἀγορὰς ... καὶ οὐκ ἀνέχονται παρακύπτειν ἔξω τοῦ σκίμποδος καὶ τῆς γωνίας. XXXIV 12: τὴν ἐν ταῖς γωνίαις φιλοσοφίαν, cf. also XXVI (322b). Cicero, *De Oratore* I 13, 56f.: on subjects like *de dis immortalibus, de pietate, de concordia*, etc., *clamabunt omnia gymnasia atque omnes philosophorum scholae sua esse haec omnia propria, nihil omnino ad oratorem pertinere. Quibus ego ut his de rebus in angulis consumendi otii causa disserant cum concessero*, etc.; *De Republ.* I 2: the greatest use of virtue is ... *earum rerum quas isti* (i.e. *philosophi*) *in angulis personant, reapse non oratione perfectio.* Epict. II 12, 17: τὸν γὰρ ποιοῦντα αὐτό (i.e. Socratic dialectics) οὐκ ἐν γωνίᾳ δηλονότι δεήσει ποιεῖν. Plut., *An Seni Resp.* 788B: an old man who is still active is a σεμνὸν θέαμα, ὁ δ'ἐν κλίνῃ διημερεύων ἢ καθήμενος ἐν γωνίᾳ στοᾶς φλυαρῶν καὶ ἀπομυττόμενος εὐκαταφρόνητος. *De Curios.* 516 B: curious people are anxious to learn τί δ'ὁ δεῖνα καὶ ὁ δεῖνα καθ'ἑαυτοὺς ἐν τῇ γωνίᾳ διελέ-γοντο. Lucian, *Deorum Conc.* 1 : Zeus calling to order the meeting of the gods says: μηκέτι τονθορύζετε, ὦ θεοί, μηδὲ κατὰ γωνίας συστρεφόμενοι, κτλ. There are, however, other aspects to this problem. Jesus retires with his disciples κατ' ἰδίαν, cf. Mk 6:32 parr.; and the school of Pythagoras is reported to have been a closed secret community, cf. E. Zeller, *Die Philosophie der Griechen* I, 1 (Leipzig, 1923⁷), p. 400 and references there.

[1] Cf. *supra*, p. 39ff. where the rest of this part of the Mandate is expounded.

[2] Apparently, τὴν παραβολὴν ἣν μέλλω σοι λέγειν refers to all illustrations which follow since it is not repeated before any of them. παραβολή is used here in a different

of each pair have an identical meaning, and thus tend to reinforce each other.[1] The first pair brings two *adunata*:[2] throw a stone up to heaven and see if you can touch it;[3] take a water pump, squirt up to heaven and see if you can make a hole in heaven.[4] Both are impossible, ἀδύνατα, and so are the earthly spirits ἀδύνατα, powerless.[5] This takes up the emphatic denial of δύναμις with regard to the earthly spirits discussed above.[6] The illustrations are useful to Hermas because he takes them not metaphorically but literally. They describe unsuccessful attempts to reach heaven and, hence, can be used to illustrate the lack of power of the earthly spirits. The other pair describes movements from above, ἄνωθεν:[7] the hail is a very small grain, but when it falls on somebody's head it hurts;[8] the drop which falls from the roof makes a hole in a stone.[9] Again, Hermas takes the

---

way from its use elsewhere in Hermas. Its usual meaning is an enigmatic vision or saying which needs to be explained in detail. Here, however, the parable functions as an illustration the meaning of which is obvious, cf. Bauer s.v. 3; F. Hauck, art. παραβολή, *Th. W. N. T.* V, p. 758f.

[1] Such use of parallel pairs is very common in the synoptic parables, cf. J. Jeremias, *Die Gleichnisse Jesu* (Göttingen, 1956[4]), p. 76ff.; it is also a well-known feature in the Lucan writings, cf. R. Morgenthaler, *Die lukanische Geschichtsschreibung als Zeugnis, Gestalt und Gehalt der Kunst des Lukas* (Zürich, 1949) *passim*.

[2] Cf. G. van der Leeuw, Adunata, *Jaarbericht Ex Oriente Lux* 8 (1942), p. 631-641.

[3] An adaptation of the proverb λίθοις τὸν Ἥλιον βάλλει (*Corp Paroem. Graec.* II 759), cf. εἰς οὐρανὸν τοξεύεις (*ibid.* I 68. 344; II 27). The explication of the paroemiographi is: ἐπὶ τῶν διακενῆς πονούντων but Hermas uses it in a literal sense and transforms it into an *adunaton*.

[4] The pump which the text refers to is the fire engine, cf. Hammer-Jensen, art. Siphon, *P. W. R. E.*, III, c. 268f., Hero Alex. I 28: οἱ δὲ σίφωνες, οἷς χρῶνται εἰς τοὺς ἐμπρησμούς. Hesych. s.v. ὄργανόν τι εἰς πρόεσιν ὑδάτων ἐν τοῖς ἐμπρησμοῖς. Plin., *Epist ad Traj.* 33, 2: (in a report on a big fire in Nicomedia) *nullus usquam in publico sipho.* Isid., *Etym.* XX 6, 9. Apollodorus, *Poliorc.* 174, 4 (*Abh. Königlicher Gesellschaft der Wiss. zu Göttingen, Philol.-hist. Klasse* 1908, p. 36f.): the ὄργανον ὃ καλεῖται σίφων is used ἔαν που ἀκρωτήριον καίηται δυσεπίβατον i.e. when the water had to be squirted up. Seneca, *Controv.* X, *praef.* 9, mentions the rhetor Musa who, speaking *de siphonibus*, used to say: 'Caelo refluunt', which in its own way comes close to Hermas' saying. Whether the latter is also some kind of a proverb is uncertain.

[5] Hermas' double use of ἀδύνατα is made clear by ἀδρανῆ, 'impotent', 'weak', which interprets the second ἀδύνατα.

[6] Cf. *supra*, p. 43ff.

[7] This takes up the use of ἄνωθεν with regard to the Spirit in 5 and 8.

[8] Probably also an adapted proverb, but it is not yet traced. It contains also the well-known motif of the small thing which has great effect, cf. Mk 4:31 parr., Mt 17:20 par.

[9] An adaption of a well-known proverb, cf. Lucretius, *De Rerum Nat.* I, 313: *stilicidi*

illustrations literally because of ἄνωθεν and so makes them serve his purpose well: what comes from above has great power. This paves the way for the final injunction: trust the Spirit from above, refrain from the other.

This concludes our treatment of the 11th Mandate as a whole. All concepts and materials which the author uses serve a single purpose, namely to picture the contrast between the prophet and the false prophet and what they stand for: on the one hand the Spirit, the church and the faithful, on the other hand, the spirit of the devil, paganism and the double-minded Christians. The subsequent chapters will fill in further details of this picture and thus enable us to view it in the wider perspective of the history of early Christianity and its environmment

---

casus lapidem cavat; other examples in A. Otto, *Die Sprichwörter und sprichwörtlichen Redensarten der Römer* (Leipzig, 1890, repr. Hildesheim, 1962) p. 156f. The point of the proverb is usually that expressed by Ovid., *Ep. ex Ponto* IV 10, 7: *tempus edax igitur praeter nos omnia perdit*, but Hermas makes it serve his purpose by stressing the idea of falling from above.

CHAPTER FOUR

PROPHECY AND DIVINATION

The issue of false prophecy is no doubt the primary concern of Hermas in the 11th Mandate. It is appropriate, then, to begin our detailed investigation here. First, we will analyse the concept or concepts of false prophecy that prevailed in the Christian church of the first and second century A.D., and try to determine the place of the false prophet as described by Hermas within this framework. Next the criteria by which false prophets are judged will be examined. As the false prophet in the 11th Mandate acts as a μάντις (2), our third concern will be that of the relationschip between prophecy and divination. Finally, we will attempt to gain a picture of his divinatory activities in the light of the pagan divination of his time.

THE CONCEPT OF FALSE PROPHECY

When we attempt to identify the false prophet of the 11th Mandate we need a framework within which to place him. A survey of the most important data on false prophets in Christian sources may serve to provide such a framework.

To begin with the New Testament, we can distinguish four types of false prophets: (a) itinerant false prophets; (b) apocalyptic false prophets; (c) pagan false prophets; (d) false teachers.

(a) The reference to false prophets in Matthew 7:15: προσέχετε ἀπὸ τῶν ψευδοπροφητῶν οἵτινες ἔρχονται πρὸς ὑμᾶς ἐν ἐνδύμασιν προβάτων, ἔσωθεν δέ εἰσιν λύκοι ἅρπαγες, refers to itinerant Christian prophets. They are branded false because they do not show forth the fruits that might be expected from them (vv. 16-20). As this is also the basic thought of vv. 21-23 these may be considered as an elaboration of v. 15f. Then v. 22 gives a description of what the false prophets do: they prophesy, they cast out demons and they perform miracles; and they think that all this shows that they are genuine prophets. But their behaviour is totally incompatible with their prophetic activities and that reveals them as false prophets. Though the content of their prophetic utterances is not disclosed, it is probable that the false prophets envisaged here are not teachers but claimed to be inspired speakers of the word of the Lord.[1]

(b) The references to apocalyptic prophets are found in Mark and Matthew, and in the Apocalypse of John. In the latter ψευδοπροφήτης occurs only in the singular and does not refer to an existing false prophet but denotes an eschatological *topos*.[2] In the first two Gospels the word occurs in Mark 13:22 // Matthew 24:24 together with ψευδόχριστοι. In Matthew 24:11 it occurs alone. Whether real false prophets are referred to is doubtful. Also here we may have to do with a *topos*. If, however, the reference is to actual prophets they are of the same type as those mentioned above under (a) because they attempt to authenticate themselves and their message by means of signs and miracles.

(c) There is one reference to a ψευδοπροφήτης who operates in the pagan world, namely Acts 13:6ff. Here the most surprising thing is that a Jewish μάγος practices his divinatory and magical trade at the court of a Roman governor, and that he is called ψευδοπροφήτης. This implies an admission of some common ground between the (Christian) prophet and the pagan diviner and shows that ψευδοπροφήτης could also be used in the conflict between Christianity and its pagan environment.[3]

(d) In 1 John the situation is totally different. Here the content of their teaching discloses the false prophets as what they are. This does not mean that the denial of Jesus Christ's coming in the flesh was the only doctrine they taught. It is quite natural to assume that the false prophets were teachers. The prophetic and the teaching ministry overlap, and Schnackenburg rightly compares the ψευδοδιδάσκαλοι in 2 Peter 2:1.[4] This does not exclude the presence of true prophets

---

[1] Cf. *supra*, p. 8f. That it refers to Jewish figures, either Zealots comparable to the false porphets which Josephus mentions as Schlatter, *Der Evangelist Mattheus* (Stuttgart, 1948), p. 251ff. thinks, or exorcists like Bar-Jesus (Acts 13:6ff.), is improbable, since in either case the phrase ἐν ἐνδύμασιν προβάτων would be inappropriate. Conceivably, this phrase refers to "die asketische Standestracht der jüdischen Propheten" (O. Böcher, Wölfe in Schafspelzen; zum religionsgeschichtlichen Hintergrund von Matth. 7, 15, *Theol. Zeitschrift* 24 (1968), p. 405-426, esp. p. 412), and serves to identify those who wear the sheep's clothing as prophets.

[2] Apoc. 16:13;19:20; 20:10. The close connection between the false prophet and the beast suggests that a typical, not an actual prophet is envisaged.

[3] Cf. H. Conzelmann, *Die Apostelgeschichte*, H. N. T. 7 (Tübingen, 1963), p. 73f.; *ad loc.*

[4] R. Schnackenburg, *Die Johannesbriefe*, H. Th. K. N. T. XIII 3 (1963²) p. 213.

among the readers of 1 John, nor does it mean that the false prophets presented their teachings "begeistert" as Schnackenburg is inclined to think.

When we turn to the postapostolic sources we can distinguish a twofold use of the word ψευδοπροφήτης: it is used (a) in a more general way, and (b) in a more specific way.

(a) The famous 11th chapter of the Didache is the first post-apostolic text to mention false prophets. It is not necessary to study this passage in detail. What concerns us here is the way in which the word ψευδοπροφήτης is used. It is applied to itinerant apostles who stay longer than one or two days in a congregation: Every apostle who comes to you should be received as the Lord. But he should not remain more than one day, and if there is some necessity, also another: τρεῖς δὲ ἐὰν μείνῃ, ψευδοπροφήτης ἐστίν. (11, 4f.). It is remarkable that the writer does not say ψευδαπόστολος¹ which would be natural after πᾶς ... ἀπόστολος.

When this is compared to 9: καὶ πᾶς προφήτης ὁρίζων τράπεζαν ἐν πνεύματι, οὐ φάγεται ἀπ᾽ αὐτῆς, εἰ δὲ μήγε ψευδοπροφήτης ἐστί, it is evident that ψευδοπροφήτης is applicable to both and that there exists no clear distinction between 'apostle' and 'prophet' in the mind of the writer.² Together with 1 John 4:1ff this means that from the end of the first century the term ψευδοπροφήτης was applicable to any teacher or preacher within the Christian community who, either by his teaching or by his conduct, betrayed himself as being false. The emphasis is increasingly being laid on 'false', and the idea of 'prophet' is in the process of losing its specific meaning.

This process is evident in Justin and Eusebius. The latter quotes Hegesippus as saying that with Theboutis began the corruption of the church by the seven heresies to which he belonged.³ After naming

His opinion that in the New Testament the false prophets never act as the antitype of the charismatic prophets of the primitive church rests on an interpretation of Mt. 7:15 which differs from that of the present writer, cf. *supra*, p. 58. It is interesting that in 2 Pet.2:1 the ψευδοδιδάσκαλοι are compared to the ψευδοπροφῆται of the Old Testament past.

¹ Cf. 2 Cor. 11:13; Apoc. 2:2.

² Cf. R. A. Kraft, *Barnabas and the Didache*, *The Apostolic Fathers, A New Translation and Commentary*, Vol. 3 (New York, 1965) p. 170f. J. P. Audet, *La Didachè, Instruction des Apôtres* (Paris, 1958). p. 441ff. does not mention this aspect of the problem.

³ *H. E.* IV 22, 5f.; ὧν καὶ αὐτὸς ἦν means that Theboutis was an adherent of the ἑπτὰ αἱρέσεις.

the groups that proceeded from the seven heresies[1] he continues (6): ἀπὸ τούτων ψευδόχριστοι, ψευδοπροφῆται, ψευδαπόστολοι, οἵτινες ἐμέρισαν τὴν ἕνωσιν τῆς ἐκκλησίας φθοριμαίοις λόγοις κατὰ τοῦ θεοῦ καὶ κατὰ τοῦ χριστοῦ αὐτοῦ.[2] This sentence is clearly meant to characterize the heretical groups named before. The absence of ψευδοδιδάσκαλοι is remarkable as this would be more fitting than any of the three words that are used. The use of ψευδόχριστοι is especially striking, but when we compare two passages in Justin the picture is clear. In Dial. 35,3 he quotes a contamination of Matthew 24:11 and 24, but reads ψευδοαπόστολοι instead of ψευδοπροφῆται as in Matthew. This may be due to the fact that a quotation of Matthew 7:15 preceeds where ψευδοπροφῆται occurs and perhaps Justin wanted to avoid repetition. At first sight the quotations seem to apply to those Christians whom Tryphon mentions who eat εἰδωλόθυτα. But, in what follows, Justin makes it refer to heretical groups called after the name of the men ἐξ οὗπερ ἑκάστη διδαχὴ καὶ γνώμη ἤρξατο. Mentioned by name are the Marcionites, the Valentinians and the followers of Basilides and Saturnilus who are also mentioned by Hegesippus. In Dial. 82, 1f. Justin says that τὰ προφητικὰ χαρίσματα had been transferred from the Jews to the Christians, and just as there had been ψευδοπροφῆται in the days of the old prophets, so παρ'ἡμῖν νῦν πολλοί εἰσι καὶ ψευδοδιδάσκαλοι, and with reference to them once again Matthew 24:11 and 24 are quoted, this time, however, with ψευδοπροφῆται. It appears that the nouns compounded with ψευδο- are almost interchangeable and have lost their own distinctive meaning.

The texts quoted above have two common elements. They quote or reflect the sayings of Jesus about the false prophets in Matthew 7:15 and 24:11, 24 — sayings which the writers see fulfilled in their own time —, and they refer to heretical teachers. Both elements are also found together in Irenaeus, A.H. III 16,8f.: omnes extra dispositionem sunt qui sub obtentu agnitionis alterum quidem Jesum intellegunt, alterum autem Christum ... qui a foris quidem oves per eam quam habent extrinsecus loquellam similes nobis apparent...intrinsecus vero lupi.

---

1 'Ἀφ'ὧν and ἀπὸ τούτων which procede the names of the various teachers and groups may mean that they belonged to them (cf. K. Lake's rendering, "Of these were ..."), or that they derived from them, preferably the latter.

2 The combination ψευδόχριστοι, ψευδαπόστολοι and ψευδοπροφῆται also Acta Petri et Pauli c. 60 (ed. Lipsius-Bonnet I, p. 205) and Mart. Petri et Pauli 39 (ib., p. 152).

With reference to them 2 John 7f. and 1 John 4:1-3 are quoted. The latter is quoted as follows: *Multi pseudoprophetae exierunt in saeculo* ... But in the next paragraph mention is made of *subdivisiones malorum magistrorum*.

Two further comments are in order. In the first place this use of ψευδοπροφήτης is not limited to Gnostic teachers. It is applicable to all whose teaching is false or heretical;[1] also Jesus' sayings about the false prophets are not applied to false teachers only but also to Montanist prophets.[2] Secondly, this equation of false prophets and false teachers may well imply a similar equation of prophecy and teaching, and suggests that prophecy as a distinctive ministry was declining.

(b) There are in Irenaeus passages which represent another area where ψευδοπροφήτης is applicable, but the concept of false prophecy is different. In *A.H.* IV 33,1 the true believer is described as follows: *vere spiritualis recipiens Spiritum Dei, qui ab initio in universis dispositionibus Dei adfuit hominibus et futura annuntiavit et praesentia ostendit et praeterita enarrat,*[3] *judicat quidem omnes, ipse autem a nemine judicatur* (1 Cor. 2:15). Then follows a long and detailed account of all who are judged by the spiritual disciple, and of their doctrine: Jews, Marcion, the disciples of Valentinus, the Gnostics who are disciples of Simon Magus, the Ebionites and *eos qui putativum inducunt*, i.e. those who introduce the idea of δόκησις, the mere appearance of Christ. Then the text continues: *Iudicabit autem et pseudoprophetas, qui non accepta a Deo prophetica gratia nec Deum timentes, sed aut propter vanam gloriam aut ad quaestum aliquem aut et aliter secundum operationem mali spiritus fingunt se prophetare, mentientes adversus Deum* (33, 6).

Obviously, the false prophets are distinguished from the other groups mentioned before;[4] but otherwise their identification is not sure. The use of terms like *prophetica gratia* and *prophetare* suggests that they specifically claimed to be inspired prophets. This looks

---

[1] Cf. e.g. Origen *in Matth. comm. ser. 47* (Lommatzsch. IV 298): *qui autem Marcionis vel alicuius eorum predicant verbum falsum, prophetae sunt antichristi eius qui est secundum Marcionem. Et alii falsi prophetae sunt mendacii illius quod est secundum Basilidem, alii autem eius quod est secundum Apellem ... qui ecclesiastice docent verbum, prophetae sunt Christi.*

[2] Cf. Euseb., *H. E.* V 16, 8: some people who heard the outburst of ecstatic utterances of Montanus, ἐπετίμων καὶ λαλεῖν ἐκώλυον, μεμνημένοι τῆς τοῦ κυρίου διαστολῆς τε καὶ ἀπειλῆς πρὸς τὸ φυλάττεσθαι τὴν τῶν ψευδοπροφητῶν ἐγρηγορότως παρουσίαν.

[3] For this tripartite formula cf. *infra*, p. 77ff.

[4] And of those who follow, namely *qui schismata operantur* (33, 7).

like a new semantic development after the gradual loss of the distinctive meaning of ψευδοπροφήτης, or, rather a regaining of the specific meaning. This has to do with the specific claim of the prophetic charisma by the false prophets. It is tempting to think of the movement of Montanus which made just that claim, and indeed we find several occurrences of ψευδοπροφήτης — or a related word — referring to the Montanists.[1] If this is true, it would point to an early stage of Montanism because the false prophets are still within the Christian church and distinguished from the schismatics.

When we compare the picture in the 11th Mandate with Irenaeus' description, there are striking parallels. The false prophet has not a πνεῦμα ἀπὸ θεοῦ δοθέν (5), i.e. no *prophetica gratia*; he elevates himself and claims for himself πρωτοκαθεδρίαν (12), which corresponds to *vanam gloriam* in Irenaeus; he accepts money for his prophecies and if he is not paid he does not prophesy at all, i.e. he prophesies *ad quaestum aliquem*.[2] The πνεῦμα which is in him is the spirit of the devil, which corresponds with *secundum operationem mali spiritus*. He says ἑαυτὸν πνευματοφόρον εἶναι (16), i.e. *fingit se prophetare*. And like the false prophets who are judged and condemned by the truly spiritual disciple, he is emptied by the congregation of men who have the divine Spirit (14). The false prophet of Hermas belongs clearly to the type of false prophets described by Irenaeus in *A.H.* IV 33, 6: people who claim the gift of prophecy but who prophesy under the influence of the spirit of the devil. It is this claim, and its denial, which distinguishes them from the false teachers whose doctrine is judged to be false. This raises the question whether the false prophet of Hermas is a Montanist. This is on chronological and geographical grounds very improbable.[3] When there are similarities the most we can say is that they are analogies, not the result of a historical relationship.

---

[1] Cf. e.g. Euseb. *H. E.* V. 16-18 *passim*; Irenaeus *A. H.* III 11, 9.

[2] For the motives of *vana gloria* and *quaestus*, cf. *supra*, p. 51ff.

[3] The outbreak of Montanism was either in 156 or in 172, cf. G. S. P. Freeman-Grenville, The Date of the Outbreak of Montanism, *J. E. H.* 5 (1954), p. 7-15. Though the latter date is now generally accepted, both dates are too late to admit of connections between Hermas and Montanism. It appears also that the beginning Montanist movement did not spread outside Asia Minor, cf. K. Aland, Bemerkungen zum Montanismus und zur frühchristlichen Eschatologie, *Kirchengeschichtliche Entwürfe* (Gütersloh, 1960), p. 139).

64 PROPHECY AND DIVINATION

The distinction between false prophets and false teachers made above is of a typological nature and not necessarily an exact description of historical facts. This appears when we compare Irenaeus' account of the Gnostic prophet Marcus in *A.H.* I 13 with the false prophets of IV 33 and Hermas. Since we deal with the terms on which the false prophets are judged we leave aside the description of Marcus' magical and prophetical activities (this will concern us presently) and turn immediately to the criteria of judgment. They are represented as the insights of the women who refuse to be initiated as prophetesses. They know, says Irenaeus, ὅτι προφητεύειν οὐχ ὑπὸ Μάρκου τοῦ μάγου ἐγγίνεται τοῖς ἀνθρώποις, ἀλλ' οἷς ἂν ὁ θεὸς ἄνωθεν ἐπιπέμψῃ τὴν χάριν αὐτοῦ, οὗτοι θεόσδοτον ἔχουσιν τὴν προφητείαν, καὶ τότε λαλοῦσιν ἔνθα καὶ ὁπότε θεὸς βούλεται, ἀλλ' οὐχ ὅτε Μάρκος κελεύει (13, 3). Again, the decisive point is from whom the gift of prophecy comes. As in Hermas and Irenaeus, in the case of the true prophet it comes from God. Whatever the claims of the false prophets may be, they have not received the Spirit of God. Whatever spirit is in them, or works and speaks through them, comes from the devil (ὑπὸ τοῦ Σατανᾶ ἐκπεμπόμενα). And the financial motive is not absent in the case of Marcus: χρημάτων πλῆθος πολὺ συνενήνοχεν. This shows that, in Irenaeus' understanding, Marcus is a prophet, or rather a false prophet of the specific type. Yet he goes on to deal with his teaching just as he does with the teaching of the other heretics. On the strength of all the evidence set forth above we may conclude that there are two concepts of false prophecy in the Christian church from the latter part of the first century A.D. onwards. The first is the more general of the two and refers not only or specifically to prophets, but to teachers as well. The noun element ψευδο- which is found in the substantives used within the area of this concept refers primarily to their utterances and their teaching, and only implicitly to themselves. The verbal meaning is predominant, but προφήτης has lost its specific force.

The second is the more specific, and stresses the specific prophetic element: the prophet, whether true or false, is inspired and commissioned. If he is inspired by the Holy Spirit and commissioned by God, he is truly a prophet. If he is inspired by the spirit of the devil, he is ψευδῶς a prophet. The nominal meaning is predominant and -προφήτης denotes the inspired speaker.

It is clear that the false prophet whom Hermas describes is of the second type. It is, however, conceivable that, like Marcus, he belongs to a group to which the first concept also applies. Already in 1865

Lipsius argued in a lengthy paper that the picture of the false prophet in Hermas fits the Gnostics perfectly.[1] Dibelius, though disagreeing with Lipsius on some points, admitted that chronologically his interpretation was very convincing.[2] Lipsius' argument is as follows: the comparison with pagan divination fits the heretical Gnostics just as in the Pseudoclementine writings the roots of false prophecy are found in paganism. Also προφητεύειν κατὰ γωνίαν or κατὰ μόνας applies to the Gnostic teachers who used to operate on an individual basis and tried to gather adherents and to form a school of followers. Occasionally, they even tried to speak in the gathered congregation, but as a rule they avoided meetings with others than their own followers. The question which people bring to the false prophet, τί ἄρα ἔσται αὐτοῖς (2) is interpreted by Lipsius in the light of Vis. III 4, 3 where it is said of the δίψυχοι that they debate in their hearts εἰ ἄρα ἔστιν ταῦτα ἢ οὐκ ἔστιν which he takes to express doubt as to the parousia and the judgement and the resurrection of the flesh.

Lipsius' view raises several questions. The first concerns the description itself of the false prophet. Does it contain allusions to Gnostic teachings? We have dealt with this question already implicitly when we discussed Snyder's interpretation of the 11th Mandate.[3] What the false prophet tells his listeners has nothing to do with teaching, because their questions do not refer to doctrine or knowledge, but to their personal future. Admittedly, the people around the false prophet are δίψυχοι, just as the people for whom the visions are revealed to Hermas (Vis. III 4, 3) but it does not follow that in both places the questions are alike.[4]

It is, however, conceivable that Hermas contains polemics against Gnosticism to such an extent that it is at least probable to see the

---

[1] R. A. Lipsius, Der Hirt des Hermas und der Montanismus in Rom, *Zeitschrift für wissenschaftliche Theologie* VIII (1865), p. 266-308, IX (1866) p. 27-81, 183-218. His views about the false prophet on p. 75ff.

[2] P. 538f.

[3] Cf. *supra*, p. 27.

[4] In *Vis.* III 4, 3 the answer is, therefore, in terms of truth (ταῦτα πάντα ἐστὶν ἀληθῆ), and here in terms of personal fate (αὐτοῖς — for questions of this nature, cf. infra, p. 83f.). For the concept of δίψυχος cf. *supra* p. 32f. Also ἀπατάω (*Mand.* XI 13: ἀπατᾷ αὐτούς) has in Hermas a moral rather than a doctrinal connotation, cf. *Sim.* VII 2, 1: καταστρέφει αὐτοὺς ἀπὸ τῆς ἀληθείας, ἀπατῶν ταῖς ἐπιθυμίαις ταῖς πονηραῖς: the turning away from the truth is effected by deceiving people by evil desires, cf. also the combination of τρυφή and ἀπάτη in *Sim.* VI *passim*, and *supra*, p. 52.

false prophet as a representative of this movement. In 136 A.D.
Valentinus came to Rome[1] and hence we may look for traces of anti-
gnostic polemics in Hermas. Lipsius quotes *Sim.* V 7, 2; VIII 6, 5
and IX 22, 1-2. The first is a warning against underestimating one's
own flesh as being mortal and misusing it in some defilement.[2] That
human flesh is mortal is not an exclusively Gnostic idea.[3] In VIII 6, 5
(ὑποκριταὶ καὶ διδαχὰς ἑτέρας εἰσφέροντες καὶ ἐκστρέφοντες τοὺς δούλους
τοῦ θεοῦ, μάλιστα δὲ τοὺς ἡμαρτηκότας, μὴ ἀφίοντες αὐτοὺς μετανοεῖν)
it is very doubtful whether Gnostic teachers are envisaged since the
main point against the hypocrites is that they do not allow the sinners
to repent.[4] Finally IX 22, 1 refers to people who are πιστοὶ μέν,
δυσμαθεῖς δὲ καὶ αὐθάδεις καὶ ἑαυτοῖς ἀρέσκοντες, θέλοντες πάντα
γινώσκειν καὶ οὐδὲν ὅλως γινώσκουσι. They want to be ἐθελοδιδάσκαλοι. This is probably an allusion to Gnostic teachers as appears
from the pointed use of γινώσκειν. But this allusion is of a very
general nature and applies to their presumptions rather than to the
contents of their doctrine.

In summary we may conclude that there is very little in Hermas
which refers to controversies with Gnostic teachers, and this makes
it very improbable that the false prophet is a Gnostic teacher who
practices divination. Only the second, not the first concept of false
prophecy applies to him.

DISTINGUISHING THE PROPHETS

After identifying the false prophet as belonging to those who specifically claim to be inspired and commissioned prophets we may well
ask the question which Hermas puts to the Shepherd: How will a
man know which of them is a prophet and which is a false prophet ? (7).

---

[1] Cf. Irenaeus *A. H.* III 4, 3: Οὐαλεντῖνος μὲν γὰρ ἦλθεν εἰς 'Ρώμην ἐπὶ 'Υγίνου. Joly,
p. 38f.

[2] *Sim* V 7, 2: βλέπε, μήποτέ σου ἐπὶ τὴν καρδίαν ἀναβῇ τὴν σάρκα σου ταύτην φθαρτὴν
εἶναι καὶ παραχρήσῃ αὐτῇ ἐν μιασμῷ τινι.

[3] This idea is often found connected with a rejection of the resurrection; for an account
of the controversies on the resurrection in the second century A. D., cf. W. C. van Unnik,
The Newly Discovered Gnostic 'Epistle to Rheginos' on the Resurrection, *J. E. H.* 15
(1964), p. 141-167, esp. p. 156-165; Van Unnik shows that the "battle had to be fought
on various fronts, ... against criticism of the pagans, against doubts among church-
members, against the opposing tenets of Gnosticism" (p. 156).

[4] Cf. Snyder, p. 123; Dibelius, p. 596, however, thinks that Gnostic teachers are
envisaged who hold that repentance is superfluous; cf. also Joly, p. 37, 277.

This question arises whenever there is doubt about a prophet. The διάκρισις πνευμάτων is the crux of all prophecy. A brief survey of the various ways of testing a prophet will follow, in order to view the ways of Hermas in their proper perspective.

There are four ways. A prophet may be tested:
(a) on the basis of the doctrine he presents;
(b) on the basis of the outcome of his prophecies;
(c) on the basis of his moral life;
(d) on the basis of the spirit which is in him.

Logically and theologically, these tests are not of the same order. The first three are tests of the results of the spirit, the fourth tests the nature of the spirit by itself.

(a) In the case of teaching prophets the doctrinal tests is indicated as soon as Christian doctrine has become sufficiently developed to serve as a criterion. This is not yet so in the earliest evidence: 1 Corinthians 12:3. ΚΥΡΙΟΣ ΙΗΣΟΥΣ is not a credal statement but a confession which expresses the core of primitive Christian faith. Paul's statement that no one can say "Jesus is Lord" except by the Holy Spirit, expresses that everyone who utters this acclamation had received the Spirit. It is not so much a criterion as a sign by which the presence of the Spirit can be observed.[1] There is evidently no danger that the content of the Κύριος - acclamation was somehow jeopardized. When this happens a criterion is needed which can be applied. This is the situation in 1 John 4:1-3. The confession that Jesus Christ has come in the flesh is a criterion by which the spirits can be tested. But this does not mean that it is an external instrument which can be applied independently, and is meant to replace the διάκρισις πνευμάτων as an act of the Spirit. The same letter stresses the fact that the church is endowed with the Spirit by referring to the ointment which the believers have received.[2] The doctrinal criterion can be applied by the church only under the guidance of the Spirit.

---

[1] Cf. Robertson and Plummer, *A Critical and Exegetical Commentary on the First Epistle of St Paul to the Corinthians* (Edinburgh, 1914), p. 261f., *ad loc.*: "every loyal Christian is inspired". T. Holz, Das Kennzeichen des Geistes, *N. T. S.* 18 (1972), p. 374: "... da wo Jesus als Kyrios bekannt wird, da muss es der Geist sein, der wirkt". Lietzmann, *op. cit.*, p. 60f., interprets the acclamation as a mark by which the true "Geistbegabter" can be recognised.

[2] Cf. 2:20: καὶ ὑμεῖς χρῖσμα ἔχετε ἀπὸ τοῦ ἁγίου, and that is why they all know the truth concerning the liar who denies that Jesus is the Christ, cf. also v. 27f. χρῖσμα

The process which in the course of the 2nd century led to the emergence of fixed creeds, is well known and need not be described here. The greater the fixity, the greater the authority of the church as an institution, and the end of this development with regard to the doctrinal testing of the prophets is well expressed in Origen's words: *qui ecclesiastice docent verbum, prophetae sunt Christi*.[1]

The doctrinal criterion is shaped and whetted in the great controversies between the church and the heretics. How difficult it is to use it when the core of the faith is not at stake can be seen in Hermas. It is not applied in the 11th Mandate because neither the prophet nor the false prophet are pictured as teachers, and only indirectly in *Sim*. VIII 6,5,[2] because no connection between the rejection of the second repentance and any creed is indicated. This is, again, an indication that Hermas lived before the great controversies. But even in the midst of those controversies, in the Montanist crisis, the doctrinal criterion proved inadequate. It is absent in the oldest accounts preserved in Eusebius.[3] Later writers acknowledge openly that, as far as the heart of the Christian faith was concerned, there were no essential points of difference between the church and the Montanists, yet are of one accord with the older witnesses in their rejection of Montanus and the prophetesses as false prophets.[4]

(b) When prophecy includes an element of prediction it may be judged on the basis of its outcome. Deuteronomy 18:21f. states: 'If you say in your heart, 'How may we know the word which the Lord has not spoken?' — when a prophet speaks in the name of the Lord, if the word does not come to pass or come true, that is a word which the Lord has not spoken'. The same principle is involved in Jeremiah 28:9: 'As for the prophet who prophesies peace, when the word of that prophet comes to pass, then it will be known that the Lord has truly

---

refers to the Spirit as the use of χρίω elsewhere (Lk. 4:18; Acts 4:27; 10:38; 2 Cor. 1:21) indicates.

1 Cf. *supra* p. 62, n. 1.
2 Cf. *supra* p. 66.
3 *H. E.* V 16-18.
4 Cf. Hippolytus, *Ref.* VIII 19: οὗτοι τὸν μὲν πατέρα τῶν ὅλων θεὸν καὶ πάντων κτίστην ὁμοίως τῇ ἐκκλησίᾳ ὁμολογοῦσι καὶ ὅσα τὸ εὐαγγέλιον περὶ τοῦ χριστοῦ μαρτυρεῖ. Epiphanius, *Panar*. 48, 1, 1: οὗτοι οἱ κατὰ Φρύγας καλούμενοι δέχονται πᾶσαν γραφήν, παλαιὰν καὶ νέαν διαθήκην, καὶ νεκρῶν ἀνάστασιν ὁμοίως λέγουσι ... περὶ δὲ πατρὸς καὶ υἱοῦ καὶ ἁγίου πνεύματος ὁμοίως φρονοῦσι τῇ ἁγίᾳ καθολικῇ ἐκκλησίᾳ.

sent the prophet'.[1] This means that at the moment when the prophecy is uttered, no testing is possible.[2] Quell thinks that it is "a theory which appears beforehand remarkably helpless to come to grips with the problem of truth and falsehood of prophetic speaking", because it is "a blunt weapon in the battle of the moment". This is true, but that is not the only reason why this principle has found little application in Christian writers of the first and second century A.D., notwithstanding the remarkable increasing emphasis on the πρόγνωσις τῶν μελλόντων in the idea of prophecy.[3]

The principle is only valid on the assumption that there is only one source of knowledge of what will happen. As soon as there is access to that knowledge by other means, it becomes useless. Confronted with a world full of oracles and diviners of all sorts, the Christians had to admit that even the devil and the demons have some knowledge of what is going to happen. They make no attempt to deny it, they try to explain and discredit it.[4] Small wonder then that in his reply to Hermas' question how to tell the true from the false prophet the

---

[1] Cf. G. Quell, *Wahre und falsche Propheten* (Gütersloh, 1952), p. 150ff.

[2] Cf. Iren. *A. H.* IV 26, 1: πᾶσα γὰρ προφητεία πρὸ τῆς ἐκβάσεως αἴνιγμά ἐστιν καὶ ἀντιλογία τοῖς ἀνθρώποις. Severianus ad 1 Cor. 14:21-25 (J. A. Cramer, *Catenae* V (Oxford, 1844), p. 272f.): ἡ δὲ προφητεία ἀπὸ τῆς ἐκβάσεως θαῦμα, οὐκ ἐν τῷ λέγεσθαι. Johann. Chrysost., *In Ep. I ad Cor. Homil.* 29 (259 A): προφητεία γὰρ οὐκ ἐν τῷ καιρῷ, ᾧ λέγεται, ἀλλ' ἐν τῷ καιρῷ τῆς ἐκβάσεως παρέχεται τῆς οἰκείας ἀληθείας τὸν ἔλεγχον.

[3] Cf. *infra*, p. 78f.

[4] Cf. e.g. Pseudoclem., *Recogn.* IV 21: *quod a vero deo dicitur sive per prophetas, sive per visiones diversas, semper verum est; quod autem a daemonibus praedicitur, non semper verum est;* Tert., *Apologeticum* 22, 9: *dispositiones dei et tunc prophetis contionantibus exceperunt et nunc lectionibus resonantibus carpunt. Ita et hinc sumentes quasdam temporum sortes aemulantur divinitatem, dum furantur divinationem;* Orig., *c. Celsum* VII 3, argues as follows: it would be possible to draw on Aristotle and his school, and on Epicurus to show that even some Greeks reject the oracles, but it must be admitted that they are not necessarily πλάσματα μηδὲ προσποιήσεις ἀνθρώπων. They are however not the work of some gods, but of δαίμονές τινες φαῦλοι καὶ πνεύματα ἐχθρὰ τῷ γένει τῶν ἀνθρώπων. This argument implies that the truth of the oracles as such cannot be denied. Cf. also Lact., *Div. Inst.* II 16, 13; Min. Felix 27, 1ff.; H. C. Weiland, *Het Oordeel der Kerkvaders over het Orakel* (Amsterdam, 1935), p. 39-54; P. Courcelle, Art. Divinatio, *R. A. C.* III c. 1245ff. J. Tambornino, *De antiquorum daemonismo* (Gieszen, 1909), p. 31-54. In the rejection of divination Plutarch, *Def. Orac.* 418 E (quoted *infra*, p. 88, n. 4) plays a great part, cf. Weiland, *op. cit.*, p. 41 n. 1. Pseudoclem., *Recogn.* VIII 60 and *Hom.* III 14, though seemingly referring to the truth of prophetic words, do not belong here but under (a), since the criterion is, in the last analysis, doctrinal.

Shepherd does not include the criterion *ex eventu*. Sometimes the false prophet does tell the truth: τινὰ δὲ καὶ ῥήματα ἀληθῆ λαλεῖ· ὁ γὰρ διάβολος πληροῖ αὐτὸν τῷ αὐτοῦ πνεύματι.[1]

(c) When the prophets cannot be distinguished on the basis of what they proclaim, they may be tested by their moral conduct. This is based on the conviction that moral integrity is the hallmark of true prophecy. According to Quell it may have been the most popular criterion in ancient Israel but certainly not the most effective, because ecstatic phenomena tend to blunt moral discernment.[2] This may explain why the criterion *e moribus* is applied only a few times in the Old Testament. In Jeremiah 23:9-15 the prophets of Jerusalem are exposed as uncommissioned by the Lord because they commit adultery.[3] On the same grounds Ahab and Zedekiah are discredited (Jer. 29:15-23). But in a religion which connects moral life and religious experience this criterion is indispensable. This is reflected in the warning that the false prophets will be known by their fruits (Matthew 7:16).[4] As to the διακρίσεις πνευμάτων (1 Cor. 12:10), Paul does not indicate how they were performed; but it is hardly conceivable that for him the καρπὸς τοῦ πνεύματος (Gal. 5:22) did play no part. The Didache expressly forbids the testing of any prophet while speaking ἐν πνεύματι but states that ἀπὸ ... τῶν τρόπων γνωσθήσεται ὁ ψευδοπροφήτης καὶ ὁ προφήτης (11,8). The true prophet must show forth τοὺς τρόπους κυρίου.[5] By itself, this phrase refers to general Christian life,[6] but the

---

[1] Cf. Clement, *Strom.* I 17, 85: εἶχον δὲ καὶ οἱ ψευδοπροφῆται τὸ κλέμμα, τὸ ὄνομα τὸ προφητικόν, προφῆται ὄντες τοῦ ψεύστου ... ἐν δὲ τοῖς ψεύδεσιν καὶ ἀληθῆ τινα ἔλεγον οἱ ψευσπροφῆται, καὶ τῷ ὄντι οὗτοι ἐν ἐκστάσει προεφήτευον ὡς ἂν ἀποστάτου διάκονοι, followed by the words of Hermas. Clement's concern, however, is not the eventual truth of predictions but the elements of truth in Greek philosophy, cf. *ib.* 87, 1: ἔστιν οὖν κἂν φιλοσοφίᾳ, τῇ κλαπείσῃ καθάπερ ὑπὸ Προμηθέως, πῦρ ὀλίγον εἰς φῶς ἐπιτήδειον χρησίμως ζωπυρούμενον, ἴχνος τι σοφίας καὶ κίνησις περὶ θεοῦ. His concept of prophecy is different.

[2] Quell, *op. cit.*, p. 142.

[3] This appears to follow from the fact that vv. 16-22 where the (false) prophets are denounced as not being sent by Jahwe are preceded by vv. 9-15, cf. Quell, *op. cit.*, p. 143f.; P. Volz, *Der Prophet Jeremia, K. A. T. herausgeg. von Ernst Sellin*, X² (Leipzig, 1928), p. 239.

[4] Cf. *supra*, p. 58.

[5] *Κυρίου* may refer to the Lord Jesus Christ, or to God, cf. Audet and Kraft *ad loc.*

[6] *Τρόπος* or *τρόποι* is found generally in the meaning 'way of life', cf. Liddell-Scott s. v. III; Lampe s.v. D4; *Const. Apost.* VIII 32, 2: ἐξεταζέσθωσαν ... αὐτῶν (sc. the catechumens) καὶ οἱ τρόποι καὶ ὁ βίος.

subsequent indications refer to a speaking ἐν πνεύματι: ordering a table, asking for money and other things. If he does this for the benefit of other people, especially the poor, he shows forth the ways of the Lord. If he does it for his own sake, he gives himself away as a false prophet.

This criterion is also predominant in the Shepherd's instruction. Not only are the positive aspects more or less specified but also the characteristics of a life incompatible with the prophetic χάρισμα are set forth in some detail. We have seen that the ζωή which is to be found with the true prophet does not go beyond what is expected from any Christian. He must show the same fruits of the Spirit as his fellow believers.[1] This has a bearing on his position in the fellowship of the Church, which will concern us in chapter VI.

The portrait of the false prophet shows several traits which have been touched upon already in the preceding chapter.[2] Some of them will be discussed at greater length when we investigate the religio-historical type of the divination which the false prophet practices.[3] The differences between Hermas and the Didache are obvious. They spring from the fact that in the latter every prophet is given more than the benefit of the doubt, whereas in Hermas the false prophet has given himself away by his divination on request. But this does not explain the most remarkable difference. Where the Didache forbids to test a prophet when he speaks ἐν πνεύματι, the Shepherd shows a διάκρισις πνευμάτων in actu, which supplements the testing on the basis of conduct. For him the latter cannot be final because, in the last analysis, it is not the man but the spirit that is in him which makes him a false prophet.

(d) The demasqué of the false prophet in the congregation is, like its counterpart, a unique feature in the 11th Mandate. It is to be distinguished from that indication of the Holy Spirit which is called ἀπόδειξις πνεύματος καὶ δυνάμεως (I Cor. 2:4), when the Spirit manifests itself convincingly by miracles. This is common enough in the New Testament and usually serves to support the preaching of the Gospel.[4] Occasionally, it may also result in the unmasking and

---

[1] Cf. *supra*, p. 49.
[2] Cf. *supra*, p. 50ff.
[3] Cf. *infra*, p. 81ff.
[4] Cf. Acts 4:29f., 5:12; Heb. 2:4. Mk. 16:17f; Cf. also τὰ σημεῖα τοῦ ἀποστόλου in 2 Cor. 12:12 and H. D. Betz, *Der Apostel Paulus und die sokratische Tradition*, p. 70ff.

overcoming of an evil spirit as is the case with the πνεῦμα πύθων in Acts 16:16-18,[1] but this happens in the missionary situation at the frontier line between the church and the pagan world. The testing of the Spirit within the fellowship of the church is another matter. However important the demonstration of Spirit and power may have been in the apostolic and post-apostolic church, as a test it is not fully adequate. Even the false prophets of Matthew 7:15-23 performed miracles.[2] The power was there, but not the Spirit. Here we are face to face with the deepest problem of prophecy in the Christian church. Even the test by the demonstration of Spirit and power is inadequate, since it fails to reveal the true nature and origin of the Spirit that is at work. Only the Spirit itself is able to carry out the διάκρισις πνευμάτων, and man only when, and to the extent that, the Spirit speaks and works through him. Such a man may rightly be called πνευματικός, and when he is truly a Spirit-man, he is at the same time not subject to the control of other people who do not have the Spirit to the extent he has it. Hence ὁ πνευματικὸς ἀνακρίνει μὲν πάντα, αὐτὸς δὲ ὑπ' οὐδενὸς ἀνακρίνεται (1 Cor. 2:15, cf. Iren. A.H. IV 33, 1). The only one to test him is another πνευματικός or a community of πνευματικοί. This is precisely the situation in Hermas. The man who claims to be a πνευματοφόρος comes in a congregation of righteous men who have the divine Spirit. The prayer of the congregation releases, as it were, the power of the divine Spirit,[3] and then the Spirit itself unmasks the false prophet and the empty spirit in him. The man is emptied and the spirit flees from him (14). This is the perfect διάκρισις πνευμάτων. There is no need of external standards but it is the Spirit itself that tests the alleged spirit-bearer.

Two comments may be in place. The unmasking of the false prophet is described in the language of the Two Spirits doctrine. The spirit of the devil flees from the false prophet, just as in the 5th Mandate the delicate Spirit leaves (ἀποχωρεῖ) when forced to live together with an evil spirit or with harshness. The man who is left is κενὸς ἀπὸ τοῦ πνεύματος τοῦ δικαίου and henceforth filled by the evil spirits.[4]

---

[1] This comes close to an exorcism, cf. Pseudoclem. Hom. IX 16, 3: ὅτι καὶ πύθωνες μαντεύονται, ἀλλ' ὑφ' ἡμῶν ὡς δαίμονες ὁρκιζόμενοι φυγαδεύονται.

[2] Cf. Const. Apost. VIII 2, 1: οὔτε πᾶς ὁ προφητεύων ὅσιος οὔτε πᾶς ὁ δαίμονας ἐλαύνων ἅγιος.

[3] The prayer is, of course, not envisaged as self-effective but as an operation of the Spirit in and together with those who pray, cf. infra, p. 124.

[4] Mand. V 2, 6f., cf. supra. p. 40.

Secondly, the divine Spirit does not operate through one single person but through the congregation. There are no parallels of such a congregational execution of the διάκρισις πνευμάτων. There is some likeness in 1 Corinthians 14:24f.: 'If all prophesy and an unbeliever or outsider enters, he is convicted by all, he is called to account by all, the secrets of his heart are disclosed; and so, falling on his face, he will worship God and declare that God is really among you', but this is not a case of testing a prophet; rather, it concerns an unbeliever who happens to be present in the congregation[1]. The διάκρισις πνευμάτων in Hermas is connected with his pneumatology and his ecclesiology. To these aspects we will turn in the next chapters.

PROPHECY AND DIVINATION

Our next concern is how the phenomenon of a soothsaying prophet in a Christian church is to be explained. Dibelius points to two factors: (a) the decline of Christian prophecy, and (b) the religious tendencies of the second century.[2] His descriptions, however, need some further qualifications in order to do justice to the rather complicated developments of history.

According to Dibelius, the Didache proves clearly that the ministry of prophecy was in the process of losing respect in the churches. This was due to the abuse which individuals made of their prophetic authority and to the growing prestige of the local church-officers over against the itinerant prophets. Even the prophetic self-consciousness of Hermas which he could have had as a proclaimer of the second repentance, awkwardly remains in the background.[3] This loss of standing may have led to degeneration from prophecy to magic and divination, the more so since a similar development had long since been completed in the surrounding pagan world.

This explanation fails to do justice to the evidence of Christian prophecy in the second century A.D. There is evidence that prophecy was present among the manifestations of the Spirit in the church in the latter part of the century and later.[4] It functioned, not only in the great personalities of the church, the apostles and their successors, but rather through many unknown members of the church.

---

[1] Cf. Conzelmann, Der erste Brief an die Korinther (Göttingen, 1969), p. 286 ad loc.
[2] P. 539f.
[3] For this see ch. VII.
[4] Cf. supra, p. 10.

This explains why so few names of Christian prophets have come down to us.[1] That Christian prophets acted like pagan μάντεις may well have had other reasons than the loss of prestige in the church. One reason is that the borderline between prophecy and divination, by itself vague enough and hard to draw, tended to become invisible, — and sometimes indeed was invisible. This requires a broader argument on the relationship between prophecy and divination.

The Old Testament rejects and forbids pagan divination in its various forms, but at the same time mentions forms of divination within Jahwism which are considered quite legitimate.[2] This shows that divination and prophecy are opposed only when the former appears in paganistic forms and applies paganistic means to obtain knowledge of what is coming. Apart from that, an element of divination — in the sense of foretelling — appears to be inherent in prophecy. When in the days of the classic prophets the emphasis shifts to 'political' prophecy, in the sense that their message concerns the people of Israel and Judah and their kings as a whole, rather than the individuals, this element is less prominent, but there is a good reason to assume that several forms of more or less private divination continued to flourish besides the main stream of prophecy.[3]

Psychologically, divination and prophecy are much closer than, perhaps, theologically. When Kaufmann writes that in the separation between the source of the decree and the source of the disclosure the essential nature of pagan divination reveals itself, because it is not his will that the god makes known but his knowledge,[4] he attempts to give a theological evaluation of the phenomenon of divination. Psychologically, the will of God and destiny are not separate worlds. Both prophecy and divination respond to the need to understand and to foresee.[5] Phenomenologically the difference may be that the prophet

---

[1] The New Testament mentions by name Agabus (Acts 11:28; 21:10) and the daughters of Philippus (Acts 21:9); in post-apostolic times we have only the names of Quadratus (Euseb. *H. E.* III 37, 1) and Ammia (*ib.* V 17, 4), apart from Montanus and some of his co-prophetesses.

[2] Cf. *supra*, p. 34ff.

[3] Cf. Fascher, p. 150. Probably the false prophets of Zech. 13:1-6 belong here, cf. present writer, *art. cit.*, p. 151.

[4] *Religion of Israel*, p. 43. According to Kaufmann in divination "the gods manifest their knowledge of matters not necessarily dependent upon them" (*ib.*).

[5] Cf. G. Devereux, *Considérations psychanalytiques sur la divination*, in: A. O. Caquot and M. Leibovici (ed.), *La Divination* (Paris, 1968), vol. II, p. 454ff.

speaks on the order of God and the diviner on human request,[1] but the fact that both functions can be performed by the same person, like e.g. Samuel, indicates sufficiently that divination and prophecy are, to a large degree, co-extensive.

When the voice of 'political' prophecy (in the sense indicated above) ceases to be heard, the divinatory element in prophecy may come to the fore again. This can be seen from Josephus' description of prophetic personalities of his time and the preceding period.[2] An indication of the general trend of this description may be found in the fact that in Josephus the word group μάντις and derivatives has lost its connotation of paganism.[3] Judas the Essene, who predicted the death of Antigonus, is called μάντις.[4] Simon the Essene is among the μάντεις called in to explain the dream of Archelaus.[5] Among the Essenes are people οἳ καὶ τὰ μέλλοντα προγινώσκειν ὑπισχνοῦνται. They use various means and are seldom, if ever, wrong in their predictions.[6] Manaëmus, who predicted to Herod that he would eventually become king, had πρόγνωσιν ἐκ θεοῦ τῶν μελλόντων.[7] Finally, Josephus' account of his own prophetic experiences is full of terms reminiscent of divination.[8] All this points to a concept of prophecy in which the divinatory element has a central place.[9] This may be, in part, the result of hellenistic influences, but is, perhaps, also due to a lack of living

---

[1] Cf. A. J. Heschel, *The Prophets* (New York, 1962), p. 458; Heschel tends to assign theological value to his phenomenological observations.

[2] Meyer, art. προφήτης, *Th. W. N. T.* VI, p. 813ff., tries to establish that the alleged absence of "Gegenwartsprophetie" in this period is the product of a rabbinic theological construction and has no foundation in the evidence. This may be true but whether all the "geschichtlichen Erscheinungsformen" which he lists and discusses are rightly called 'prophetic' is to be doubted. This question, however, is beyond the scope of the present investigation.

[3] Cf. his account of Balaam; *Ant.* IV 104ff. (Balaam is μάντις ἄριστος τῶν τότε. Moses honoured him ἀναγράψας αὐτοῦ τὰς μαντείας 157).

[4] *Bell. Jud.*, I 78-80.

[5] *Ib.* II 112f.

[6] *Ib.* II 159.

[7] *Ant.* XV 373f.

[8] *Bell. Jud.* III 351-354: συμβάλλειν, ἔνθους, τὰ μέλλοντα εἰπεῖν·

[9] The contemporary false prophets whom Josephus mentioned are, however, in a certain sense 'political', or 'Messianic' prophets because their predictions concerned the coming of the national deliverance, cf. *Ant.* XVIII 85ff.; XX 97; *Bell. Jud.* II 261; VI 286; Meyer, *art. cit.*, p. 825.

prophecy in those times.¹ The concept of prophecy is liable to a shift of emphasis toward divination.

In the classic description of Christian prophecy in 1 Corinthians 12 and 14 no trace of this trend is found.² Prophecy is a church-centered charisma and serves the οἰκοδομή of the congregation.³ Part of this charisma is also the revealing of secrets, especially the secrets of the human heart before God,⁴ and prophecy is exercised congregationally.⁵ But the first Christian prophet who has become known to us by name, Agabus, is mentioned because he predicted the great famine in the days of Claudius.⁶ The same prophet is mentioned in Acts 21:10f. when he foretells Paul's arrest. This shows that the divinatory element was also present in Christian prophecy at an early stage.⁷ Yet this divinatory element is not the same thing as divination on request. It is, as it were, embedded in the life of the church and serves the well being and the mission of the church. Divination is rejected as pagan.⁸ The rising tide of apocalyptic prophecy in the church adds a new dimension to the function of prophecy.⁹ By virtue of its nature it

---

¹ This applies also to prophecy in Qumran where נבא occurs only referring to the Old testament prophets and is never applied to a member of the community, not even the Teacher of Righteousness, cf. H. Braun, *Qumran und das Neue Testament* I (Tübingen, 1966), p. 14.

² 1 Cor. 12 and 14 is the oldest account; 1 Thess. 5:19 is no more than a reference. The presence of prophets in the church which Mt. 10:41 and perhaps 23:34 appear to suggest, may have to be placed earlier, but the scant evidence allows no safe conclusions as to their place and function in the church, cf. *supra*, p. 11.

³ Cf. *supra*, p. 13.

⁴ Cf. 1 Cor. 14:24; Iren. *A. H.* 6, 1: *quemadmodum et multos audimus fratres in ecclesia, prophetica habentes charismata, et per Spiritum universis linguis loquentes et absconsa hominum in manifestum producentes ad utilitatem, et mysteria Dei enarrantes.* The same concept of prophecy is found in Origen., *Comm in Eph.* 4:11-12 (*J. T. S.* 3 (1902), p. 414): προφήτην ἀπίστους ἐλέγχοντα καὶ ἀνακρίνοντα (τοιοῦτος γάρ ἐστιν ὁ τῆς καινῆς διαθήκης προφήτης). Both statements recall Paul's words.

⁵ This applies also to 1 Thess. 5:19.

⁶ Acts 11:28. Friedrich, *Th. W. N. T.* VI, p. 849 f., n. 425, thinks that Agabus' prophecy of a great famine referred to the apocalyptic *topos* of a famine in the last days (cf. Mk. 13:8 par., Mt. 24:7; Lk. 21:11; Apoc. 6:6) and was de-eschatologised and historised by Luke, but he offers no evidence.

⁷ Acts 15:32 reflects a concept of prophecy closer to that of 1 Cor. 14, cf. E. Earle Ellis, The Role of the Christian Prophet in Acts, in W. Ward Gasque and R. P. Martin (editors), *Apostolic History and the Gospel, Essays presented to F. F. Bruce* (Exeter, 1970), p. 55-67, esp. p. 56f.

⁸ Cf. Acts 16:16ff., *Did.* 3, 4.

⁹ The oldest full fledged literary document of apocalyptic prophecy (in the sense indicated *supra*, p. 13f.) is the Apocalypse of John, but apocalyptic prophecy is, of

is concerned with the future and as such it contains an element of prediction. Again this is not divination, but divinatory prophecy proclaiming God's design for the consummation of salvation. Yet it also represents a shift from the immediate present to the future as the object of prophecy.

These brief remarks on the varieties of prophecy in the first century may serve as a starting point for a description of subsequent developments. In a well documented paper, W.C. van Unnik has pointed to the tripartite formula, *That which is, that which has been, that which will be*, which is frequently used in the second century texts to characterize the content as prophetic,[1] The oldest appearence of this formula in a Christian text is Apocalypse 1:19, but it is also found in writings of a different nature. When we attempt to classify the materials from Christian sources collected by Van Unnik it appears that the formula is used (a) in apocalyptic texts, (b) in Gnostic texts, and (c) in texts relating to the prophets of the Old Testament and their authority with regard to the present.[2] It is significant that the majority of the places belongs to (c). Van Unnik remarks "that this requirement (i.e. the knowledge of past, present and future) is not mentioned in passages which deal with the distinction between true and false prophets like Hermas, *Mand.* XI". In the second century crisis with regard to prophetism "the present formula is never used ..., the criteria being quite different".[3] This observation leads us to the crucial point. The description of the true prophet by the tripartite formula implies that in order to command authority with regard to the present and the future, prophecy must have proved its veracity in the past. This is clear in Theophilus, *Apol.* 2, 9: the prophets of the Hebrews and the Sibylla predicted τά τε πρὸ αὐτῶν γεγενημένα καὶ τὰ κατ᾽ αὐτοὺς γεγονότα καὶ τὰ καθ᾽ ἡμᾶς νυνὶ τελειούμενα· διὸ καὶ πεπείσμεθα καὶ περὶ τῶν μελλόντων οὕτως ἔπεσθαι, καθὼς καὶ τὰ πρῶτα ἀπήρτισται.[4]

course, much older, cf. P. Vielhauer, *Apokalyptik des Urchristentums*, in Hennecke-Schneemelcher, *Neutestamentliche Apokryphen* (Tübingen, 1964³), II, p. 428ff.

[1] A Formula describing Prophecy, *N. T. S.* 9 (1963), p. 86-94.

[2] (a) Apocalyptic texts: Apoc. 1:19; (b) Gnostic texts: *Apocr. Joh.*, opening section; Hippolytus, *Ref.* V 7, 20, 29 (Naassenes); (c) of O. T. prophets: Barnabas 1, 7; 5, 3; Theophilus, *Apol.*, 1, 14; 2, 9, 33; Irenaeus *A. H.* IV 33, 1; Pseudoclem., *Hom.* II 6, 1; Hippolytus, *De antichristo* 2; there are several places more where, if not the exact wording yet the same idea is found.

[3] *Art. cit.*, p. 89f.

[4] Cf. also Pseudoclem., *Hom.* II, 10, 1: ἐὰν ἡμῖν ᾖ τι προειρηκὼς ὁ εἰς τέλος ἐγνώκαμεν

The formula rests on the foundation of the criterion *ex eventu*.
The divinatory element in prophecy is gaining weight. This is also
supported by various definitions of prophecy and prophets occurring
in Christian texts. Suffice it to quote two examples. In *A.H.* IV 20, 5,
Irenaeus accuses those who distinguish between the invisible Father
and the God who had been seen by the prophets, that they have no
idea whatsoever of prophecy, and continues: *Nam prophetia est
praedictio futurorum, hoc est eorum quae post erunt praesignificatio.*
In the closing chapters of his *Refutatio*, Hippolytus calls upon the
prophets as his last witnesses, as it were, and introduces them with
the following words: δίκαιοι ἄνδρες γεγένηνται φίλοι θεοῦ· οὗτοι προφῆται κέκληνται διὰ τὸ προφαίνειν τὰ μέλλοντα (X 33).[1]
It is true that in these and other texts prophecy as prediction is
embedded in the framework of the divine revelation-history, but the
very fact that it could be defined in these terms is highly significant,
because these definitions could not be applied to "Gegenwartsprophetie".
The Christian writers who used them must have been aware that their
terminology stemmed from pagan divination. Cicero defines divination
as *praesensio et scientia rerum futurarum* (*De Divin.* I 1), and as *earum
rerum quae fortuitae putantur praedictio atque praesensio* (*ib.* I 9).[2]
This is the most general definition and is not affected by the Stoic
predilection for divination.[3] This general definition is taken over by
Irenaeus apparently without realising that its use might help to
blur the distinction between Christian prophecy as it existed in the
churches, and divination. This was the more striking since there
was a spectacular revival of pagan divination in the second century
A.D.[4] The same is true of the tripartite formula. Apart from philosophical contexts, Van Unnik refers to Ovid, *Metam.* I 517f. where Apollo
is described as the god by whom ... *quod eritque, fuitque estque patet,*

γεγενημένον, καλῶς αὐτῷ ἐκ τῶν ἤδη γεγενημένων καὶ τὰ ἐσόμενα ἔσεσθαι πιστεύομεν, οὐ
μόνον ὡς γινώσκοντι, ἀλλὰ καὶ προγινώσκοντι; Hippolytus, *De Antichristo* 2.
  [1] Cf. also Justin, *Dial.* 7, 1; 39, 2 (where the prophetic Spirit is called πνεῦμα προ-
γνώσεως); Origen, *c. Celsum* I, 36. For later evidence cf. Lampe s.v. προφήτης I B.
  [2] *Quae fortuitae putantur* instead of *futurarum* is used in order to avoid the dilemma
of fate and prediction, cf. A. S. Pease *ad. loc.* p. 68. Cf. also Lucian, *Hes.* 1: τὴν τῶν
μελλόντων προαγόρευσιν; 8 (μαντικὴ) ... ἧς τὸ ἔργον τὰ ἄδηλα καὶ οὐδαμῇ οὐδαμῶς φανερὰ
προγιγνώσκειν.
  [3] Cf. O. Gruppe, *Griechische Mythologie und Religionsgeschichte* (München, 1906)
II, p. 1471ff.
  [4] Cf. *infra*, p. 79f.

and to Vergil, *Georg.* IV, 392f. about Proteus: ... *novit namque omnia vates, quae sint, quae fuerint, quae mox ventura trahantur*, which probably go back to Greek examples.[1] How easily such general, all-embracing formulae may be adjusted to divination in a more direct and narrow sense appears from a London Papyrus where a magician prays that when people come to him he may know τὰ ἐν ταῖς ψυχαῖς ἀπάντων ἀνθρώπων ..., ὅπως αὐτοῖς ἐξαγγείλω τὰ προγεγονότα αὐτοῖς καὶ ἐνεστῶτα καὶ τὰ μέλλοντα αὐτοῖς ἔσεσθαι ... καὶ ἀπαγγείλω αὐτοῖς πάντα ἐξ ἀληθείας.[2] The insertion of αὐτοῖς brings us in the sphere of divination for individuals just as in the 11th Mandate people ask the false prophet in Hermas τί ἄρα ἔσται αὐτοῖς (2). This example shows what happens to prophecy — defined as prediction of the future — when it is detached from the context of salvation-history and applied to the personal fate of individuals. This evidence shows sufficiently that the crisis of prophecy to which the 11th Mandate witnesses was due, not only to the loss of prophetic authority in the church, but also to the increasing emphasis on the divinatory element in Christian prophecy. The introduction and the spread of the tripartite formula itself is another witness to the same process. The formula may have been useful to claim prophetic authority, it fails when it is applied to distinguishing the diviner from the prophet because its foundation is the criterion *ex eventu* which underlies both prophecy and divination.

THE CHRISTIAN μάντις.

The second factor to which Dibelius points to explain the phenomenon of false prophecy is the religious tendencies of the second century. This century presents an interesting picture of conservatism, revival of old forms, criticism of old traditions, and new influences from the East. They have been described several times and there is no need to repeat or summarise those descriptions.[3] Divination in its various forms

---

[1] *Art. cit.*, p. 92, referring to Homer, *Iliad* A 70; Hesiod., *Theogon.* 38; *Orph. Hymn.* 25, 4f.: (Proteus) ἐπιστάμενος τά τ᾽ ἐόντα ὅσσα τε πρόσθεν ἔην ὅσα τ᾽ ἔσσεται ὕστερον αὖτις.

[2] *P. G. M.* V 294f. (Preis. I 190); Reitzenstein, *Hellen. Mysterienreligionen*, p. 239f., compares 1 Cor. 14:24, but there the situation is different because the prophets in the congregation do not prophesy on request but spontaneously.

[3] Cf. e.g. J. Geffcken, *Der Ausgang des griechisch-römischen Heidentums* (Heidelberg, 1929, repr. Darmstadt, 1963), ch. 1; Nilsson, *Geschichte der griechischen Religion*, vol. II², p. 311ff.; E. R. Dodds, *Pagan and Christian in an Age of Anxiety* (Cambridge, 1965). J. Ferguson, *The Religions of the Roman Empire* (London, 1970).

held an important place. Not only the official oracles flourished but also private divination and dream-interpretation. Astrology was beginning to make its way into the hellenistic world.[1] What was the Christian reaction to this? In order to appreciate it two things must be remembered. The Christians were people of their own time. They shared the ideas of the ancient world about the possibility of divination. They too believed that man could receive from God knowledge of what was to come.[2] They had many examples of this in their own tradition. They knew of dreams boding the future.[3] They knew of prophets who announced what was to happen.[4] But this same tradition uncompromisingly rejected pagan divination in which they could see only the work of demons.[5] Apart from that, it soon became customary to consider the various forms of pagan divination as superseded and overcome.[6]

This is what may be called the official point of view, no doubt sincerely believed by those who adhered to it. Yet underneath the surface the situation is different. The Didache already explicitly forbids several forms of divination and magic, apparently not without good reason.[7] The Shepherd of Hermas warns against consulting the

---

[1] For the oracles cf. Nilsson, op. cit., p. 467-485; for oneiromancy cf. Dodds, op. cit., p. 38-52; for astrology cf. F. Cumont, Astrology and Religion among the Greeks and Romans (repr. New York, 1960), p. 42-56.

[2] Cf. supra, p. 69, n. 4.

[3] Cf. Gen. 31:10; 37:1-10; 40:5-23; 41:1-32; Dan. 2:1-45; 4:4ff., all relating dreams which require explanation. Mt. 1:20-24; 2:12,13, 19-22 relate dreams which are self-explaining and are more like the nightly visions of Paul in Acts 16:9; 18:9; 23:11; 27:23, cf. Lindblom, Gesichte und Offenbarungen, p. 27ff.; E. Benz, Paulus als Visionär (Mainz 1952), p. 91-94; id., Die Vision (Stuttgart, 1969), p. 104-130.

[4] Cf. Acts 11:28; 21:11.

[5] Cf. supra, p. 74f.

[6] The oldest place where this is found is Clem. Alex., Protreptikos II 11, 1 who warns not to bother about the old oracles because they have withered away and have been reduced to silence; cf. also Eusebius, Praep. Evang. IV 2, 8 (134d), V 16, 2 (205b); 17, 13f. (208a). Athanasius, De Incarn. Verbi 47,1: νῦν δὲ ἀφ' οὗ Χριστὸς καταγγέλλεται πανταχοῦ, πέπαυται καὶ τούτων (i.e. the oracles) ἡ μανία, καὶ οὐκ ἔστιν ἔτι λοιπὸν ἐν αὐτοῖς ὁ μαντευόμενος; the same is said about the demons, the gods and magic! Cf. Weiland, op. cit., p. 14f. and references there. It is, however, worth noting that this triumphant note is not found in 1st and 2nd century documents.

[7] 3, 4: μὴ γίνου οἰωνοσκόπος, ἐπειδὴ ὁδηγεῖ εἰς τὴν εἰδωλολατρίαν, μηδὲ ἐπαοιδὸς μηδὲ μαθηματικὸς μηδὲ περικαθαίρων, μηδὲ θέλε αὐτὰ βλέπειν μηδὲ ἀκούειν· ἐκ γὰρ τούτων ἁπάντων εἰδωλολατρία γεννᾶται; cf. also Knopf, H. N. T., p. 14f. ad loc. It is noteworthy that none of these terms belongs to the vocabulary of inspirational divination but to that of inductive divination and magic.

false prophet. In both injunctions the word εἰδωλολατρία is found.[1] There appears to have been here and there an undercurrent of divination within the Christian church, more reminiscent of the religious ideas outside the church than of the theological arguments of its teachers. Since the latter are much better represented in our sources than the adherents of the former, it is not surprising that there are not many traces of Christian divination left. Yet there may have been more Christian μάντεις than we expect. A casual remark of Chrysostomus is significant in this connection. In his homily on 1 Corinthians 14:20ff. he elaborates the differences between the prophets and those speaking in tongues. Paul does not mean to say, he explains, that a prophet may not speak when there is no one who judges his prophecy (ὁ διακρίνων) as he forbids speaking in tongues without interpretation. Prophecy is αὐτάρκης. But this does not mean that the listener is not protected. There is the congregation to judge, ὥστε μὴ παρεμπεσεῖν μεταξὺ μάντιν: no μάντις will be able to intrude under the pretence of being a prophet.[2] Even in the 4th century the opposite of the prophet was the diviner.

A picture of the Christian μάντις is to be gained on the basis of the direct evidence in Christian sources and with the aid of analogous material from pagan sources. The latter is not as rich as might be expected in view of the renewed interest in oracles and divination in the second century A.D. It is tempting to compare the false prophet in Hermas with the θεῖοι ἄνδρες of that time, such as Alexander of Abonuteichos or Apollonius of Tyana; but the Christian μάντις operates on a much smaller scale. He is, so to speak, a "small time" diviner. There are, of course, similarities, as already noted, or yet to be noted. But his overall picture is different. A very striking and illuminating parallel, however, is found in Apuleius' description of a Chaldaean diviner, operating in Corinth.[3] It deserves to be quoted at some length.

The Chaldaean, whose name is Diophanes, *arcana fatorum stipibus emerendis edicit in vulgum.* He tells people at their request what day

---

[1] This makes the injunctions all the more stringent, cf. *supra,* p. 34f.

[2] Johann. Chrysost., *In Ep. 1 ad Cor. Homil.* 36 (338 CD).

[3] *Metam.* II 12, 3 - 14, 6. It follows a story of divination by means of a *lucerna,* and the explanation of that form of empyromancy by relating it to the heavenly fire;with both the story of the Chaldaean, notwithstanding the word *nam* in its opening clause, has nothing to do.

to choose for a marriage which will turn out to be stable; which day is good for the merchant, the traveller, or for a sea-voyage. But he does not just name a day. His answer to the man who tells the story about him contains *multa ... et oppido mira et satis varia; nunc enim gloriam satis floridam, nunc historiam magnam et incredundam fabulam et libros me futurum.* This is a good specimen of answering people κατὰ τὰς ἐπιθυμίας αὐτῶν, and for a good wage! He performs his divinations in public, *frequentis populi circulo conseptus.*[1] But inadvertently he gives himself away as an impostor. When a certain merchant named Cerdo asked him to name him a day favourable for a journey and he had named a day, a young man appeared who turned out to be a good friend of the diviner; after mutual kissing and embracing he asked the diviner how he had fared on his journey from Euboea to Corinth. Then Diophanes, *ille Chaldaeus egregius mente viduus necdum suus*, told his sad story: the ship on which he sailed was shipwrecked and what little material help they received from benevolent people was taken by a band of robbers who even killed his own brother before his eyes. Not until Cerdo took back his money and ran away and the bystanders began to laugh did he realise that he had given himself away as one who, though foretelling other people their future, had failed to foresee his own.

When we compare this amusing story with Hermas' account of the Christian μάντις, some comments may be made. In the first place, Diophanes is called *Chaldaeus* but there are no traces of astrology in the story. We must distinguish between the Chaldaeans as professional astrologists and astronomists of the past, and the itinerant Chaldaean diviners who practice divination by various means.[2] The former are also devoted to philosophy and are often pictured as superhuman. Yet even they are not only philosophers and astronomists. The well-known account of Diodorus ascribes to them the use of other means of divination, and several forms of magic as well.[3] The latter generally

---

[1] Cf. *supra*, p. 31.

[2] Cf. Baumstark, art. Chaldaioi, *P. W. R. E.* III 2059; he distinguishes between "die halbmystischen Chaldaioi" and "der Unfug sich chaldaeisch nennenden Wanderpropheten". For the former cf. e.g. Strabo XVI 1, 6 (739): ἀφώριστο δ'ἐν Βαβυλωνίᾳ κατοικία τοῖς ἐπιχωρίοις φιλοσόφοις, τοῖς Χαλδαίοις προσαγορευομένοις, οἳ περὶ ἀστρονομίαν εἰσὶ τὸ πλέον· προσποιοῦνται δέ τινες καὶ γενεθλιαλογεῖν, οὓς οὐ καταδέχονται οἱ ἕτεροι. Cf. also W. J. W. Koster, art. Chaldäer, *R. A. C.* II c. 1006-1021, esp. 1013-1018.

[3] II 29, 2-3: (οἱ Χαλδαῖοι) πρὸς γὰρ τῇ θεραπείᾳ τῶν θεῶν τεταγμένοι πάντα τὸν τοῦ ζῆν χρόνον φιλοσοφοῦσι, μεγίστην δόξαν ἔχοντες ἐν ἀστρολογίᾳ. ἀντέχονται δ' ἐπὶ πολὺ καὶ

do have a bad reputation and we may presume that they did also practice divination and magic of all kinds.[1] There are no clear distinctions between Χαλδαῖος, μάγος and μάντις.[2] This explains the absence of any reference to astrology in the story of Diophanes, and, at the same time, enables us to use this story as a close parallel to the Christian μάντις.

In the second place, the similarity between Diophanes and the Christian μάντις refers also to the nature of the questions. People ask, τί ἄρα ἔσται αὐτοῖς (2). Commenting upon this phrase, Dibelius quotes Plutarch, Defect. Orac. 413 B: the Cynic Didymus complains about the shameful and ungodly questions which people nowadays put to the oracle. Some test it as if they were sophists; others ask questions about treasures or inheritances or unlawful marriages.[3] This biting criticism resembles that of asking and answering questions κατὰ τὰς ἐπιθυμίας τῆς πονηρίας αὐτῶν, rather than indicating the content of the questions which people ask when they come to the oracles and to the false prophets. Those questions deal with their personal situation

---

μαντικῆς, ποιούμενοι προρρήσεις περὶ τῶν μελλόντων, καὶ τῶν μὲν καθαρμοῖς, τῶν δὲ θυσίαις, τῶν δ' ἄλλαις τισὶν ἐπῳδαῖς ἀποτροπὰς κακῶν καὶ τελειώσεις ἀγαθῶν πειρῶνται πορίζειν. ἐμπειρίαν δ' ἔχουσι καὶ τῆς διὰ τῶν οἰωνῶν μαντικῆς, ἐνυπνίων τε καὶ τεράτων ἐξηγήσεις ἀποφαίνονται. οὐκ ἀσόφως δὲ ποιοῦνται καὶ τὰ περὶ τὴν ἱεροσκοπίαν ἄκρως ἐπιτυγχάνειν νομίζοντες.

[1] In this respect Diodorus' account appears to reflect contemporary practice, rather than old tradition. Baumstark, loc. cit. understands in Diog. Laert., Proem. 6 (τοὺς δὲ Χαλδαίους περὶ ἀστρονομίαν καὶ πρόρρησιν ἀσχολεῖσθαι) πρόρρησιν to refer to inspirational divination, but this is not sure.

[2] Cf. Lucian, Hermot. 6: μαντικὸς ὢν ἢ χρησμολόγος τις ἢ ὅσοι τὰς Χαλδαίων μεθόδους ἐπίστανται. Macrob. 4: among those who live long are καὶ οἱ καλούμενοι δὲ μάγοι, γένος τοῦτο μαντικὸν καὶ θεοῖς ἀνακείμενον παρά τε Πέρσαις καὶ Πάρθοις. Josephus, Ant. X 216: τοὺς μάγους refers to τοὺς Χαλδαίους καὶ τοὺς μάγους καὶ τοὺς μάντεις in 195. Hesychius s.v. Χαλδαῖοι· γένος μάγων πάντα γινωσκόντων. Dio Chrysostomus XXXVI 41: οὓς οἱ Πέρσαι μάγους ἐκάλεσαν ... οὐχ ὡς Ἕλληνες ἀγνοίᾳ τοῦ ὀνόματος οὕτως ὀνομάζουσιν ἀνθρώπους γόητας, also reflects contemporary understanding. For the low appreciation of the Chaldaeans cf. Cato, Agric. V 4: (vilicus) haruspicem, augurem, hariolum, Chaldaeum nequem consuluisse velit. Columella XI 1, 31; Gellius, Noct. Att. XIV 1, 2: (from a summary of Favorinus' work adversus istos qui sese Chaldaeos seu genethliacos appellant) disciplinam istam Chaldaeorum tantae vetustatis non esse quantae videri volunt neque eos principes eius auctoresque esse quos ipsi ferant, sed id praestigiarum atque offuciarum genus commentos esse homines aeruscatores et cibum quaestumque ex mendaciis captantes.

[3] Τὸν τρίποδα καταπιμπλάμενον αἰσχρῶν καὶ ἀθέων ἐπερωτημάτων ἃ τῷ θεῷ προβάλλουσιν οἱ μὲν ὡς σοφιστοῦ διάπειραν λαμβάνοντες οἱ δὲ περὶ θησαυρῶν ἢ κληρονομιῶν ἢ γάμων παρανόμων διερωτῶντες.

and future,[1] and they will have been much more like the questions
which we find in the story of Diophanes and also in some Magical
Papyri. From the latter, a few examples may be quoted: should I
stay in Bacchias? Am I allowed to marry Tapetheus? Shall I recover
from this illness? Is the governor angry with me or does he investigate
about me because I write Valerius' accounts? Are you agreed that
he goes to town? Is it to my adventage to buy a slave from Tasarapion.[2]

In the third place, the Chaldaean who did not foresee his own future
is not an isolated phenomenon. From Homer on there are stories of
diviners who were ignorant of their own fate.[3] A classic example is
Prometheus.[4] Josephus quotes a story from Hecataeus in which the
Jew Mosollamus, a bowman, shoots a bird which is being observed
by a seer, and says: οὗτος τὴν αὐτοῦ σωτηρίαν οὐ προϊδὼν περὶ
τῆς ἡμετέρας πορείας ἡμῖν ἄν τι ὑγιὲς ἀπήγγελλεν.[5] Cicero quotes
Ennius who denounces the superstitious seers, qui sibi semitam non
sapiunt alteri monstrant viam.[6] In a Berlin papyrus of the second century
A.D. the commander of an army which had sacked Delphi scoffs
at the prophet for not having foreseen his own fate.[7] Needless to say
that this theme was eagerly taken up by the Christian critics of the
oracles.[8] In a certain sense this same criticism is also true of the false
prophet of the 11th Mandate: he walks into the meeting of the gathered
congregation without realising what is going to happen to him.

---

[1] Cf. the insertion of αὐτοῖς in the tripartite formula, supra, p. 79.

[2] P. G. M. XXX, XXXI (Preis. II 155ff.): χρηματισόν μοι ἢ μείνω ἐν Βακχιάδι ; —
εἰ οὐ δίδοταί μοι συμβιῶσαι Ταπεθεῦτι Μαρρείους οὐδ' οὐ μὴ γένηται ἄλλου γυνή ; — ἢ μὲν
σοθήσω ταύτης ἧς ἐν ἐμοὶ ἀσθενίας ; — εἰ οὐ μέλλι ὁ νομάρχης ἐναυτοῦ ἀγανακτῖ ἢ ἐξετάζι τὰ
κατ' ἐμέ, ὅτι τὰ πιττάκια Οὐαλερίου ἐγὼ γράφω. — εἰ συμφέρει μοι ἀγοράσαι παρὰ Τασα-
ραπίωνος, ὃν ἔχει δοῦλον ... ; cf. also P 1 (ib., p. 189, Christian !).

[3] Cf. Homer, Iliad B 858f.: Ἔννομος οἰωνιστής· ἀλλ' οὐκ οἰωνοῖσιν ἐρύσσατο κῆρα
μέλαιναν. Apoll. Rhod., Argonautica II 816: Ἴδμονα, μαντοσύνῃσι κεκασμένον· ἀλλά μιν
οὔτι μαντοσύναι ἐσάωσαν. Vergil, Aeneid. IX 328: (Rhamnes augur) ... non augurio
potuit depellere pestem. Ovid, Metamorph. V 146f.: Aethionque sagax quondam ventura
videre, tunc ave deceptus falsa.

[4] Cf. Aeschylus, Prometheus 85ff.: ψευδωνύμως σε δαίμονες Προμηθέα καλοῦσιν· αὐτὸν
γάρ σε δεῖ προμηθέως ὅτῳ τρόπῳ τῆσδ' ἐκκυλισθήσῃ τέχνης. Cf. also 267, 335f., 473ff.

[5] Josephus, c. Apion. I 201-204.

[6] De Divin. I 58.

[7] W. Schubart, Aus einer Apollon-Aretalogie, Hermes 55 (1920), p. 190, l. 35ff. :
σὺ δὲ τοῖς ἄλλοις ἅπασιν ἃ δεῖ προλέγων ἃ σὲ δεῖ παθεῖν οὐκ ἔγνως.

[8] Cf. Weiland, op. cit., p. 33f.

A further step towards a more complete picture of the Christian μάντις can be taken when we compare him again with Irenaeus' story of the Gnostic prophet Marcus with which it has much in common. As set forth above[1], the common element refers to the concept of false prophecy, but it concerns also the false prophets themselves. In Hermas the false prophet is unequivocally described as a μάντις. As to Marcus, Irenaeus says that the women whom he forced to prophecy, venture to speak ληρώδη καὶ τὰ τυχόντα πάντα, i.e. any silly thing that comes to their mind; but this reveals very little, as it is clearly meant to be depreciatory. There is no reason to suppose that it points to some form of glossolalia.[2] Reitzenstein takes προφητεύειν in a rather general sense and interprets it as, "eine bestimmte Art erbaulicher Rede",[3] but there is no support for this judgment in the text. More light is shed by Irenaeus' own comment in A.H. I 13,3: εἰ οὖν Μάρκος μὲν κελεύει ... καὶ ἀλλήλοις ἐγκελεύεσθαι τὸ προφητεύειν καὶ πρὸς τὰς ἰδίας ἐπιθυμίας ἑαυτοῖς μαντεύεσθαι, κτλ. These words suggest that for him προφητεύειν and μαντεύεσθαι were identical, at least in the context of Marcus' prophetic activities. In view of Irenaeus' own definition of prophecy as praedictio futurorum[4] we may suggest that προφητεύειν, understood in malam partem, is tantamount to divination.

What kind of divination was this? There is no reason to think of inductive divination. On the contrary, if such divination was performed by technical means, the sources would not have failed to tell it.[5] This leaves the wide field of inspirational divination. We can, however,

---

[1] Cf. supra, p. 64f.

[2] Weinel, Wirkungen, p. 75f., doubts whether Irenaeus knew what glossolalia was, referring to A. H. III 12, 1. 15; V 6, 1, but even if he had known he would not easily have attributed it to heretics or called its utterances ληρώδη. Possibly the latter has the same connotation of heretical or pagan nonsense as ληρωδία in Epiphanius, Panar. 21, 6; 31, 1; 36, 6 and elsewhere.

[3] Poimandres p. 222 n. 1. He criticises Bonwetsch (Zeitschrift für kirchliche Wissenschaft und kirchliches Leben 1884, p. 471 n. 1) who judges that Marcus' practices rested on an identification of divination and prophecy. Reitzenstein refers to the hellenistic concept of prophecy as found in the Hermetic literature.

[4] A. H. IV 20, 5; cf. supra, p. 78.

[5] For the distinction between inductive and intuitive, or inspirational divination cf. Hopfner, art. Mantike, P. W. R. E. XIV 1, c. 1258-1262; W. R. Halliday, Greek Divination (1913, repr. Chicago, 1967), p. 54ff. Inductive divination could more easily be identified as pagan and has received the most severe denunciations, cf. Courcelle, art. Divinatio, R. A. C. III, c. 1249f.

define the type of divination which Hermas describes, more closely when we take up the clue suggested by the statement that the devil fills the false prophet with his own spirit.[1] At this point we must, again, compare Irenaeus *A.H.* I 13. It is to Marcus that the false prophet is rightly compared, but the angel of the prophetic spirit who fills the true prophet and is κείμενος ἐπ᾽ αὐτῷ unmistakably resembles the δαίμων πάρεδρος through whom Marcus was said to prophesy.[2] At first sight it appears as if Hermas borrows a well-known concept of hellenistic divination to describe what happens when the prophet is inspired by the Holy Spirit, and fails to see that this concept could be put to a much better use to describe and unmask the divination of the false prophet. But two things must be noticed: (1) Hermas does not use the concept of the δαίμων πάρεδρος to explain the inspiration of the false prophet, because in his demonology there is no place for such an intermediary agent; (2) in the view of the ancient Christian writers divination through a δαίμων πάρεδρος was fundamentally also from the devil.

(1) Hermas does not use the word δαίμων.[3] δαιμόνιον occurs *Mand.* II 3 and *Sim.* IX 22, 3; 23:5, where it refers to some form of a human behaviour, namely καταλαλιά and αὐθάδεια, identifying as it were a certain sin. This is equivalent to the identification of a sin with a πνεῦμα[4] and it shows that the demonology of Hermas is virtually a part of his dualistic pneumatology. Only twice this pneumatology is connected with the devil. *Mand.* IX 9 (ἡ διψυχία θυγάτηρ ἐστὶ τοῦ διαβόλου), 11 (ἡ δὲ διψυχία ἐπίγειον πνεῦμά ἐστι παρὰ τοῦ διαβόλου) and XI 17 (ἀπὸ τοῦ διαβόλου ἔρχεται, sc. τὸ πνεῦμα τὸ ἐπίγειον καὶ κενόν) describe this connection: the bad spirits originate from the devil, and they act as if they were more or less personal beings.[5] This is also true of the empty spirit in the false prophet.[6]

---

[1] Cf. *supra*, p, 70.

[2] Cf. Dibelius, p. 541. For the angel of the prophetic spirit cf. *infra*, p. 104ff.

[3] Except *Mand.* V 2, 8 in ms A, but all other mss have πνεύματος.

[4] Cf. e.g. *Mand.* V 2, 8: ὀξυχολίας, τοῦ πονηροτάτου πνεύματος; X 1, 2: ἡ λύπη πάντων τῶν πνευμάτων πονηροτέρα ἐστίν.

[5] Cf. e.g. *Mand.* III 5 (ὃς ἂν ... ἀφέξεται τοῦ πονηροτάτου πνεύματος); V 1, 2 (the Holy Spirit in you will be pure μὴ ἐπισκοτούμενον ὑπὸ ἑτέρου πονηροῦ πνεύματος 1, 3 (id. πνίγεται ... ὑπὸ τοῦ πονηροῦ πνεύματος).

[6] Cf. *Mand.* XI 6.11.14.17. Yet in this same text Hermas describes the inspiration of both the false prophet and the true prophet in terms of filling; in this context the spirit is strictly instrumental and not personal. This shows the fluidity of his thinking.

There is one place which seemingly offers a parallel *in malam partem*
to the angel of the prophetic spirit. This is *Mand*. VI, which relates
the theme of the two angels, one of righteousness and one of evil.
But a comparison of the vocabulary of *Mand*. V (the two spirits)
with that of *Mand*. VI shows that the angels have the same characteristics as the spirits and that the theme of the two angels adds no new
element to Hermas' demonology.¹ They are virtually identical with
πνεύματα and not beings between God and the devil on the one side
and the spirits on the other.

(2) This explanation of why Hermas does not resort to a δαίμων
πάρεδρος to explain the inspiration of the false prophet does not
mean that this concept has no relevance for the divination of the
false prophet. For the ancient Christian writers there were not two
distinct ways of divination, one through the δαίμων πάρεδρος and
one directly from the devil. All divination was from the devil, whether
under his direct inspiration or through demons or through other
means. How little such distinctions meant is clear when we compare
the end of Irenaeus' description of Marcus with its beginning. It begins
with the δαίμων πάρεδρος and it ends with πνεύματα ... ὑπὸ τοῦ Σατανᾶ
ἐκπεμπόμενα, both referring to the same events, though from a different perspective. And Hippolytus does not mention the δαίμων πάρεδρος
at all, but ascribes Marcus' prophecy to demons.²

What then is the reason why Irenaeus mentions the δαίμων πάρεδρος
so explicitly? This may be inferred from the words: εἰκὸς δὲ αὐτὸν
καὶ δαίμονα τινὰ πάρεδρον ἔχειν, δι᾽ οὗ αὐτός τε προφητεύειν δοκεῖ,
καὶ ... προφητεύειν ποιεῖ. The opening word of this sentence,
εἰκός, implies that the δαίμων πάρεδρος is an inference of Irenaeus,
and serves to typify Marcus' prophetic activities. They are such that
a δαίμων πάρεδρος must be assumed to work through him. Naming
this demon was tantamount to characterizing the prophet and what
he did, and made further details unnecessary.

---

¹ The angel of righteousness is τρυφερός (VI 2, 3) like the Holy Spirit in *Mand*.
V 1, 3; the angel of evil is ὀξύχολος (2, 4) like the evil spirit in V 2, 8. Cf. also O. F.J.
Seitz, Two Spirits in Man, an Essay in Biblical Exegesis, *N. T. S.* 6 (1959-60), p. 82-95,
esp. p. 89f. A comparable text is *Test. Jud.* 20, 1: δύο πνεύματα σχολάζουσι τῷ ἀνθρώπῳ
τὸ τῆς ἀληθείας καὶ τὸ τῆς πλάνης cf. Dib., p. 522.

² *Ref*. VI 41: ποτὲ μὲν αὐτὸς ἐνομίζετο προφητεύειν, ποτὲ δὲ καὶ ἑτέρους ἐποίει· ὅτε μὲν
καὶ διὰ δαιμόνων ταῦτα ἐνεργῶν, ὅτε δὲ καὶ κυβεύων ὡς προείπομεν. Hippolytus also appears to connect the influence of the demons with the eucharist which Marcus admin-
isters.

In order to recapture these details, we must go to those sources which can bring to life for us the δαίμων πάρεδρος and, in the process, help us to gain a fuller picture of Marcus and the false prophet in Hermas. This search, however, will lead us again to the world of pagan divination.

The δαίμων πάρεδρος is mentioned several times with regard to certain Gnostics.[1] A passage in Justin mentions οἱ λεγόμενοι παρὰ τοῖς μάγοις ὀνειροπομποὶ καὶ πάρεδροι among other things as an argument for survival after death,[2] and it is indeed παρὰ τοῖς μάγοις that it is found most frequently. But this is probably a secondary development. The primary association was with divination.

For the purpose of our investigation it is sufficient to note that in Greek religion demons appear as a collectivity in the plural and in the singular as a personal demon, connected with individuals.[3] In hellenistic and Roman times the demons were connected with oracles and divination.[4] We have already seen what opportunities for serious

---

[1] Cf. Iren. A. H. I 23, 4: the disciples of Simon and Helena μαγείαις ἐπιτελοῦσι καὶ ἐπαοιδαῖς φίλτρα τε καὶ ἀγώγιμα καὶ τοὺς λεγομένους ὀνειροπομποὺς δαίμονας ἐπιπέμπουσι πρὸς τὸ ταράσσειν οὓς βούλονται. ἀλλὰ καὶ παρέδρους τοὺς λεγομένους ἀσκοῦσιν ib. 24, 5: utuntur autem et hi (i.e. Saturninus and Basilides) magia et imaginibus et incantationibus et invocationibus et reliqua universa periergia; ib. 25, 3: the Carpocratians practice τέχνας ... μαγικὰς ... καὶ ἐπαοιδὰς φίλτρα τε καὶ χαριτήσια, παρέδρους τε καὶ ὀνειροπομποὺς καὶ τὰ λοιπὰ κακουργήματα. Eusebius H. E. IV 7, 9: the Carpocratians are σεμνυνόμενοι τοῖς κατὰ περιεργίαν πρὸς αὐτῶν ἐπιτελουμένοις φίλτροις ὀνειροπομποῖς τε καὶ παρέδροις τισὶ δαίμοσιν καὶ ἄλλαις ὁμοιοτρόποις τισὶν ἀγωγαῖς.

[2] Apol. 18, 3. It occurs in the same function Tert., De Anima 28, 5: scimus etiam magiae licere explorandis occultis per catabolicos et paredros et pythonicos spiritus, cf. Waszink ad loc., p. 362f. It is worth noting that the idea of the πάρεδρος itself is sometimes applied to the devil, cf. Sulpic. Severus, Dial. 3, 8, 3: quod intellexerit egisse se semper adsidentis sibi diaboli voluntatem.

[3] Cf. M. P. Nilsson, op. cit., I², p. 216-222; II², p. 210-218; E. des Places, La Religion grecque (Paris, 1969), p. 113-117; W. Foerster, art. δαίμων, Th. W. N. T. II, p. 1-10.

[4] This connection is primarily a concern of the philosophers and not of popular religion. Probably the earliest evidence is Plato, Symp. 202e where τὸ δαιμόνιον is described as μεταξὺ ... θεοῦ τε καὶ θνητοῦ ... ἑρμηνεῦον καὶ διαπορθμεῦον θεοῖς τὰ παρ' ἀνθρώπων καὶ ἀνθρώποις τὰ παρὰ θεῶν ... διὰ τούτου καὶ ἡ μαντικὴ πᾶσα χωρεῖ (cf. Epinomis 984e δαίμονας, ἀέριον ... γένος ... τῆς ἑρμηνείας αἴτιον). Here, the demons have a mediating function between gods and men. This idea was developed by the Stoa, probably by Posidonius (cf. Cicero, De Divin. I 30, 64: quod plenus aër sit immortalium animorum in quibus tamquam insignitae notae veritatis appareant; cf. also Pease ad loc. and Nilsson, op. cit. II², p. 265), and taken up by Plutarch (cf. Def. Orac. 418 E τὸ μὲν ἐφεστάναι τοῖς χρηστηρίοις ... μὴ θεοὺς ... ἀλλὰ δαίμονας ὑπηρέτας θεῶν; cf. also R. Flacelière in his edition of De Pyth. Orac. (Paris, 1962), p. 16-19; Nilsson, op. cit. II², p. 409ff.),

criticism this connection offered to the Christian writers, from the Apologists on. They understood δαίμων as δαιμόνιον, i.e. *in malam partem*.¹ The concept of a δαίμων πάρεδρος as the source of divination is to be understood as a development of the idea of a personal demon. This idea originates from the identification of the individual's soul with a δαίμων.² Plato mentions a δαίμων σύνοικος³ and this idea was further developed in the course of time.⁴ The ill-reputed ventriloquist (ἐγγαστρίμυθος) Eurycles is said to have prophesied through a demon that was in him.⁵ The δαίμων πάρεδρος belongs to this type of personal divinatory demons. In the so-called Berlin Magical Papyrus he is described as δαίμων ὃς τὰ πάντα μηνύσει σοι ῥητῶς καὶ συνόμιλος καὶ συναριστῶν ἔσται σοι καὶ συγκοιμώμενος.⁶ The seer has no knowledge of his own, he depends on the δαίμων for his divination.⁷ When

---

and by Apuleius (cf. *Apologia* 43, 2 (ed. Valette): *quamquam Platoni credam inter deos atque homines natura et loco medias quasdam divorum potestates intersitas easque divinationes cunctas et magorum miracula gubernare*; and on this text F. Regen, *Apuleius Philosophus Platonicus* (Berlin, 1971), p. 3-22, who shows that Apuleius' appeal to Plato is only indirectly justified).

¹ Cf. *supra*, p. 69, n. 4. The Septuagint does not have δαίμων (only Is. 65:11), the New Testament has it only once (Mt. 8:31) and in the Apostolic Fathers it is found only Hermas, *Mand.* V 2,8 v.l. (cf. *supra*, p. 86, n. 4. In the same literature δαιμόνιον is used only *in malam partem*.

² Cf. des Places, *op. cit.*, p. 115, who sees the origin of the concept in the Heraclitean saying ἦθος ἀνθρώπῳ δαίμων (Fr. 119 Diels-Kranz).

³ *Tim.* 90c; cf. *Phaed.* 107d: ὁ ἑκάστου δαίμων, ὅσπερ ζῶντα εἰλήχει.

⁴ Cf. Nilsson, *op. cit.* II², p. 210ff. H. Hanse, *"Gott haben"* in der Antike und im frühen Christentum (Berlin, 1939), p. 11ff.,

⁵ Cf. Schol. ad Aristoph. *Vespae* 1016ff.: οὗτος (i.e. Eurycles) ὡς ἐγγαστρίμυθος λέγεται 'Αθήνησι τἀληθῆ μαντευόμενος διὰ τοῦ ἐνυπάρχοντος αὐτῷ δαίμονος; Schol. ad Plat., *Soph.* 252 c: Εὐρυκλῆς γὰρ ἐδόκει δαίμονά τινα ἐν τῇ γαστρὶ ἔχειν τὸν ἐγκελευόμενον περὶ τῶν μελλόντων λέγειν· ὅθεν καὶ ἐγγαστρίμυθος ἐκαλεῖτο; cf. Tambornino, *op. cit.*, p. 59f.

⁶ *P. G. M.* I 1f. (Preis. I, p. 2). The text is uncertain in some places. Reitzenstein, who was the first to use this papyrus for the purpose of interpreting Marcus and his prophetesses (*Poimandres*, p. 226ff.; *Hellen. Mysterienreligionen*, p. 27, 35) emphasized the mystical nature of the union between the δαίμων πάρεδρος and the person with whom he dwelt, and compared the ἱερὰ λῆψις παρέδρου with the prophetic initiation of the women by Marcus. But the difference is that the former is a magical rite to gain the πάρεδρος and in the case of Marcus the initiative is on the other side. Whether the basic pattern of the συνουσία of the demon is that of a ἱερὸς γάμος (*Poimandres*, p. 228; H. Leisegang, *Pneuma Hagion*, p. 33ff.) is another matter and beyond the scope of this study.

⁷ In Pap. VII 1011 (Preis. II p. 44f.) the seer is warned to give no answer before the angel comes into him (μηδενὶ δοὺς ἀπόκρισιν).

the δαίμων comes the seer is told: ἐρώτα αὐτόν, περὶ οὗ θέλεις, περὶ μαντείας, περὶ ἐποποιίας, περὶ ονειροπομπείας ... περὶ κατακλίσεως, περὶ πάντων ὅσων ἐστὶν ἐν τῇ μαγικῇ ἐμπειρίᾳ (328ff., p. 18). The 'magic experience' is in this context apparently restricted to divination.[1] The divinatory event itself is as follows: ἐὰν δέ τίς σε ἐρωτήσῃ τί κατὰ ψυχὴν ἔχω; ἤ·τί μοι ἐγένετο ἤγε μέλλει γενέσθαι; ἐπερώτα τὸν ἄγγελον, καὶ ἐρεῖ σοι σιωπῇ· σὺ δὲ ὡς ἀπὸ σεαυτοῦ λέγε τῷ ἐπερωτῶντί σε. (175-178, p. 10). It is this last point which led Irenaeus to surmise that Marcus prophesied through a δαίμων πάρεδρος. The magical diviner is urged to behave in such a way that people think him to speak ὡς ἀφ' ἑαυτοῦ, and this is exactly what Marcus does too. He does not disclose the source of his prophecies, but speaks and acts as if by virtue of his own χάρις. This is a common characteristic of diviners of this type. Diophanes does not ask a god but gives his answers straightaway. This distinguishes them from all oracular diviners: both prophets and μάντεις alike are supposed to transmit the word or the answer of the god they serve. Even a man like Alexander of Abonuteichos did his utmost to maintain the idea that Asclepius was the one who answered the questions.[2] The so-called αὐτόφωνοι purported to be spoken directly by the god himself.[3]

The situation in the 11th Mandate is similar, though this similarity is somewhat obscured by the idiom of the Two Spirits doctrine. The false prophet is not openly accused of speaking ἀφ' ἑαυτοῦ but the question is shifted from the men to the spirits in them, and the claim of the false prophet to speak ἀφ' ἑαυτοῦ is implicitly rejected by the somewhat uncalled for statement: πᾶν πνεῦμα ἀπὸ θεοῦ δοθὲν ... ἀφ' ἑαυτοῦ λαλεῖ πάντα (5).

This behaviour of the private diviners will have its roots in the need to enhance their prestige and renown. They could not derive their authority from some time-honoured and celebrated oracle, but depended on their own resources. This explains their self-recommendation. The Christian μάντις is fundamentally in the same position. He is

---

[1] Elsewhere (96-129, p. 8) a long list of what the δαίμων πάρεδρος may accomplish is given: he brings women and men, he takes away, he throws up winds from the earth, he brings gold, silver, copper, fire water, wine, etc. The passage ends: δουλεύσει σοι ἱκανῶς εἰς ἃ ἂν ἐπινοήσῃς, ὦ μακάριε μύστα τῆς ἱερᾶς μαγείας.

[2] Cf. Lucian, Alex. 19: προλέγει πᾶσι τοῖς ἀφικομένοις ὡς μαντεύσεται ὁ θεός.

[3] Ib., 26: ὑπέσχετο καὶ λαλοῦντα παρέξειν τὸν θεόν, αὐτὸν ἄνευ ὑποφήτου χρησμῳδοῦντα.

not accepted by the church, and hence has to claim that he himself
is important. He does this by saying ἑαυτὸν πνευματοφόρον εἶναι,
whereas the prophet is identified as ὁ ἄνθρωπος ὁ ἔχων τὸ πνεῦμα τὸ
θεῖον.[1]
This picture of the false prophet, drawn with the aid of analogies
and inferences, brings us to the borderline between the church and the
pagan world and shows how easily prophecy could change into divination and assume pagan forms. This is understandable enough in the
first centuries of the Christian era. But less obvious is the fact that
phrases and concepts stemming from the same pagan sources are used
to describe events and acts whose genuine Christian nature cannot
be doubted. Peterson's analyses of the Visions of Hermas have shown
convincingly to what extent they use concepts and pictures from hellenistic divination.[2] When this is the case the διάκρισις πνευμάτων
cannot be understood by determining the origin of the concept, but
by a careful analysis of what the hellenistic forms and pictures are used
for. Only then is it possible to distinguish the spirits.[3]

One other point is yet to be discussed. Hermas does not explicitly
describe the behaviour of the false prophet as a μάντις, nor does he
bother to pay attention to his state of mind when acting as a μάντις.
He is not interested in the psychology of divination but in distinguishing the spirits.

Yet there are a few details which may give us some clue as to the
psychological state of mind of the false prophet, namely the words
which we left undiscussed in chapter III: καὶ εὐθὺς ἰταμός ἐστι καὶ
ἀναιδὴς καὶ πολύλαλος (12).[4] Of these words ἀναιδής, 'shameless',
is the most general and hence occurs more often than the other two.
ἰταμός 'reckless' and πολύλαλος 'talkative' are very uncommon in
Jewish and Christian Greek.[5] We must look elsewhere in order to under-

---

1 Cf. also *supra*, p. 51, on the self-recommendation of false prophets.
2 Cf. *supra*, p. 21.
3 Cf. Peterson, *Frühkirche*, p. 270.
4 Cf. *supra*, p. 52.
5 Πολύλαλος only Job 11:2 Symm. = ὁ τὰ πολλὰ λέγων in LXX; πολυλαλία only Pseudoclem., *Hom.* XVIII, 11, 3: ἐκ πολυλαλίας γὰρ ἐνίοτε εὐστοχεῖ τις πρὸς τὸ ἀληθές, οὐκ εἰδὼς
ὃ λέγει. Though the context is different these words remind of the true words which
the false prophet speaks occasionally, in Hermas. ἰταμός only Jer. 6:23: ἰταμός ἐστιν
καὶ οὐκ ἐλεήσει and 27 (50): 42 — referring to the cruel and merciless people from
the north. It is worth noting that in Is. 56:11 Symm. ἰταμός is used where the Septuagint
has ἀναιδής. ἰταμία occurs only Jer. 30:10 (= 49:16 Mas.) and 30:20 (= 49:4 Mas.);

stand their meaning here. ἰταμός and ἀναιδής are semantically
closely related.¹ They often contrast with words like αἰδώς and
εὐλάβεια and σωφροσύνη.² The recklessness and shamelessness which
they denote may refer to various spheres of life but often they are
accompanied by a somewhat over-excited state of mind. This may
be due to physical reasons as in Lucian's caricature of certain Cynic
philosophers who give no little amusement to those who watch them,
ὁπόταν ὑπὸ τῆς τυχούσης αἰτίας ἐπιζέσῃ μὲν αὐτοῖς ἡ χολή, πελιδνοὶ
δὲ τὴν χροιὰν βλέπωνται, ἰταμόν τι καὶ παράφορον δεδορκότες, καὶ
ἀφροῦ, μᾶλλον δὲ ἰοῦ, μεστὸν αὐτοῖς ᾖ τὸ στόμα.³ But more often
there are other incentives, among them the wine. Aristotle tries
to explain why so many famous men, like Empedocles, Plato and
even Socrates, are μελαγχολικοί, by comparing the effect of the wine:
ὁ γὰρ οἶνος ὁ πολὺς μάλιστα φαίνεται παρασκευάζειν τοιούτους οἵους
λέγομεν τοὺς μελαγχολικοὺς εἶναι καὶ πλεῖστα ἤθη ποιεῖν πινόμενος,
οἷον ὀργίλους, φιλανθρώπους, ἐλεήμονας, ἰταμοὺς ... παραλαβὼν γὰρ
ἀπεψυγμένους ἐν τῷ νήφειν καὶ σιωπηλοὺς μικρῷ μὲν πλείων ποθεὶς
λαλιστέρους ποιεῖ ... ῥητορικοὺς καὶ θαρραλέους, προϊόντας δὲ πρὸς
τὸ πράττειν ἰταμούς⁴. Sexual desire is another. In Menander's *Epi-
trepontes* a girl rehearses what she will say to a young man about
their sexual relationship, and says ὡς δ' ἀναιδὴς ἦσθα καὶ ἰταμός

---

in the former place it renders Hebrew זדון which occurs in Deut. 18:22: 'when a prophet
speaks in the name of the Lord, if the word does not come to pass or come true, that is
a word which the Lord has not spoken; the prophet has spoken it *presumptuously*',
but here the Septuagint has ἀσέβεια and Symm. and Theod. ὑπερηφανία. Conceivably,
ἰταμός may also have this connotation of presumptuousness in our place in Hermas.

¹ Cf. e.g. Demosth., c. *Aristog.* 24 (777): πάντα τὰ σεμνὰ καὶ καλὰ ... τῶν αἰσχρῶν
περίεστιν, τῆς ἀναισχυντίας, τῆς θρασύτητος, τῆς ἀναιδείας. Ἰταμὸν γὰρ ἡ πονηρία καὶ
τολμηρὸν καὶ πλεονεκτικόν. Lucian, *Vit. Auct.* 10f., where ἰταμόν χρὴ εἶναι is resumed
by ἦν μόνον ἡ ἀναίδεια ... παρῇ; Plut., *Pelop. et Marc.* 1 (277E) where ἰταμός, παράβολος
and τολμηρός are used synonymously; Ael. Aristides 31, 5 (Keil), where θρασύ, ἰταμόν
and αὔθαδες appear together.

² Cf. Luc., *Vit. Auct.* 10: αἰδὼς δὲ καὶ ἐπιείκεια καὶ μετριότης ἀπέστω. Plato, *Politicus*
311a: τὰ μὲν γὰρ σωφρόνων ἀρχόντων ἤθη σφόδρα μὲν εὐλαβῆ καὶ δίκαια καὶ σωτήρια, δρι-
μύτητος δὲ καί τινος ἰταμότητος ὀξείας καὶ πρακτικῆς ἐνδεῖται. id., *Leges* VI 773a (ἰταμός
vs. κόσμιος). These quotations show that ἰταμός is not always used *in malam partem*,
as also Plut., *Galba* 25; *Fab.* 19; *Cato Minor* 44.

³ *Fugit.*, 19.

⁴ *Problemata* 30, 1 (953 a b); cf. Plut., *Quaest. Conv.* VII 715 E: πολλοῖς δ'ἰταμότητα
θάρσους συνεργὸν ὁ ἄκρατος (sc. οἶνος), οὐ βδελυρὰν οὐδ' ἄκρατον ἀλλ' εὔχαριν καὶ πιθανήν,
προστίθησιν, ὥσπερ καὶ τὸν Αἰσχύλον ἱστοροῦσι τὰς τραγῳδίας ἐμπίνοντα ποιεῖν. Eur. Fr.
265 Nauck: νῦν δ' οἶνος ἐξέστησέ με.

τις¹. As so often it is Plutarch who presents us with the physiological or psychological explanation. Young people are καὶ ὀξεῖς καὶ ἰταμοὶ περί τε τὰς ὀρέξεις διάπυροι καὶ οἰστρώδεις αἵματος πλήθει καὶ θερμότητι². Elsewhere, following Plato, he speaks of ὁ ἐρωτικὸς ἐνθουσιασμός³. What wine and love have in common is that they make people warm and hilarious and reckless in words and deeds.⁴ But this is not confined to them. A similar experience is that of ὁ μαντικὸς ἐνθουσιασμός. In a lengthy discussion of the part played by the soul in divination Plutarch posits that its potential divinatory disposition may become effective when it comes under the influence of τὸ μαντικὸν ῥεῦμα καὶ πνεῦμα. This πνεῦμα may approach the body καθ' ἑαυτὸ δι'ἀέρος or through running water. What happens when it has entered the body is described as follows: θερμότητι γὰρ καὶ διαχύσει πόρους τινὰς ἀνοίγειν φανταστικοὺς τοῦ μέλλοντος εἰκός ἐστιν, ὡς οἶνος ἀναθυμιαθεὶς ἕτερα πολλὰ κινήματα καὶ λόγους ἀποκειμένους καὶ λανθάνοντας ἀποκαλύπτει. This is the state of mind which is called ἐνθουσιασμός, the state of mind ὅταν ἔνθερμος ἡ ψυχὴ γενομένη καὶ πυρώδης ἀπώσηται τὴν εὐλάβειαν ἣν ἡ θνητὴ φρόνησις ἐπάγουσα πολλάκις ἀποστρέφει καὶ κατασβέννυσι τὸν ἐνθουσιασμόν⁵.

It may seem a little far-fetched to stretch the words ἰταμὸς ... καὶ ἀναιδὴς καὶ πολύλαλος to carry the associations and connotations set forth above. But we should not overlook the brachylogical nature of this description. Hermas is not interested in the inner experiences of the false prophet but in what proceeds from them, his perceptible behaviour. Yet he did not choose the depreciative terms used to describe this behaviour at random. This becomes clear when once again

---

¹ Ed. v. Leeuwen 352f. = Körte 310. Cf. also Plut., *Conj. Praec.* 140 C; *Amat.* 767 B; *Non posse suaviter* 1094 A; Heliodorus, *Aethiopiaca* I 9, 3 (of a stepmother in love with her stepson): ἰταμώτερον προσῄει καὶ θερμότερα ἦν τὰ φιλήματα τοῦ πρέποντος.

² *Virt. Mor.* 450 F.

³ *Pyth. Orac.* 406 B, referring to Plato, *Phaedrus* 245 b. It appears that ἐνθουσιασμός is not restricted to divinatory inspiration but may have wider application, cf. also *Amat.* 758 E — 759 D.

⁴ Plut., *Quaest. Conv.* I E (622 D E): τῷ μεθύειν τὸ ἐρᾶν ὅμοιόν ἐστι· ποιεῖ γὰρ θερμοὺς καὶ ἱλαροὺς καὶ διακεχυμένους. Plato, *Tim.* 60 a: τὸ μὲν τῆς ψυχῆς μετὰ τοῦ σώματος θερμαντικὸν οἶνος. Aristotle, *loc. cit.* (cf. p. 92, n. 4). Plut., *Quaest. Viv.* VII (715 F); some people have an inventive nature which is ἐν τῷ νήφειν ἀτολμοτέρα καὶ πεπηγυῖα but ὅταν εἰς τὸ πίνειν ἔλθωσιν, ὥσπερ ὁ λιβανωτός, ὑπὸ θερμότητος ἀναθυμιῶνται.

⁵ *Def. Orac.* 432 D-F.

we turn to Irenaeus' story of Marcus and his prophetesses. At the end he concludes: τοιαῦτα ... πνεύματα (namely those who are commanded by men and speak when they want) ἐπίσαθρα καὶ ἀδρανῆ ἐστι (i.e. unstable and impotent), τολμηρὰ δὲ καὶ ἀναιδῆ. This is strongly reminiscent of ἰταμὸς καὶ ἀναιδής. The same words are found in the description of the prophesying women who speak τολμηρῶς and whose soul is τολμηρὸν καὶ ἀναιδές. But there is still a closer link between the two documents. Both the false prophet of Hermas and the prophesying women are said to be inspired by a κενὸν πνεῦμα. This is a very rare expression and its very rarity suggests that there is some direct connection between Hermas and Irenaeus. The latter borrowed it because he felt the close affinity between the false prophet and Marcus and his adherents.[1] If this interpretation is correct we may proceed one step further and examine whether the description of the prophetesses in Irenaeus supplies the connecting link between Hermas and the hellenistic ideas about divinatory inspiration.

When the woman, whom Marcus wants to prophesy, hesitates and answers: οὐ προεφήτευσα πώποτε καὶ οὐκ οἶδα προφητεύειν, Marcus makes some further invocations and repeats his formula ἄνοιξον τὸ στόμα σου adding: λάλησον ὅ τι δήποτε, καὶ προφητεύσεις. We may safely assume that this is an interpretative quotation. Then the woman yields her resistence, because she is χαυνωθεῖσα καὶ κεπφωθεῖσα by what has been said, i.e. excited and deceived.[2] Her state of mind is described as διαθερμανθεῖσα τὴν ψυχήν, 'with overheated soul'. At first it seems as if Irenaeus is explaining this psychologically, as due to the thrill of expectation which makes her heart beat frantically (ὑπὸ τῆς προσδοκίας τοῦ μέλλειν αὐτὴν προφητεύειν, τῆς καρδίας πλέον τοῦ δέοντος παλλούσης), but this is immediately replaced by another explanation. The woman speaks κενῶς καὶ τολμηρῶς, ἅτε ὑπὸ κενοῦ τεθερμαμμένη πνεύματος. This is not some ad hoc explanation, but corroborated by a quotation from some one called ὁ κρείσσων ἡμῶν, apparently indicating some person with authority for Irenaeus and his readers.[3]

---

[1] Cf. supra, p. 41f.

[2] Χαυνωθεῖσα may mean 'softened', 'weakened' (cf. Lampe, P. G. L. s.v. and Test. Zab. 2, 4) or 'puffed up' (Harvey, cf. L-Sc. s.v. II), or 'excited' (Klebba, cf. Euseb., H. E. V 16, 8: ὡς ἁγίῳ πνεύματι καὶ προφητικῷ χαρίσματι ἐπαιρόμενοι καὶ οὐχ ἥκιστα χαυνούμενοι. The Latin version of Irenaeus has: seducta et elata, reversing the order), The last appears to be preferable. Κεπφωθεῖσα is best understood as 'deceived', 'ensnared' cf. Lampe, P. G. L. s.v. and Prov. 7:22 LXX.

[3] Cf. supra, p. 42, n. 1.

Apart from κενόν, Irenaeus' explanation fits Plutarch's description of the ἐνθουσιασμός exactly but it takes the common key word 'warm' (ἔνθερμος, τεθερμαμμένη) in a vituperative sense. They now serve to identify for those who know Marcus and his women followers as paganistic 'enthusiasts'. And even in Hermas the picture of a similar 'enthusiastic' μάντις in the Christian church, drawn by a Christian author hides behind the succinct description of his behaviour.

So far we have only found evidence referring to the state of mind of those concerned. When we attempt to translate this into the terms of reference set forth above,[1] the 'enthusiasm' of the women appears to mean that they have lost control over what they say completely. That they also have lost consciousness is improbable. As to the false prophet, the veiled indications do not permit further conclusions, save that he showed forth considerable excitement.

This is the picture of the Christian μάντις which Hermas draws in the 11th Mandate. Almost every detail of this picture can be explained when the picture is compared with that of similar diviners of various kinds in the hellenistic world. In most cases, these diviners meet with severe criticism in the hellenistic world. The Christian μάντις is in no way superior to his pagan colleagues. One would almost forget that he operates within the church and that his following consists of church members. Yet this is unmistakably the case. The writer is clearly intent on bringing out how deeply this form of paganism had made its way into the Christian community and not just some form of foretelling which only remotely resembled pagan divination but one which could be identified as hellenistic divination in one of its lower forms.[2]

Two additional remarks are to be made. The description of the ἐνθουσιασμός in Plutarch, Def. Orac. 432 F has been used by W. C. van Unnik to elucidate 1 Thessalonians 5:19: τὸ πνεῦμα μὴ σβέννυτε.[3] As in Plutarch the φρόνησις often turns off and quenches the ἐνθουσιασμός, so the Christians in Thessalonica are admonished not to quench the Spirit by human considerations and human shame lest they appear as mad in the eyes of other people. But Van Unnik remarks that the comparison of Paul with Plutarch does not mean that Paul would have given the same explanation of Christian enthusiasm.

---

[1] Cf. supra, p. 19.
[2] For the meaning of 'lower' in this connection, cf. infra, p. 171f.
[3] W. C. van Unnik, "Den Geist löschet nicht aus", N. T. 10 (1968), 255-269.

When this is kept in mind, his elucidation of 1 Thessalonians 5:19 is convincing. But when our interpretation of the background of the words which characterise the false prophet (derived ultimately from the same place in Plutarch!) is correct, inevitably the two conclusions must be balanced against one another. In 1 Thessalonians 5:19 Christians are warned not to let themselves be guided by their εὐλάβεια to quench the Spirit, in Hermas we find a prophet who, inflamed by another spirit, has put off his εὐλάβεια and speaks and appears ἰταμὸς καὶ ἀναιδὴς καὶ πολύλαλος. Once again we are confronted with the problem of hellenistic concepts being put to an opposite use in Christian texts and once again we must conclude that the question cannot be dealt with in terms of Christian borrowing and hellenistic lending. No διάκρισις πνευμάτων is possible by simply tracing the origin of a certain idea or picture.[1] The Christian authors, however, do not seem to have been bothered by this problem because they were both Christian and hellenistic. The fact that they were Christians did not gainsay the fact that, sociologically and psychologically, they remained hellenistic. They were aware of the deep cleft between them and their non-Christian fellow men and they did not hesitate to denounce pagan religion and its intrusions into their own ranks. Yet it is also true that they did not hesitate to use ideas and phrases of their pagan environment to express their own religious experience.

Van Unnik's remark: "Phänomenologisch betrachtet, bestand eine große Aehnlichkeit zwischen den christlichen Geistesäußerungen und dem griechischen Enthusiasmus",[2] leads us to the second point. This statement seems to need further qualification. When our interpretation of the false prophet's behaviour is correct it follows that the difference between his 'enthusiasm' and the Christian prophet's "Geistesäußerungen" must have been perceptible to the congregation, and that phenomenologically there will have been little resemblance between the two prophets. In the case of glossolalia the resemblance which Van Unnik mentions may have been considerable, but for Hermas' two prophets some reservations appear in order. This raises the question whether the true prophet was an 'enthusiast' or not. To him and his ministry we now turn.

---

[1] Cf. *supra*, p. 91.

[2] *Art. cit.*, p. 269; he compares 1 Cor. 14:23: οὐκ ἐροῦσιν ὅτι μαίνεσθε to Euripides, *Bacch.* 298f.: τὸ γὰρ βακχεύσιμον καὶ τὸ μανιῶδες μαντικὴν πολλὴν ἔχει.

CHAPTER FIVE

PROPHECY AND THE SPIRIT

The Marks of the Prophet

In the context of a διάκρισις πνευμάτων the designation 'the true prophet' which we use without second thought, appears only rarely in early Christian literature.[1] Contrasted to the ψευδοπροφήτης is not the ἀληθοπροφήτης,[2] but ὁ προφήτης without further qualification. He is the man who has the Spirit from above and he can be distinguished from the man who has the earthly spirit by the standards discussed in the preceding chapter. As we have noticed there,[3] the testing by a doctrinal standard or by the outcome are not applied in Hermas because they are not relevant to the problem under consideration. Relevant are the other two and the description of the prophet therefore begins with his Christian moral life. He is gentle, quiet and humble; he refrains from all wickedness and from all evil and worthless desire of this age, and he makes himself more needy than all other people. As set forth in ch. III, the way of life described by these words and phrases is not peculiar to πνευματικοί but characteristic of all Christians.[4] The prophet is not a Christian of exceptional moral behaviour but an ordinary Christian who meets the standards which apply to all. If he does not meet them, he is not fit to act as a prophet at all. There is nothing like a προφητικὴ τάξις in the church of Hermas.[5]

What follows concerns the prophet as a prophet. Three negative statements are given to distinguish him from the false prophet: (1) he

---

[1] Cf. *Did.* 13, quoted *supra*, p. 8f. The phrase ὁ ἀληθὴς προφήτης in the Pseudo-clementine writings is a different matter: it is a messianic title and refers only to Jesus, cf. e.g. *Hom.* XVIII, 7, 6 where Peter says of himself: προφήτου ἀληθοῦς μαθητὴς ὤν, οὐ προφήτης, cf. also VII, 11, 3; *Recogn.* III, 45. Cf. Friedrich, art. προφήτης, *Th. W. N. T.* VI, p. 860f.

[2] Like ἀληθόμαντις (Aesch. *Agam.*, 1241) contrasting with ψευδόμαντις (*ib.* 1195). Cf. also Josephus, *Ant.* IX 23: Elijah prays for fire to fall from heaven ἐπὶ πείρᾳ τοῦ προφήτης ἀληθὴς ὑπάρχειν.

[3] Cf. *supra*, p. 68f.

[4] Cf. *supra*, p. 49f.

[5] For the place of the prophet in the church cf. *infra*, p. 151ff.

does not answer when a question is put to him; (2) he does not speak κατᾰμόνας. (3) the Spirit does not speak when a man wishes to speak. These points deserve some further investigation.

(1) That the prophet does not answer questions appears to be an important point because it is, in a slightly different form, already stated in 5: πᾶν ... πνεῦμα ἀπὸ θεοῦ δοθὲν οὐκ ἐπερωτᾶται ἀλλὰ ... ἀφ' ἑαυτοῦ λαλεῖ πάντα.[1] What is said in 5 of the Spirit, is said of the prophet in 8. The prophet cannot be consulted. This is a remarkable criterion which is not used elsewhere in distinguishing prophets. It plays no part in the Montanist crisis in the latter part of the second century.[2] It does not fit any of the four criteria discussed in ch. IV.[3] It has to do with the prophet's behaviour as a prophet, the prophetic situation, as distinct from his inspiration. It is all the more amazing since in the Old Testament consulting God through a priest or a prophet was a very common procedure.[4] To the present writer's knowledge this caused no embarrassment to early Christian exegetes either because they paid no attention to it.[5] The one occasion when an exegete deals with the question explicitly it is made clear that consulting God implies going to an priest and putting the question to him.[6]

More important is that this criterion apparently plays no part in the Christian polemics against the oracles, though this would have

---

[1] Snyder's rendering of ἐπερωτᾶται "need be asked" seems not quite to make the point which was so important to Hermas, namely that the prophet *cannot* be consulted. It is worth noting that in John 16:13 it is emphasized that the Spirit does not speak ἀφ' ἑαυτοῦ just as Jesus did not speak of himself (7:17; 12:49; 14:10); both speak what they had heard from the Father. Here the Spirit is viewed as strictly instrumental whereas in Hermas the Spirit appears to operate more independently

[2] The decisive criterion appears to have been that of ecstasis, cf. P. de Labriolle, *La Crise Montaniste* (Paris, 1913), p. 162-175, 555-560.

[3] Cf. *supra*, p. 67ff.

[4] Cf. *supra*, p. 35, n. 2. It caused neither the Septuagint translators nor Josephus any embarrassment. The latter sometimes inserts a reference to a human mediator where the Septuagint does not mention it, cf. *Ant.* VI 122 (1 Sam. 14:37); 271 (1 Sam. 23:2, 4); VII 7 (2 Sam. 2:1); 72 (2 Sam. 5:19, 23).

[5] Neither Origen nor Theodoretus deal with it in their commentaries on Joshua, Judges, Samuel and Kings.

[6] Joh. Chrysost., *In c. XXV Gen. Hom.* L (MPG 54, 448): ἐπορεύθη πυθέσθαι παρὰ κυρίου. Τί ἐστιν· ... ἔδραμεν ἐπὶ τὴν ἀληθῆ γνῶσιν καὶ ἐπὶ τὸν ἱερέα τὸν τοῦ θείου θεραπευτήν ... καὶ γὰρ καὶ ἑτέρωθι ἄγγελον καλεῖ τὸν ἱερέα ἡ θεία Γραφή, δεικνῦσα ὅτι ἐκεῖνα φθέγγεται ἅπερ ἂν ἐνηχήσῃ ἡ τοῦ Πνεύματος χάρις.

been the most natural occasion to use it.[1] Here then we have a criterion of genuine prophecy which is, as it were, Hermas' own contribution to the διάκρισις πνευμάτων in the Christian church of the second century. But this criterion does not come from nowhere. It is the application of another, more generally accepted, criterion to the specific prophetic situation in Hermas. This situation is such that a prophet must be distinguished from a μάντις: that is, one who speaks καθώς ὁ κύριος βούλεται (9) must be distinguished from one who speaks καθώς αὐτοὶ βούλονται (2). The general principle involved is that stated in 2 Petr. 1:21: οὐ γὰρ θελήματι ἀνθρώπου ἠνέχθη προφητεία ποτέ, ἀλλὰ ὑπὸ πνεύματος ἁγίου φερόμενοι ἐλάλησαν ἀπὸ θεοῦ ἄνθρωποι.[2] This principle which is also valid in the prophetic situation of the classic prophets of the Old Testament,[3] is here modified in the sense that it refers, not to the impulse of the prophet, but to the wishes of people who come to the prophet. This modification was indicated because in divination asking questions is a matter of course.[4]

A glance at Hermas' use of the verb ἐπερωτάω may reveal something about the meaning this principle had for him. It is remarkable that he is the only early Christian writer (apart from the evangelists) to use it frequently.[5] Apart from *Mand.* XI, where it always refers to asking questions either of the prophet or of the false prophet, it occurs 19 times when Hermas asks for further information and/or explanation about what is revealed to him. This feature is not uncommon in apocalyptic literature.[6] But in one respect Hermas is different

---

[1] When diviners are compared with prophets, they are contrasted to the prophets of the Old Testament (cf. Weiland, *op. cit.*, p. 54-61) to whom the criterion of not answering requests did not apply.

[2] For the general nature of this statement cf. Windisch, *Die kathol. Briefe, H. N. T.* 15³, p. 91, *ad loc.*; Lindblom, *Gesichte und Offenbarungen*, p. 162f.

[3] It is implied in the prophetic formulae כה אמר יהוה, נאם יהוה etc., cf. Lindblom, *Prophecy*, p. 108ff. Only seldom is the Spirit mentioned as the source of the prophet's inspiration (Hos. 9:7; Mic. 3:8; Is. 61:1; Ezek. 11:5), probably due to the opposition of the classical prophets to the manifestations of the ecstatic nᵉbi'im, cf. E. Jacob, *Théologie de l'Ancien Testament* (Neuchatel, 1955), p. 101.

[4] Cf. *supra*, p. 83f.

[5] It is found only at 2 Clem. 12, 2 and Justin, *Dial.* 50, 1 apart from its occurrence in O. T. quotations (Justin, *Dial.* 24, 3; 119, 4; 131, 1; *Apol.* 49, 2).

[6] Cf. e. g. Dan. 7:16ff.; 8:15-19; 9:20-23; Zech. 1:18f.; 4:11; 5:6, 10; 6:4; 1 Enoch 21, 3f.; 24, 5f.; 53, 4; 61, 2f.; 4 Ezra 4, 1ff.; 7, 1ff.; 10, 29ff.; *Test. Levi* 2, 6-9; 5, 1-7. In Baruch the seer is in direct dialogue with God, cf. e.g. 3, 1 - 5, 4, but cf. 55, 3 where Ramiel who presides over the true visions appears to reveal the interpretation of the vision. For the use of ἐπερωτάω in Greek oracular idiom cf. *supra*, p. 36. n. 1.

from most others. His questions often meet with severe criticism and rebuke from the revealer. In *Vis.* III 3,2 the πρεσβυτέρα addresses Hermas after he had asked for an explanation of the vision of the tower, as follows: μηκέτι μοι κόπους πάρεχε περὶ ἀποκαλύψεως· αἱ γὰρ ἀποκαλύψεις αὗται τέλος ἔχουσιν· πεπληρωμέναι γάρ εἰσιν. ἀλλ' οὐ παύσῃ αἰτούμενος ἀποκαλύψεις·ἀναιδὴς γὰρ εἶ. After identifying herself as the church she allows Hermas to ask further questions (ὃ ἂν οὖν θελήσῃς ἐπερώτα περὶ τοῦ πύργου, 3). A little further, after the church had finished her exegesis, Hermas is unashamed enough to ask another question (ἀναιδευσάμενος ἔτι αὐτὴν ἐπηρώτησα, 7, 5).[1] In *Sim.* V 4, 2 the angel replies to a long list of questions: αὐθάδης εἶ λίαν εἰς τὸ ἐπερωτᾶν. οὐκ ὀφείλεις, φησίν, ἐπερωτᾶν οὐδὲν ὅλως· ἐὰν γὰρ σοι δέῃ δηλωθῆναι, δηλωθήσεται. A similar expression follows when Hermas adds another request for an explanation: πανοῦργος εἶ καὶ αὐθάδης, ἐπερωτῶν τὰς ἐπιλύσεις τῶν παραβολῶν (5, 1).[2] These are very hard judgments indeed! The words ἀναιδής, αὐθάδης and πανοῦργος recall the false prophet who is ἰταμὸς καὶ ἀναιδής![3] It is also worth noting that Hermas does not only ask for explanations but also for revelations, but the answer is that revelations will be granted to him who must receive them! It appears as if Hermas is aware of the impropriety of his inquisitiveness *vis à vis* the divine revealers. This awareness is understandable when it is seen against the background of the principle that no divine spirit complies with human questions, and shows what the principle meant to Hermas.

(2) The prophet does not speak καταμόνας i.e. in a small group.

---

[1] Ἔτι goes with ἐπηρώτησα (Dibelius), rather than with ἀναιδευσάμενος (Lake, Snyder). In the latter case ἀναιδευόμενος would have been appropriate, cf. *Vis.* III 8, 9 (τὸν πύργον ἔτι οἰκοδομούμενον) V 4 (ἔτι λαλοῦντος αὐτοῦ) to *Mand.* IV 4, 1; *Sim.* V 5, 4; VI 4, 1 (ἔτι μοι τοῦτο δήλωσον).

[2] In other places Hermas is chided as foolish and/or stupid (μωρός, ἀσύνετος, ἄφρων), cf. *Vis.* III 6, 5; 8, 9; *Mand.* X 1, 2; XII 4, 2; *Sim.* VI 4, 3; 5, 2; IX 12, 1; 14, 4, but this is a criticism of a different order since it rebukes not the asking as such but the content of the questions. It is closer to such passages as Mk. 4:13; 7:18; Jn. 3:10; 14:9; 4 Ezra 4, 10f.; *Epist. Apostolorum*; 17 (28); 22 (33); 24 (35) transl. Duensing (Bonn, 1925); *Corp. Herm.* 1, 20, and is better understood as a literary device to lend a new impulse to the dialogue than as an expression of the inaccessibility of the divine to man (cf. Dibelius p. 458, *ad Vis.* III 2, 3).

[3] For these words cf. *supra*, p. 91ff. They appear somehow to be reserved for the false prophet and for Hermas when he asks questions! For πανοῦργος cf. also Betz, *Der Apostel Paulus und die sokratische Tradition*, p. 104ff.

This contrasts with the false prophet who κατὰ γωνίαν προφητεύει (13),[1] whereas the prophet λαλεῖ εἰς τὸ πλῆθος. This has a bearing upon the prophet's place in the church and will be dealt with in that context.[2]

(3) The prophet does not speak when a man wants to speak. This rendering contains the same ambiguity as the Greek text which is open to several interpretations: οὐδὲ ὅταν θέλῃ ἄνθρωπος λαλεῖν, λαλεῖ τὸ πνεῦμα τὸ ἅγιον may mean, (a) "nor does the holy Spirit speak whenever a man wishes to speak" (Snyder), i.e. when a man wants to speak as a prophet, or (b) 'nor does the holy Spirit speak whenever a man wants him (i.e. the prophet or the Spirit, preferably the latter) to speak'. Interpretation (a) takes ἄνθρωπος to denote the prophet as a man and distinct from the Spirit in him. This, however, is improbable since he is referred to twice as ὁ ἄνθρωπος.[3] The second interpretation has in view a situation in which other people want the prophet to speak ἐν πνεύματι. This is related to, but not identical with, the fact that he does not answer questions. The common element in both is that prophecy does not act upon outside incentives. But the rule of not answering questions was due to the situation of conflict between prophet and μάντις whereas the situation of not speaking when other people want it, is not. There must be another reason why this rule is introduced in the description of the prophet with such obvious emphasis. Before starting a search for this reason it may be useful to attempt to penetrate somewhat deeper into the meaning of the rule itself by comparing it to the general principle of prophecy laid down in 2 Pet. 1:21 and quoted on p. 99. There the will of a man (ἀνθρώπου) is clearly that of the prophet. As prophecy is not a question of ἰδίας ἐπιλύσεως, its content is not τὸ ἴδιον of the prophet.[4] The need of a divine interpretation is shown by pointing to the divine origin of the prophetic message. The Spirit of God is, as it were, set off against the will of the prophet. This, however, is a situation which is incompatible with Hermas' understanding of the Spirit. When the prophet speaks it is either the Spirit of God which speaks through him or an earthly

---

[1] Cf. *supra*, p. 54.

[2] Cf. *infra*, p. 123ff.

[3] The absence of the article would be very awkward if ἄνθρωπος had the same referent as ὁ ἄνθρωπος in 9. Lake has the same interpretation as Snyder, but takes the clause as explaining why the prophet does not speak καταμόνας; this is very unlikely.

[4] Cf Philo, *Quis Rer. Div. Haer.* 259: προφήτης γὰρ ἴδιον μὲν οὐδὲν ἀποφθέγγεται, ἀλλότρια δὲ πάντα ὑπηχοῦντος ἑτέρου quoted by Windisch *ad loc.*

spirit. Distinguishing the prophets is not finding out who has the Spirit and who speaks of his own accord but distinguishing the Spirit of God and the earthly spirit. Even if there is, in a sense, a permanent identification of the prophet and the Spirit,[1] it is impossible for the latter to become subject to the will or control of the former. This, however, is not restricted to the area of prophecy but applies to Christian life in general. Human conduct is determined by spiritual powers. Ill temper, ὀξυχολία, is a πνεῦμα,[2] and also grief, λύπη,[3] and double-mindedness.[4] On the other hand there is a close relationship between μακροθυμία, patience, and the Spirit, to the extent that it is sometimes called πνεῦμα.[5] The same is true of cheerfulness, ἱλαρότης,[6] and of πίστις,[7] and probably also of ἀλήθεια.[8] None of these are subject to the will of the believer. What he can do is to treat the Spirit in a wrong way. By lying one may bring grief to the reverent and true Spirit.[9] When ill temper enters, the Holy Spirit, which is delicate, is discomforted and seeks to leave the place.[10] The Spirit is grieved by ill temper and double-mindedness and will depart from man.[11]

These few indications may suffice to show that, in Hermas' understanding, it is never possible for man to control the Spirit.[12] Consequent-

---

[1] Cf. 12: δύναται οὖν πνεῦμα θεῖον μισθοὺς λαμβάνειν καὶ προφητεύειν; οὐκ ἐνδέχεται τοῦτο ποιεῖν θεοῦ προφήτην. This identification causes the writer considerable trouble when he has to explain the situation, in which the Spirit is inactive, cf. infra, p. 111ff.

[2] Mand. V 1, 3f.: ἀμφότερα τὰ πνεύματα refers to ὀξυχολία and μακροθυμία.

[3] Ib., X 1, 2: ἡ λύπη πάντων τῶν πνευμάτων πονηροτέρα ἐστίν.

[4] Ib., IX 11: ἡ δὲ διψυχία ἐπίγειον πνεῦμά ἐστι παρὰ τοῦ διαβόλου.

[5] Ib. V 1, 2: ἐὰν μακρόθυμος ἔσῃ, τὸ πνεῦμα τὸ κατοικοῦν ἐν σοὶ καθαρὸν ἔσται.

[6] Ib., X 3, 1 f.: ἔνδυσαι τὴν ἱλαρότητα, and τὸ πνεῦμα τὸ ἅγιον τὸ δοθὲν τῷ ἀνθρώπῳ ἱλαρόν.

[7] Ib., IX 11: ἡ πίστις ἄνωθέν ἐστιν παρὰ τοῦ κυρίου καὶ ἔχει δύναμιν μεγάλην.

[8] Ib. III 1-4: ἀλήθεια is identified with τὸ πνεῦμα τῆς ἀληθείας or τὸ πνεῦμα ... ἀληθές. Cf. also the names of the virgins in Sim. IX 15, 2: Πίστις, Μακροθυμία, Ἱλαρότης, Ἀλήθεια, while the virgins are called ἅγια πνεύματα in 13, 2.

[9] Mand. III 4; cf. also 2: οἱ ψευδόμενοι ἀθετοῦσι τὸν κύριον καὶ γίνονται ἀποστερηταὶ τοῦ κυρίου, μὴ παραδιδόντες αὐτῷ τὴν παρακαταθήκην ἣν ἔλαβον which expresses the same thought by means of a different picture.

[10] Ib., V 1, 3: ἐὰν δὲ ὀξυχολία τις προσελθῇ, εὐθὺς τὸ πνεῦμα τὸ ἅγιον, τρυφερὸν ὄν, στενοχωρεῖται ... καὶ ζητεῖ ἀποστῆναι ἐκ τοῦ τόπου Cf. also 2, 5f.

[11] Ib., X 2, 4: ἀμφότεραι αἱ πράξεις (διψυχία and ὀξυχολία) λυποῦσι τὸ πνεῦμα.

[12] The statement that the spirits of the prophets are subject to the prophets (1Cor. 14:32) refers to the order in the congregation, not to the fundamental relationship between the Spirit and the prophet.

ly, the general principle of prophecy is, again, applicable only indirectly. Are we justified in stating that this adjustment is due, not only to Hermas' understanding of the Spirit but also to a peculiar situation in the church of Hermas ? If so, this situation is to be distinguished from the issue of divination which caused the rule that the prophet does not answer questions. There are no direct indications in Hermas that a situation existed in which a group of people or an individual tried to compel a person to act as a prophet. But this is precisely what we find in Irenaeus' account of the Gnostic prophet Marcus, who tries to do exactly this. The considerations of the women who object to their attempted initiation into prophecy[1] concur with Hermas' statement. The judgment which Irenaeus himself passes on this attempt brings out the underlying principle very neatly: εἰ οὖν Μάρκος μὲν κελεύει, ἢ ἄλλος τις, ὡς εἰώθασιν ἐπὶ τοῖς δείπνοις τοῦ κλήρου οὗτοι πάντοτε παίζειν καὶ ἀλλήλοις ἐγκελεύεσθαι τὸ προφητεύειν καὶ πρὸς τὰς ἰδίας ἐπιθυμίας ἑαυτοῖς μαντεύεσθαι, ἔσται ὁ κελεύων μείζων τε καὶ κυριώτερος τοῦ προφητικοῦ πνεύματος, ἄνθρωπος ὤν, ὅπερ ἀδύνατον.[2]

This is also the principle which underlies Hermas' statement. The agreement between the two documents is too strong to be a coincidence, all the more so since it is not restricted to this point. It almost seems as if Irenaeus, who knew the book of Hermas,[3] found in the latter's description of the false prophet a suitable model for his interpretation of Marcus' prophetic experiments. If it is permissible to deduce from Irenaeus' description a conclusion as to the situation in Hermas, the statement that the Spirit does not speak when someone wants the prophet to speak reflects a situation in the church of Hermas in which an alleged πνευματοφόρος tried to confer his gift on other people.

The three negative statements which we have been studying so far, are, so to say, the background on to which the portrait of the prophet is to be projected. This portrait consists of two parts: (a) the prophet and the Spirit, and (b) the prophet and the church.

THE PROPHET AND THE SPIRIT

Hermas' description of the inspirational experience of the prophet, succinct though it may be, is a precious document in the history of

---

[1] Iren. A. H. I 13, 3 quoted *supra*. p. 13.
[2] *Ib*.
[3] Cf. A. H. IV 20, 2, and *infra*, p. 170, n. 3.

Christian prophecy before the Montanist crisis. It deserves to be examined very carefully. It runs as follows: ὅταν οὖν ἔλθῃ ὁ ἄνθρωπος ὁ ἔχων τὸ πνεῦμα τὸ θεῖον εἰς συναγωγὴν ἀνδρῶν δικαίων τῶν ἐχόντων πίστιν θείου πνεύματος, καὶ ἔντευξις γένηται πρὸς τὸν θεὸν τῆς συναγωγῆς τῶν ἀνδρῶν ἐκείνων, τότε ὁ ἄγγελος τοῦ πνεύματος τοῦ προφητικοῦ ὁ κείμενος ἐπ' αὐτῷ πληροῖ τὸν ἄνθρωπον καὶ πλη-σθεὶς ὁ ἄνθρωπος ἐκεῖνος τῷ πνεύματι τῷ ἁγίῳ λαλεῖ εἰς τὸ πλῆθος καθὼς ὁ κύριος βούλεται (9).

Syntactically and semantically, this passage presents no problems, apart from the phrase ὁ κείμενος ἐπ' αὐτῷ to which we will turn in due time. The key word in this passage is τὸ πνεῦμα which occurs four times in different connections: τὸ πνεῦμα τὸ θεῖον, τὸ πνεῦμα τὸ προφητικόν and τὸ πνεῦμα τὸ ἅγιον. A full appreciation of the work of the Spirit is possible only when the specific features of the passage have been clarified and when it is viewed in the perspective of Hermas' pneumatology as a whole.[1]

(1) *The angel of the prophetic Spirit*

The inspiration of the prophet is presented as an act, not of the Spirit but of the angel of the prophetic Spirit. His appearance in the description is considered by Dibelius and Opitz as a complication of the event.[2] It is also quite unexpected since the preceding section of the text represents the Spirit as being given by God without an inter-mediary. But the angel is not another example of the fluidity and the lack of consistence in Hermas' way of thinking, but, when seen in the proper perspective, turns out to have a very definite function in the description. Paradoxically, the angel is mentioned as if he had been in the picture all the time. The text even suggests that there is a per-manent relationship between him and the prophet. This relationship is expressed by the phrase ὁ κείμενος ἐπ' αὐτῷ, or πρὸς αὐτόν.[3]

---

[1] In the context of this study, Hermas' pneumatology cannot be dealt with in its totality, but only in so far as it is relevant to the subject of prophetic inspiration.

[2] Dib., p. 541; H. Opitz, *Ursprünge frühkatholischer Pneumatologie* (Berlin 1960), p. 113.

[3] 'Επ' αὐτῷ is the better attested reading; it is found in P⁰ˣ and appears to have been the reading of E (*qui super eum est*) and L² (*qui superimpositus est ei*); πρὸς αὐτόν is found only in A. Dibelius and Lake accept it. Harnack rejected it after the discovery of P⁰ˣ (cf. *infra*, p. 125, n. 2) in favour of ἐπ' αὐτῷ which is adopted also by Whittaker, Joly and Snyder (Dibelius erroneously refers to the P⁰ˣ reading as ἐπ' αὐτόν; the same error is found in Bauer s.v. κεῖμαι 1b).

But there is also another permanent relationship, viz. that between the Spirit and the prophet, expressed by the words: ὁ ἄνθρωπος ὁ ἔχων τὸ πνεῦμα τὸ θεῖον. When the two are balanced against each other, both appear to pertain to the same situation: that of the prophet before the moment of his inspiration. The statement about the angel views this situation, as it were, from the point of view of the Spirit, the other statement is from the angle of the prophet. These rather general indications need further substantiation in order to bring out the finer points.

The phrase ὁ κείμενος ἐπ' αὐτῷ is open to various interpretations. The ancient translations seem to betray a certain perplexity as to its meaning.[1] The crux of the phrase is κείμενος. When the other passages in which κεῖσθαι ἐπί occurs in Hermas are taken into account, the meaning might be, 'who is in charge of'[2] This seems to be Snyder's interpretation. He translates, "who is assigned to him". This interpretation, however, is not altogether satisfactory because it would require the genitive rather than the dative,[3] and in Hermas κεῖσθαι ἐπί never describes the relationship of an angel to an human being.[4] In the case of such a relationship Hermas is said to have been handed over, or entrusted to, the angel,[5] and this suggests that Hermas is subordinate to the angel. This is also true of the prophet and the angel of the prophetic Spirit.

Joly's translation, "qui est près de lui", though less correct semant-

---

[1] E appears to mean, 'which is on him', since τὸν ἄνθρωπον τὸν λέγοντα ἑαυτὸν πνευματοφόρον εἶναι (16) is rendered, *hominem qui dicit: Spiritus super me est; super-impositus* (L²) is mostly used in a literal meaning, which would result here in, 'which is placed upon him'. L¹ (*nuncius sanctus divinitatis*) is a simplification.

[2] *Mand.* IV 1, 8: αὕτη ἡ πρᾶξις ἐπὶ γυναικὶ καὶ ἀνδρὶ κεῖται ("is valid for both wife and husband"); VI 1, 1: κεῖνται ... ἐπὶ δικαίῳ καὶ ἀδίκῳ ("they i.e. the powers of faith, fear and selfcontrol, relate to righteousness and unrighteousness"): *Sim.* VI 3,2: the angel of punishment is κείμενος ἐπὶ τῆς τιμωρίας 'is in charge of'. Cf. also Thegri τὸν ἄγγελον τὸν ἐπὶ τῶν θηρίων ὄντα (*Vis.* IV 2, 4, cf. ὁ τῶν ζῴων ἔφορος δαίμων ... ὁ ἐφεστηκὼς αὐτοῖς in Jambl., *Myst.* III 16 (136,8 - 137,1 Parthey; the edition used in this and all subsequent quotations is that of Des Places (Paris, 1966) who keeps Parthey's pagination)), and the angel of repentance who says ἐγώ ... ἐπὶ τῆς μετανοίας εἰμί (*Mand.* IV 2, 2).

[3] Cf. Bauer s.v. ἐπί I 1 b a.

[4] Κεῖσθαι referring to a personal relationship is not found in the Septuagint, the New Testament, the Apostolic Fathers or the Apologists.

[5] Cf. *Vis.* V 3.4: γίνωσκω ᾧ παρεδόθην, ... ἐκεῖνος ἦν ᾧ παρεδόθην.

ically,[1] refers to another aspect of the relationship of the angel to the prophet. It is probably chosen because elsewhere an angel is said to live with Hermas,[2] and it is quite in order to suppose that this idea applies also to the angel and the prophet.

On the basis of this circumstantial evidence, rather than on strictly semantic grounds, we may conclude that the angel of the prophetic Spirit is in charge of, and responsible for, the prophet, and is his steady companion.[3] He belongs to the type of the guardian angel which is so frequent in Jewish angelology.[4] Yet he is identified as the angel of the prophetic Spirit and our next concern is therefore to investigate the relationship between the angel and the Spirit.

The phrase ὁ ἄγγελος τοῦ πνεύματος τοῦ προφητικοῦ is a peculiar expression which is not found anywhere else in early Christian literature. Its peculiarity is the combination of its elements, the angel and the Spirit. If the latter were equivalent to prophecy, the phrase could be understood on the analogy of ὁ ἄγγελος τῆς μετανοίας[5] and the angel would belong to the type of the angels who perform tasks which are assigned to them.[6] His task would be to preside over prophecy.[7] This is certainly an aspect of the angel but prophecy is not identical with the Spirit of prophecy. There is more to the angel of the prophetic Spirit than that he is a guardian angel whose area of responsibility is prophecy. This becomes clear when we examine the concept of the prophetic Spirit more closely. The phrase τὸ πνεῦμα τὸ προφητικόν is different in structure from all Hermas' uses of πνεῦμα followed by an adjective. Elsewhere the adjective denotes a quality of the Spirit but here an area to which the action of the Spirit relates.[8] Behind it

---

[1] It would imply that κείμενος is equivalent to ὤν which is the case only when it is used metaphorically, cf. e.g. 2 Macc. 4, 31. 34.

[2] Cf. Vis. V 2: ἵνα μετὰ σοῦ οἰκήσω τὰς λοιπὰς ἡμέρας τῆς ζωῆς σου. Mand. IV 2, 1: ἵνα μετ' ἐμοῦ πάντοτε κατοικῇς, namely the angel of repentance; 4, 3: εἰς τὸν οἶκόν σου κατοικήσω; VI 2, 2: ἀμφότεροι ἄγγελοι μετ' ἐμοῦ κατοικοῦσιν.

[3] Lake's rendering, "then the angel of the prophetic spirit rests upon him", is contrary to the meaning of the phrase which denotes a permanent situation and not an event. Lake has changed the syntactic pattern accordingly.

[4] Cf. J. Michl, art. Engel II (jüdisch), R. A. C. V, c. 74f.

[5] Vis. V 7, cf. Mand. IV 2, 2: ἐγὼ ἐπὶ τῆς μετανοίας εἰμί.

[6] Cf. Michl, art. cit., c. 67f., 71f.

[7] Like the angel Remiel who in Baruch 55, 3 is said to preside over the true visions, but cf. infra, p. 109.

[8] Cf. Mand. V 2, 6 (τρυφερόν); Mand. III 2 (ἄψευστον). τὸ ἅγιον πνεῦμα or τὸ θεῖον πνεῦμα are of a different order because they identify the Spirit as divine.

we may assume the well known Jewish phrase 'Spirit of prophecy' which is found so often in the Targumim as a rendering of 'Spirit of God' or 'Spirit of Jahwe' and referring to the Spirit in the Old Testament.[1] This is also found in Christian sources. Here it is used for the first time by Justin to introduce quotations from the Old Testament and to identify them as prophecies which are now fulfilled in Christ.[2] Hence the prophetic Spirit can be identical with the prophetic word.[3] But Justin's introduction of the Old Testament prophets shows that the concept of the prophetic Spirit refers to the original inspiration of the prophets: ἄνθρωποι οὖν τινες ἐν 'Ιουδαίοις γεγένηνται θεοῦ προφῆται. δι' ὧν τὸ προφητικὸν πνεῦμα προεκήρυξε τὰ γεγενήσεσθαι μέλλοντα πρὶν ἢ γενέσθαι (Apol. 31,1). At the same time the term may acquire the general meaning of the Holy Spirit: ἐκεῖνόν (i.e. τὸν θεόν) τε καὶ τὸν παρ' αὐτοῦ υἱὸν ἐλθόντα ... πνεῦμά τε τὸ προφητικὸν σεβόμεθα καὶ προσκυνοῦμεν (Apol. 6, 2).[4] The prophetic Spirit is the Holy Spirit in relation to prophecy, and the angel is the angel of the Holy Spirit in relation to prophecy.

Now we can proceed another step and examine the concept of the angel of the Holy Spirit. This is, again, a rather uncommon concept which is not found elsewhere in Hermas. It occurs, however, in another Christian writing of the second century A.D., the *Ascension of Isaiah*,[5] together and alternating with 'Spirit', 'Holy Spirit' and 'angel of the Spirit'. The idiom of this writing throws considerable light on Hermas. In 3, 16f. the angel of the Holy Spirit, together with Michael, the prince of the holy angels, opens the grave of Christ and they carry him on their shoulders.[6] In 7, 23 the angel of the Holy Spirit carries

---

1 Cf. Strack-Billerbeck II, p. 127-134 and P. Schäfer, *Die Vorstellung vom Heiligen Geist in der rabbinischen Literatur* (München, 1972), p. 21ff.

2 Cf. e.g. *Apol.* 32, 2: μέχρι τῆς φανερώσεως 'Ιησοῦ Χριστοῦ, τοῦ ἡμετέρου διδασκάλου καὶ τῶν ἀγνοουμένων προφητειῶν ἐξηγητοῦ. ὡς προερρέθη ὑπὸ τοῦ θείου ἁγίου προφητικοῦ πνεύματος διὰ τοῦ Μωυσέως μὴ ἐκλείψειν ἄρχοντα ἀπὸ 'Ιουδαίων, ἕως ἂν ἔλθῃ ᾧ ἀπόκειται τὸ βασίλειον.

3 Cf. e.g. *Dial.* 77, 2f. where Is. 8:4 is quoted twice, introduced by ὁ προφητικὸς λόγος and τὸ προφητικὸν πνεῦμα successively.

4 Cf. also *Apol.* 13, 3: πνεῦμά τε προφητικὸν ἐν τρίτῃ τάξει ὅτι μετὰ λόγου τιμῶμεν ἀποδείξομεν.

5 For this writing, cf. J. Flemming - H. Duensing, Die Himmelfahrt des Jesaja, in Hennecke-Schneemelcher, *Neutestamentliche Apokryphen* II³, p. 454ff. The following quotations are from the Christian parts of the book.

6 Probably the angel of the Holy Spirit is here the same as the angel of the Church which is in heaven. In *Evang. Petri* 36 the guards see δύο ἄνδρας κατελθόντας ἐκεῖθεν (i.e.

to heaven those who love the Most High and his Beloved after their death.[1] In 11,4 the angel of the Spirit appears in the world in order to inform Joseph about Mary's pregnancy.[2] Sometimes he appears together with the Lord, i.e. Christ;[3] in one place together with the Father and Christ.[4] In most places there is reference to the inspiration of one or more prophets by the Holy Spirit.

In 1, 7 the prophet invokes in an oath 'the Spirit who speaks in me'; in 3,19 it is predicted 'that many who believe in Him (i.e. Christ) will speak in the Holy Spirit' and in 26f. it is said that in the last days 'the Holy Spirit will withdraw from many' and that 'there will not be many prophets nor people who speak words of power'.[5] In 6, 6-10 the voice of the Holy Spirit is heard speaking through Isaiah.[6] In 9,36 the Lord appears with a second angel, and when Isaiah asks who this angel is he is told, 'this is the angel of the Holy Spirit who has spoken through you and the other righteous men'. In 10, 6 God is called 'the Most High ... who will be called by the Holy Spirit through the mouth of the righteous men Father of the Lord'.

On balance, it appears that in the case of prophetic inspiration it is the Holy Spirit that is usually mentioned, and not the angel whereas in the other places the angel of the (Holy) Spirit prevails. The exceptions to this rule are 8, 18 where, understandably, in a trinitarian context the Holy Spirit is named, and 9,36. In the latter case, the naming of the angel is understandable because it is an identification of the 'second angel'. The angel, then, is the Holy Spirit when the Spirit is not speaking through the prophets or active in the life of men. The angel stresses the supranatural aspects of the Spirit; when the

---

from heaven) πολὺ φέγγος ἔχοντας καὶ ἐγγίσαντας τῷ τάφῳ, probably two angels (cf. ἄνδρες δύο in Lk. 24:4), cf. E. Tisserant, L'Ascension d'Isaie (Paris, 1909), p. 14. For a different opinion cf. L. Vaganay, L'Evangile de Pierre (Paris, 1930), p. 294.

[1] Cf. also Test. Abr. 14, 6: Michael brings the soul of Abraham to heaven. Elsewhere this is done by unnamed angels, cf. Lk. 16:22; Test. Asser. 6, 4-6; Test. Job 52, 2-10; Michl, art. Engel VII, R. A. C. V, c. 245.

[2] Cf. Mt. 2:13: ἄγγελος κυρίου φαίνεται κατ' ὄναρ τῷ 'Ιωσήφ.

[3] 9, 39f.; 11, 33 (cf. Tisserant, p. 210 ad loc.); 10, 4.

[4] 8, 18 but here the Holy Spirit is named, not the angel.

[5] This Tisserant's translation; Duensing, op. cit., p. 458 renders: "solche, welche Gewisses reden".

[6] In 6 and 8 it is said that all heard the voice of the Holy Spirit; in 10 that Isaiah spoke through the Holy Spirit.

Spirit is mentioned alone, its operation in the human sphere is stressed.[1]

In the light of this evidence the unexpected introduction of the angel of the prophetic Spirit in Hermas is less strange than may appear at first sight. Like the angel of the Holy Spirit, the angel of the prophetic Spirit refers to a situation in which the Spirit is not acting but is latent. This situation exists till the moment of the inspiration. When the prophet is filled with the Holy Spirit the angel disappears, and the prophet speaks as the Lord wills.

There is, however, one point of difference between the angel of the prophetic Spirit in Hermas and the angel of the Holy Spirit in the *Ascension of Isaiah*. The former is the steady companion of the prophet, the latter is the Spirit when not in contact with the prophets, the Spirit in heaven. The former is, in a sense, immanent, the latter is transcendent. This phenomenological difference is significant. Otherwise, the two writings do not show many traces of relatedness and it is not possible to argue that one derived the idea of an angel of the Spirit from the other. Both used an idea which, though not in evidence elsewhere, must have been current in apocalyptic circles, but they put it to a different use. Hermas used it as a way of expressing the latent and — as it were — inactive presence of the Holy Spirit. This is an aspect of the angel of the prophetic Spirit for which no analogy can be found in Jewish or Jewish-Christian angelology. Hence, there is reason to surmise that Hermas used yet another model to complete for him the picture of the angel of the prophetic Spirit at this particular juncture.

Most commentators refer to the angel Remiel who in Baruch 55, 3 is said to preside over the true visions.[2] But this appears to be little more than a title because he does not send a vision to Baruch, but is sent to him rather to explain the vision of the cloud from the sea. His task is that of the *angelus interpres*, not that of a double of the Spirit.[3] Remiel is not the complementary model for the angel of the prophetic Spirit.

---

[1] The two remaining places where the Spirit is mentioned, 6, 17 and 11, 40 have no bearing on the question of the angel of the Holy Spirit.

[2] Thus Harnack, Weinel, Dibelius, Joly and Snyder. Cf. *supra*, p. 106, n. 7.

[3] The same situation in 63, 6: Remiel who speaks with you. Elsewhere Remiel has quite different functions: in 4 Ezra 4, 36 he is in charge of the dead, probably also Enoch 20, 8, cf. P. Bogaert, *Apocalypse de Baruch* (Paris, 1969), I, p. 428-438; II, p. 106.

There is, however, such a model; but it is found outside, or perhaps rather in the confines of Christianity. As noticed above (p. 86), the angel of the prophetic Spirit resembles the δαίμων πάρεδρος through which the Gnostic Marcus was said to prophesy. Dibelius who was the first to point to this, states only that the angel of the prophetic Spirit is "eine Art δαίμων πάρεδρος nur im guten Sinn".[1] It is worthwhile to take up this clue in order to see whether it throws any light on the angel of the prophetic Spirit.

The δαίμων πάρεδρος and its history have been described already in ch. IV[2] As to his relationship to the seer it is to be noted that he is permanently with him.[3] Yet when the seer needs him he must call him and when he enters, ask him the questions that are put to him, order him to do the things the seer wants him to do. When the demon has done his due he may go away.[4] Apart from the times he is called upon by the seer, the δαίμων πάρεδρος is present but inactive. This is precisely the aspect of the angel of the prophetic Spirit for which no analogy could be found in Jewish-Christian angelology. It is a matter of course that the relationship between the seer and the demon is the opposite of that between the angel and the prophet. In the former it is the seer who, by means of his magic, is in command, in the latter the angel, but otherwise the relationship is analogous.

So much for the composite picture of the angel of the prophetic Spirit. It is a curious blending of Jewish, Christian and hellenistic elements. There is no reason to assume that it was designed artificially and that Hermas borrowed consciously the various elements which went into the making of this picture. The fact that the angel of the prophetic Spirit is mentioned in the context of a conflict between Christian prophecy and pagan divination rules out this possibility. When, however, a Christian δαίμων πάρεδρος appears on the scene it is apparent that this idea is, as it were, common property which can

---

[1] *Ad loc.*, p. 541.

[2] Cf. *supra*, p. 88ff.

[3] Cf. *supra*, p. 89, n. 6, and *P. G. M.* I 80 (Preis. I, p. 6): ὅπως ἀκίνητός σου τυγχάνων μείνῃ; 174 (*ib.* 10): ἀποδημοῦντί σοι συναποδημήσει; 178ff. (*ib.*) (when you are dead) σοῦ δὲ τὸ πνεῦμα βαστάξας εἰς ἀέρα ἄξει σὺν αὐτῷ.

[4] Cf. *ib.* 180ff.: ὅταν δὲ θέλῃς τι πρᾶξαι. εἰς ἀέρα λέγε τὸ ὄνομα μόνον καὶ 'ἐλθέ', καὶ ὄψῃ αὐτόν, καὶ ἐγγύς σου ἑστῶτα καὶ λέγε αὐτῷ· 'ποίησον τοῦτο τὸ ἔργον', καὶ ποιεῖ παραυτὰ καὶ ποιήσας ἐρεῖ σοι· τί ἄλλο βούλει; σπεύδω γὰρ εἰς οὐρανόν. ἐὰν δὲ μὴ ἔχῃς παραυτὰ ἐπιτάξαι, λέγε αὐτῷ· 'πορεύου, κύριε', καὶ ἀπελεύσεται. *Ib.* 328f. (p. 18): ὅταν εἰσέλθῃ, ἐρώτα αὐτόν, περὶ οὗ θέλεις, περὶ μαντείας ... κτλ.

be used on both sides of the borderline between Christianity and paganism. We must place Hermas near that borderline as we have seen in ch. III: his attacks on divination and magic as forms of idolatry betray clearly how conscious he was that he and his fellow Christian lived close to that borderline. Yet the angel of the prophetic Spirit shows that they shared the experience of all people who live in borderlands. They are conscious of that which distinguishes them from the people on the other side and they have, unwittingly, much in common with them.

(2) *Filled with the Spirit*

The angel of the prophetic Spirit is immediately an indication of the existence of the problem of the 'inactive' presence of the Spirit, and of the way in which this problem is solved. It does not, however, reveal the deepest level of the problem itself and its implications. In this section we will attempt to probe this level and to reach a more complete assessment of the implications.

Starting point of our investigation is the clause: ὁ ἄγγελος τοῦ πνεύματος τοῦ προφητικοῦ πληροῖ τὸν ἄνθρωπον καὶ πλησθεὶς ὁ ἄνθρωπος τῷ πνεύματι τῷ ἁγίῳ λαλεῖ ... καθὼς ὁ κύριος βούλεται. This is, as it were, Hermas' version of the general principle of prophecy mentioned earlier in this study: ὑπὸ πνεύματος ἁγίου φερόμενοι ἐλάλησαν ἀπὸ θεοῦ ἄνθρωποι (2 Pet. 1:21). Inspiration is a divine commission; no prophet can speak καθὼς ὁ κύριος βούλεται unless he has this divine commission. This is a common characteristic of all biblical and Christian prophecy, whether this commission is expressed in terms of the word of God, coming to a prophet, of or the Spirit coming upon, or filling him.[1]

There is, however, a distinction between Hermas and other authors who use the concept of *Geisterfüllung*: in Hermas, the man who is going to be filled with the Spirit is identified as ὁ ἄνθρωπος ὁ ἔχων τὸ πνεῦμα τὸ θεῖον. This is another complication in the description of the inspiration event and one that is less easy to understand than the angel. It seems as if the author is at pains to emphasize that the fact that the prophet is filled with the Spirit does not mean that he was empty before. This is an idea which would never occur to, for instance, Luke. In his understanding all believers have received the

---

[1] Cf. *supra*, p. 99.

Holy Spirit but this does not prevent him from writing: καὶ ἐπλήσθ-ησαν ἅπαντες τοῦ ἁγίου πνεύματος.[1] There must have been a reason for Hermas to emphasize so strongly that it is the man who has the divine Spirit who is going to be filled with the Holy Spirit.[2]

This reason is twofold. In the first place, Hermas' dualistic pneumatology implies that being emptied of the Spirit is tantamount to being full of the spirit of the devil and vice versa. In the 11th Mandate it is emphasized that the false prophet and his adherents are characterized by a state of emptiness.[3] Any possible thought that the prophet would have been empty before he is filled with the Holy Spirit is to be avoided at all costs!

But this is only part of the explanation. There is yet another side to it as is revealed by the fact that the phrase τὸ πνεῦμα τὸ θεῖον, or τὸ πνεῦμα τῆς θεότητος occurs only in Mand. XI and there greatly outnumbers the expression τὸ πνεῦμα τὸ ἅγιον.[4]

Elsewhere in Hermas the latter is the current denotation of the Spirit of God,[5] but this function is here taken over by the former. The Holy Spirit appears in our text only twice: οὐδὲ ὅταν θέλῃ ἄνθρωπος λαλεῖν, λαλεῖ τὸ πνεῦμα τὸ ἅγιον (7), and πλησθεὶς ... τῷ πνεύματι τῷ ἁγίῳ λαλεῖ, sc. the prophet (9). It is the Spirit that speaks through the prophet. This differentiation recalls the similar use of the Holy Spirit in the Ascension of Isaiah where it always appears when prophetic speaking is referred to.[6] In the prophetic situation, the Spirit is operative as the Holy Spirit, apart from that situation it is present as the divine Spirit, or as a Spirit which comes from the

---

[1] Acts 4:31. For the question whether the Spirit was an incidental loan or a permanent possession cf. J. M. E. Hull, The Holy Spirit in the Acts of the Apostles (London, 1967), p. 120-124, who points out that the question is not correctly stated. Instead, he suggests the term, "permanent loan".

[2] He is, however, not the only one who has the divine Spirit; all faithful members of the church have it, cf. infra, p. 123ff.

[3] Cf. 3: αὐτὸς γὰρ κενὸς ὢν κενὰ καὶ ἀποκρίνεται κενοῖς. This is repeated almost verbatim in 13. For the relevance of this idea for the διάκρισις πνευμάτων, cf. supra, p. 39f.

[4] It occurs ten times against twice τὸ πνεῦμα τὸ ἅγιον. τὸ θεῖον πνεῦμα is the language of hellenistic Judaism (cf. Bauer s.v. θεῖος 1a) and is not found in Christian texts before Hermas (cf. Lampe, s.v. θεῖος A5).

[5] It occurs 21 times against once τὸ πνεῦμα τοῦ θεοῦ (Mand. X 2, 6 where it takes up τὸ πνεῦμα τὸ ἅγιον in the preceding clause).

[6] Cf. supra, p. 107ff.

divine Spirit. But how can a man who has the divine Spirit conceivably be filled with the Holy Spirit? This is an idea which is as difficult to comprehend as the thought that the prophet was empty of the Spirit till the moment of the inspiration. If Hermas had used a different image to describe the inspiration event than that of filling, the differentiation between θεῖον and ἅγιον would hardly be noticeable. If he had not identified the prophet so emphatically as the man who has the divine Spirit but simply as the prophet, nobody would have thought that he came to the congregation empty of the Spirit. It is the combination of the two which makes the picture so intangible. Any explanation that is to come forth must explain first and foremost this combination.

To begin with, the use of the idea of *Geisterfüllung* has to be examined briefly.[1] In biblical texts it occurs for the first time in Exodus 28:3; 31:3; 35:31; and Deuteronomy 34:9. These texts refer to a permanent endowment with a Spirit of ability, intelligence, craftmanship or wisdom, not to prophetic inspiration. A similar use is found in wisdom literature.[2] The first application of this concept to prophetic inspiration is found in Jesus Sirach.[3] It occurs also in Philo,[4] and, in the New Testament, in the Lucan writings.[5] In the apostolic and post-apostolic literature it occurs sparingly.[6] Yet none of the texts mentioned offers

---

[1] For a use of this concept without reference to prophetic inspiration cf. *infra*, p. 157, n. 5.

[2] Cf. *Sap Sal.* 1, 7: πνεῦμα κυρίου πεπλήρωκεν τὴν οἰκουμένην, where πνεῦμα is identical with σοφία. Sirac. 39, 6: πνεύματι συνέσεως ἐμπλησθήσεται (A, S: ἐμπλήσει) (subj. κύριος) αὐτόν. Cf. also the LXX renderings of Prov. 15:4 ὁ δὲ συντηρῶν αὐτὴν (i.e. τὴν γλῶσσαν) πλησθήσεται πνεύματος (which may go back to a reading different from the Masoretic text with which it has only רוח in common), and of Is. 11:3: ἐμπλήσει αὐτὸν πνεῦμα φόβου θεοῦ (which can be traced to the Hebrew when ריח is changed into רוח; in both places the image of being filled by the Spirit is a distinctly new element.

[3] 48:12: Ἐλισαιε ἐνεπλήσθη πνεύματος αὐτοῦ (i.e. of Elijah; A reads ἁγίου); it goes back to 2 Kings 2:15: 'The spirit of Elijah rests on Elisha'.

[4] Though the wording is somewhat different the idea is the same, cf. *De Decal.* 175 (Moses the most perfect of the prophets) ὃν ἐπικρίνας ἀριστίνδην καὶ ἀναπλήσας ἐνθέου πνεύματος ἑρμηνέα τῶν χρησμῳδουμένων εἵλετο. *Vita Mosis* I 277: (Bileam) ἔνθους ... γίνεται, προφητικοῦ πνεύματος ἐπιφοιτήσαντος; *ib.* I, 175: (Moses) ἔνθους γίνεται καταπνευσθεὶς ὑπὸ τοῦ εἰωθότος ἐπιφοιτᾶν αὐτῷ πνεύματος. Cf. also Fascher, p. 152-160.

[5] Lk. 1:15, 67; Acts 2:4; 4:8, 31; 9:17; 13:9.

[6] Eph. 5:18; Ign., *Magn.* 8, 2: the Old Testament prophets were ἐνπνεόμενοι ὑπὸ τῆς χάριτος αὐτοῦ; Justin, *Dial.* 7, 1: the prophets were ἁγίῳ πληρωθέντες πνεύματι. 3: οἱ ἀπὸ τοῦ πλάνου καὶ ἀκαθάρτου πνεύματος ἐμπιμπλάμενοι ψευδοπροφῆται. *Mart. Polyc.* 7, 3: πλήρης ὢν τῆς χάριτος τοῦ θεοῦ; Iren. *A. H.* III 10, 3: *Zacharias ... novello spiritu adimpletus*, takes up Lk. 1:67; cf. also Epiph., *Panar.* 48, 3.

anything like an analogy with Hermas, and it is very unlikely that
the explanation we seek is to be found in the Hebrew-Christian sphere.
But the idea of inspiration by *Geisterfüllung* is also well represented
in Greek sources. The famous passage in Pollux, *Onomasticon* I, 15,
which lists numerous synonyms with regard to divinatory inspiration,
opens εἰ δέ που καὶ πνεῦμα εἴη μαντικόν ... This shows that the
underlying and generally known conception is that of a prophetic
πνεῦμα flowing into a man.[1] Yet Pollux does not recommend πληρωθῆναι πνεύματος but πληρωθῆναι θεοῦ, probably because he thought
the former κακόφωνον like ἐπιπνευσθῆναι which is branded as such
explicitly.[2] Be that as it may, the underlying conception is clear
enough and, in one form or another, is found abundantly elsewhere
in the relevant sources, with or without actual occurence of the words
πνεῦμα and πληροῦν.[3] It is used particularly with reference to oracles,
and it is in this context that we find a complex of ideas which may
help to clarify the problem of the divine and the Holy Spirit in Hermas.
This requires a somewhat broader argument.

In his dialogue on the obsolescense of the oracles (*De Defectu Oracul-
orum*) Plutarch deals with the question how it is possible that prophetic
inspiration can cease to function. This leads in the latter part of the
dialogue to a discussion on the cause and the power which the gods
use when they inspire the prophets and prophetesses (περὶ τῆς αἰτίας
... καὶ δυνάμεως αἷς χρώμενοι ποιοῦσι κατόχους τοῖς ἐνθουσιασμοῖς
καὶ φανταστικοὺς τοὺς προφήτας καὶ τὰς προφήτιδας (431B).[4] Lam-
prias, who represents the writer in this dialogue, claims for the
human ψυχή the same δύναμις by virtue of which the demons are
able to know and reveal the future in advance. But this faculty is
not always active because the souls are joined with the bodies. It is
restored to its proper function when the prophet reaches the state
which is called ἐνθουσιασμός and defined as κρᾶσις καὶ διάθεσις τοῦ
σώματος ἐν μεταβολῇ γιγνομένου (432D). This disposition is often

---

[1] Cf. H. Leisegang, *Der Heilige Geist* I, 1 (Leipzig, 1919, repr. Darmstadt, 1967),
p. 122f., where Pollux is quoted in full.

[2] As Leisegang points out, none of the listed words and phrases contains the syllable
πνευ, which intimates that Pollux thought this κακόφωνον. This judgment is not shared
by other writers who use πνεῦμα with various adjectives, cf. Kleinknecht, art. πνεῦμα
Th. W. N. T. VI, p. 343.

[3] Cf. Leisegang, *op. cit.*, p. 132ff., Kleinknecht, *art. cit.*, p. 343-349.

[4] The mss have ᾗ χρώμενοι, but this does not alter the meaning, since in that case
αἰτία and δύναμις are a hendiadys.

open to the body of itself (ἐξ αὐτοῦ). But sometimes the earth helps by sending up τὸ μαντικὸν πνεῦμα καὶ ῥεῦμα, which when it enters the body creates that κρᾶσις καὶ διάθεσις and thus rouses the μαντικὴ δύναμις of the soul (432 D E). This event is explained in various ways. Like wine, the πνεῦμα may, by its warmth, open certain passages through which impressions of the future may be transmitted. Or the warmth may make the soul dry since "the dry soul is the best" according to Heraclitus. Or, the πνεῦμα may by a certain chilling and compacting render the prophetic element of the soul tense and keen. Or, the prophetic vapour (μαντικὴ ἀναθυμίασις) may, like tin when alloyed with copper, fill the vacant spaces in the soul and cement it by fitting itself in (433 A). These are learned explanations which come from various sources.[1] They do not affect the underlying idea that the prophetic πνεῦμα has οἰκεῖόν τι ταῖς ψυχαῖς καὶ συγγενές. The relationship between the πνεῦμα and the soul is similar to that between the light and the eye. As the latter needs the light in order to use its power of vision, so ψυχῆς τὸ μαντικὸν ... δεῖται τοῦ συνεξάπτοντος οἰκείου καὶ συνεπιθήγοντος (433D). This psychology of prophecy is presented in the framework of the theory that the πνεῦμα μαντικόν is a vapour which rises from the earth. This theory, which comes from Aristotle, serves to explain the decline of the oracle but, at the same time, causes the writer considerable trouble when the part played by the gods and the demons is considered. But this framework need not concern us here as it does not determine the psychology of prophecy.[2] The inspiration process does not work automatically in the sense that whenever the πνεῦμα touches the soul the μαντικὴ δύναμις starts to operate immediately. This δύναμις must be in a state of proper adjustment (ἁρμοστῶς ἔχειν, 438 A). When this is not the case, no ἐνθουσιασμός will happen, or a wrong one will follow and this can have very serious consequences as is shown by the story of a Pythia who went down into the oracle ἄκουσα καὶ ἀπρόθυμος and as a result was filled by a dumb and bad spirit (ἀλάλου καὶ κακοῦ πνεύματος οὖσα πλήρης, 438 B). She died a few days later. Indicative of this state of proper adjustment are the sacrifices which precede the consultation. When they are favourable then the ἐνθουσιασμός is bound to come.

---

[1] Cf. Flacelière's edition (Paris, 1947), p. 252f. n. 241-248.

[2] For this theory and the story of the chasm, cf. P. Amandry, *op. cit.*, p. 215-239, E. R. Dodds, *The Greeks and the Irrational* (London, 1951), p. 72ff., R. Flacelière, *Devins et oracles Grecs* (Paris, 1965), p. 68ff.

In his dialogue *De Pythiae Oraculis* Plutarch returns to the subject of prophetic inspiration.[1] This time the demons and the vapour are left out. Apollo is considered to be the sole author of the divination. The role of the priestess is considered at length because the form of her oracles has changed from poetry to prose. It is not the god who speaks through her: οὐ γάρ ἐστι θεοῦ ἡ γῆρυς οὐδὲ ὁ φθόγγος οὐδὲ ἡ λέξις οὐδὲ τὸ μέτρον, ἀλλὰ τῆς γυναικός· ἐκεῖνος δὲ μόνας τὰς φαντασίας παρίστησι καὶ φῶς ἐν τῇ ψυχῇ ποιεῖ πρὸς τὸ μέλλον· ὁ γὰρ ἐνθουσιασμὸς τοιοῦτόν ἐστιν (397C). The ἐνθουσιασμός is apparently a μεῖξις κινήσεων δυοῖν, as the soul is affected by external impulses and by its own nature (404F). This nature of the soul (ὡς πέφυκε) is an essential part of the inspiration for the god does not implant the μαντικὴ δύναμις but, like Eros with regard to poetry and music, ἐνυπάρχουσαν (sc. δύναμιν) κινεῖ καὶ ἀναθερμαίνει λανθάνουσαν καὶ ἀργοῦσαν (405 F). ὁ μαντικὸς ἐνθουσιασμὸς ... χρῆται τῇ ὑποκειμένῃ δυνάμει καὶ κινεῖ τῶν δεξαμένων ἕκαστον καθ' ὃ πέφυκεν (406 B). This is the same psychology of inspiration, though with somewhat different emphasis due to the subject of the dialogue.

That this is not just an idea of Plutarch but a more generally accepted belief is shown by the fact that two centuries later Jamblichus uses it in his explanation of oracular divination.[2] This is the more remarkable since Jamblichus stresses repeatedly the supranatural character of divination. It depends on the divine initiative. The fact that in dreams the truth often lights up of its own accord, ἔξωθέν τε δείκνυσιν ἀπὸ θεῶν οὖσαν τὴν μαντείαν καὶ ταύτην αὐτεξούσιον ὅταν βούληται καὶ ὡς ἂν ἐθέλῃ μετ' εὐμενείας τὸ μέλλον ἀναφαίνουσαν.[3]

The prophetic inspiration does not proceed from the soul or from the body; or from a combination of soul and body. The real cause of the divine madness are τὰ καθήκοντα ἀπὸ τῶν θεῶν φῶτα καὶ τὰ ἐνδιδόμενα πνεύματα ἀπ' αὐτῶν καὶ ἡ ἀπ' αὐτῶν παροῦσα παντελὴς ἐπικράτεια ... ἐξορίζουσα δὲ πάντῃ τὴν οἰκείαν ἡμῶν παρακολούθησιν

---

[1] With Flacelière (cf. his edition of *De Pyth. Orac.* (Paris, 1962), p. 17) it is assumed that this dialogue is later than *De Def. Orac.*

[2] It is worth noting that, apart from Plutarch's Delphian dialogues, Jamblichus' *De Mysteriis* is the only work to have come down to us which attempts to explain these oracular phenomena.

[3] III 23 (155, 18-156, 3 Parthey). This sounds almost like Hermas where the spirit is ἄνωθεν and ἀπὸ θεοῦ δοθέν and the prophet speaks ὅταν θελήσῃ αὐτὸν ὁ θεὸς λαλῆσαι.

καὶ κίνησιν.¹ When the presence of the divine fire and an unspeakable form of light fills a man completely, he is in a state ὡς μηδεμίαν οἰκείαν ἐνέργειαν δύνασθαι διαπράττεσθαι.² But this does not mean that οἰκεία ἐνέργεια plays no part at all. Some people δι᾽ ἀτονίαν τε τῆς οἰκείας ἐνεργείας ἢ τῆς ὑπαρχούσης αὐτοῖς δυνάμεως ἔνδειαν οὐ δύνανται τῶν θεῶν τυγχάνειν.³ The ἐνέργεια and δύναμις which must be present and in order, must have a πρὸς τοὺς θεοὺς οἰκειότης or ὁμοιότης in much the same way as sounds which are consecrated each to a certain god. When a παρουσία of the gods happens, that part of men which has τὴν τυχοῦσαν πρὸς αὐτοὺς ὁμοιότητα receives a κατοχὴ τελεία καὶ πλήρωσις τῆς κρείττονος οὐσίας καὶ δυνάμεως.⁴

The difference between Plutarch and Jamblichus so far is that the soul plays a less prominent part in the expositions of the latter. It does not have in itself a power to prophesy which only has to be roused, but only the faculty to respond to the divine in such a way as to become an ὄργανον to be used by the gods.⁵ But there is yet another point of difference which is very relevant to the problem in Hermas. Jamblichus distinguishes between the inspiration by a πνεῦμα and the event which he calls χωρεῖν τὸν θεόν. This is illustrated by the story of the oracle in Colophon which gives oracles δι᾽ ὕδατος. On certain nights, after much preliminary ritual, the prophet drinks from a well and then starts to prophesy. Popular opinion has it that a prophetic πνεῦμα passes through the water but Jamblichus thinks that this is not an adequate explanation: τὸ θεῖον ... ὡς παρέχον ἔξωθεν καὶ ἐπιλάμπον τὴν πηγήν, πληροῖ δυνάμεως αὐτὴν ἀφ᾽ ἑαυτοῦ μαντικῆς. The difference between his opinion and the popul-

---

¹ III 8 (115, 16 - 117, 12 Parthey).

² III 6 (113, 8 - 12 Parthey). Cf. also III 27 (166, 5-15 Parthey): θείας ἄρα μαντικῆς οὐδέν ἐστι σπέρμα ἐν ἡμῖν ἐκ φύσεως ... πρὸς τοῦτο ἰσχυρῶς μάχεσθαι δεῖ, ἐάν τις ἐξ ἡμῶν εἶναι λέγει τὴν μαντικήν.

³ III 31 (176, 13 - 177, 6 Parthey). This is the case with ἀλιτήριοι (offenders) who jump to the divine things without law and order; eventually they cling to the evil spirits who fill them with the worst inspiration (πληρούμενοί τε ἀπ᾽ αὐτῶν τῆς κακίστης ἐπιπνοίας). This recalls the false prophet in Hermas.

⁴ III 9 (118, 16 - 119, 9 Parthey), in a discussion of the effect of music in divination. The response of the soul to music is explained by the fact that before being united with the body, the soul heard the divine harmony and remembers that harmony as soon as it hears melodies which preserve τὸ θεῖον ἴχνος τῆς ἁρμονίας and πρὸς αὐτὴν φέρεται καὶ οἰκειοῦται (120, 7-14 Parthey).

⁵ Porphyry had maintained ὡς ἡ ψυχὴ γεννᾷ δύναμιν φανταστικὴν τοῦ μέλλοντος but Jamblichus calls this δεινὴν παρανομίαν ... εἰς ὅλην θεολογίαν (III, 22; 152, 8-13 Parthey).

ar idea is that the latter assumes that the μαντικὴ δύναμις is only temporarily and partly in the water; whereas Jamblichus thinks that it is completely, permanently and fully present in the water. What follows is very interesting and clarifying with regard to Hermas: οὐ μέντοι τοῦ γε θεοῦ πᾶσά ἐστιν ἡ ἐπίπνοια ἥντινα παρέχει τὸ ὕδωρ, ἀλλ' αὕτη μὲν ἐπιτηδειότητα μόνον καὶ ἀποκάθαρσιν τοῦ ἐν ἡμῖν αὐγοειδοῦς πνεύματος ἐμποιεῖ, δι' ἣν δυνατοὶ γιγνόμεθα χωρεῖν τὸν θεόν.[1] The inspiration by the πνεῦμα in the water is only preliminary. It is to be followed by another experience viz. χωρεῖν τὸν θεόν.[2] This experience is the presence of the god, superior to the former inspiration through the water, and flashing in from above.[3] It does not keep away from any person who has enough affinity to it to receive it. Keyword in this clause is οἰκειότης 'affinity', which refers to the same state as ἐπιτηδειότης above.[4] This inspiration πάρεστι δ' εὐθὺς καὶ χρῆται ὡς ὀργάνῳ τῷ προφήτῃ.

Such then is Jamblichus' theory of inspiration with regard to the oracle of Colophon. In a somewhat different form this same theory

---

[1] III 11 (125, 3-7 Parthey). The αὐγοειδὲς πνεῦμα is the same as τὸ αἰθερῶδες καὶ αὐγοειδὲς ὄχημα which is περικείμενον τῇ ψυχῇ in III 14 (132, 12 Parthey). This is not a prophetic πνεῦμα κατιόν (cf. III 6; 112, 10: τὸ κατιὸν πνεῦμα καὶ εἰσκρινόμενον, and Porphyry apud Eus., Praep. Ev. V 8, 12) but rather the 'astral body' which is attached to the soul either permanently or during the soul's sojourn in the body. It must be cleansed before it can receive the divine φαντασίαι. For the various theories of the astral body cf. E. R. Dodds, Proclus, the Elements of Theology (Oxford, 1963), p. 313-321, and Des Places, ad Jambl. III 14 (p. 117, n. 3).

[2] The phrase occurs also V 23 (233, 8 - 10 Parthey) ἐδέξατό τινα ἀπ'αὐτῆς (i.e. τῆς θείας κοινωνίας) θείαν μοῖραν καὶ ἡ γῆ, ἱκανὴν οὖσαν χωρῆσαι τοὺς θεούς, and ib. (234, 13 Parthey): the sacrifice of a certain material which shares the nature of the gods awakes them and χωρεῖ τε αὐτοὺς παραγιγνομένους καὶ τελείως ἐπιδείκνυσι. Apparently it denotes a mystical experience which may sometimes include divination.

[3] Ib.: ἄλλη δ'ἐστιν ἡ τοῦ θεοῦ παρουσία καὶ προτέρα ταύτης καὶ ἄνωθεν ἐναστράπτουσα. ἄλλη refers to the difference between χωρεῖν τὸν θεόν and ἡ ἐπίπνοια ἥντινα παρέχει τὸ ὕδωρ. προτέρα here denotes rank, not sequence since the lesser inspiration has to prepare and to cleanse the recipient before the inspiration which makes him prophesy.

[4] Ib.: τῶν ἐχόντων διὰ τῆς οἰκειότητος συναφὴν πρὸς ἑαυτήν. οἰκειότης, or the synonym ὁμοιότης does not denote a natural endownment or quality which some people have and others don't; it must be acquired (cf. I 15; 48, 1 Parthey τὴν ... ὁμοιότητα ... κτώμεθα) by theurgic means. For the connection between fitness and likeness cf. Sallustius, Concerning the Gods and the Universe XV, p. 28, 11f. Nock: πᾶσα ἐπιτηδειότης μιμήσει καὶ ὁμοιότητι γίνεται, and Nock's comment in the Prolegomena, p. XCVIIIf.

is applied to Delphi. The prophetess yields herself entirely to the divine
πνεῦμα and is filled with the divine light emanating from the divine
fire. Thus inspired and enlightened, she seats herself on the seat of
the god and is united with the firm μαντικὴ δύναμις. Yet the consummation of the experience is, again, the presence of the god who is
described as ἕτερος ὢν καὶ τοῦ πυρὸς καὶ τοῦ πνεύματος.[1] It is
significant that Jamblichus never speaks of the μαντικὴ δύναμις
of the soul. It belongs to the gods, not to man. He is anxious to show
that ἡ μαντικὴ τῶν θεῶν δύναμις is separated from any earthly or
human faculty, yet present everywhere τοῖς μεταλαμβάνειν αὐτῆς
δυναμένοις.[2] To vouchsafe this apartness and to stress the necessity
of proper preparation, he even assigns to the time-honoured inspirational events of the renowned oracles a place in the preparatory experiences.

Despite the many differences between Plutarch and Jamblichus
which are due to their respective theologies, the substructure appears
to be the same. Prophetic inspiration presupposes the presence of some
potentiality of the soul, be it a μαντικὴ δύναμις or an ὁμοιότης πρὸς
τοὺς θεούς, which is somehow related to the power of inspiration.
This substructure is very similar to the picture which Hermas presents.
The potentiality which is present in the prophet is not a μαντικὴ
δύναμις or an ὁμοιότης πρὸς τὸν θεόν but τὸ πνεῦμα τὸ θεῖον itself
which is related to τὸ πνεῦμα το ἅγιον with which the prophet is
filled at the moment of inspiration. The substructure of Hermas'
concept of prophecy is that a man must have the divine Spirit in him
if the prophetic Spirit is to speak through him. Once again, we notice
the presence of hellenistic elements in Hermas' composite picture of
prophetic inspiration. Here also there is no reason to assume that he
derived consciously those elements from hellenistic sources. They
will have been common property like the idea of the δαίμων πάρεδρος.
But this time it can be seen clearly to what purpose the hellenistic
elements are used. They help to bring out something which could not
sufficiently be brought out by the conceptual and imaginative means

---

[1] III 11 (126, 5 - 127, 2 Parthey). The subsequent account of Branchidae is less consistent. The fulfillment with the divine light, the foretelling of the future and the
reception of the god appear as parallel events, but at the same time the acts with which
each of them is connected (the holding of the rod, the sitting on the axle, the wetting
of the feed, the inhaling of the vapour) are explicitly mentioned as means by which
the prophetess prepares herself for the ὑποδοχὴ τοῦ θεοῦ. This shows that even here
the structure is the same.

[2] III 12 (129, 4 Parthey).

of the Jewish-Christian traditions. Hermas' deepest concern in composing the complex fabric which depicts the inspiration of the prophet is to bring out that the man whom God wants to speak as a prophet is under the constant guidance and the quiet influence of the Spirit. Were this not so, he would be empty of the Spirit and, consequently, under the influence of evil spirits. The influence of the divine Spirit, however, makes him fit to speak καθὼς ὁ κύριος βούλεται when the moment of inspiration has come and the angel of the prophetic Spirit fills him with the Holy Spirit.

The unmistakable presence of hellenistic elements raises the question whether Hermas' concept of prophecy is, perhaps, hellenistic too. This question emerges naturally as long as we think in terms of borrowing.[1] That this is not the proper question can be shown when we turn to yet another aspect of prophecy.

In Jamblichus' account of the inspiration-events of the oracles it is stressed repeatedly that οἱ ἐνθουσιῶντες loose their self-consciousness. In Colophon, for instance, ἡ τοῦ θεοῦ παρουσία ... χρῆται ὡς ὀργάνῳ τῷ προφήτῃ οὔτε ἑαυτοῦ ὄντι, οὔτε παρακολουθοῦντι οὐδὲν οἷς ἢ ὅπου γῆς ἐστιν· ὥστε καὶ μετὰ τὴν χρησμῳδίαν μόγις ποτὲ ἑαυτὸν λαμβάνει.[2] This is an example of the most extreme form of ecstasy and belongs to category (1) in our preliminary classification.[3] Does the 11th Mandate show any traces of a similar inspiration experience?

It is difficult to gain an impression of the state of mind of the prophet when he is πλησθεὶς τῷ πνεύματι τῷ ἁγίῳ. Weinel thinks that the divine Spirit and the earthly spirit cannot be distinguished by the form of their speaking, presumably because, if they could, there would have been no need for further criteria.[4] This is true only in so far as both use understandable speech but there may yet have been a discernable difference in their prophetic behaviour. In ch. IV we have seen that in the false prophet there are traits of 'enthusiasm' in the popular sense.[5] It is conceivable that the picture of the prophet contains ele-

---

[1] Cf. *supra*, p. 16f.
[2] III 11 (125, 11-14); cf. also 4 (110, 16): οὐ παρακολουθοῦσιν ἑαυτοῖς ἐνθουσιῶντες; 6 (113, 13); 8 (117, 5f).
[3] Cf. *supra*, p. 19.
[4] *Wirkungen*, p. 88f.
[5] Cf. *supra*, p. 91ff.

ments which allow inferences to be drawn as to his state of mind. But nothing in this picture refers particularly to the prophetic situation.[5] Yet it is possible that those words, which contrast clearly with the words denoting the false prophet's excitement, have some bearing upon his behaviour as a prophet. Where the false prophet is ἰταμὸς καὶ ἀναιδὴς καὶ πολύλαλος, the true prophet is πραΰς καὶ ἡσύχιος. This combination occurs on two other places in Hermas. In *Mand.* V 2,3 μακροθυμία is described as παραμένουσα διαπαντὸς πραεῖα καὶ ἡσύχιος. Now μακροθυμία is sometimes described as a πνεῦμα and hence πραΰς καὶ ἡσύχιος may denote an attitude which is spiritual par excellence. This is confirmed by *Mand.* VI 2, 3 where the angel of righteousness is called τρυφερὸς καὶ αἰσχυντηρὸς καὶ πραΰς καὶ ἡσύχιος. This angel is also representing the Spirit and what is characteristic of him is characteristic of a man who has the Spirit. We may conclude, then, that the two words πραΰς καὶ ἡσύχιος refer also to the prophet's prophetic behaviour as contrasted to that of the false prophet who is ἰταμὸς καὶ ἀναιδὴς καὶ πολύλαλος. But the prophet's state of mind in no way resembles the experience of the prophet of Colophon and similar prophets.

All this shows that Hermas' concept of prophecy is not hellenistic. It is a thoroughly Christian concept even if the substructure of his concept of inspiration must be explained with the aid of elements and ideas stemming from hellenistic divination.

There is yet another feature in the 11th Mandate which confirms the Christian nature of prophecy to which it witnesses. This is the part played by the congregation. To this subject the next chapter is devoted.

CHAPTER SIX

PROPHECY AND THE CHURCH

The inspiration of the prophet by the Holy Spirit takes place when the man who has the divine Spirit appears in the congregation of righteous men who have faith in the divine Spirit. When these men pray to God, the Spirit is, as it were, released and turns the man into a prophet who speaks καθὼς ὁ κύριος βούλεται. When on the other hand the false prophet comes into this same congregation, the earthly spirit in him flees from him, driven out by the Holy Spirit, which is released by the prayer of the congregation.

There is no other text in which the role of the church in the prophetic event and its counterpart is so clearly and so impressively described as in these few lines in the 11th Mandate. They state explicitly that, to function properly, prophecy is dependent upon the proper functioning of the church. What we mean by 'proper' will become clearer when the text is scrutinized in detail.

The prophet comes into a συναγωγὴ ἀνδρῶν δικαίων τῶν ἐχόντων πίστιν θείου πνεύματος. Hermas' use of the word συναγωγή is restricted to the 11th Mandate, and in this text to the two situations described above. Its meaning is no doubt that of gathered congregation or, meeting, like in Ignatius, Polyc. 4, 2,[1] and, probably, James 2:2,[2] to quote two earlier texts. Since the prophet does not speak κατα μόνας (8), or κατὰ γωνίαν (13), it is clear that συναγωγή refers to a meeting of the whole congregation and not some private group gathered around the prophet. Rather, the latter is characteristic of

---

[1] Πυκνότερον συναγωγαὶ γινέσθωσαν.

[2] Εἰς συναγωγὴν ὑμῶν may mean 'your meeting', or 'your meeting-place", probably the former. For συναγωγή in this meaning cf. Harnack, ad loc., p. 115-119, and Schrage, art. συναγωγή, Th. W. N. T. VII, p. 839. Harnack's conclusion, "ex usu vocis συναγωγή apud Hermam obvio minime concludi posse, scriptorem Christianum e Judaeis fuisse vel coetus Judaeo-Christianos hic respexisse", is correct, as is clearly shown by the Συναγωγὴ Μαρκιωνιστῶν in Deir Ali (Lebaba), mentioned in an inscription quoted by Schrage, and by the fact that the word is also used outside Judaism and Christianity as a technical term for periodical corporate meetings, cf. Dibelius, Der Brief des Jakobus, p. 124 and references there.

the false prophet and his double-minded adherents. Prophecy needs the whole congregation if it is to function properly.

The congregation is defined as consisting of 'righteous men'. In 3 τῶν δικαίων refers to the church members in general, but here the meaning appears to be more specific, namely that of church members in good standing. This meaning applies also to other passages in Hermas where the phrase οἱ δίκαιοι refers to Christians in contrast with heathen and former believers who went astray.[1] The phrase συναγωγὴ ἀνδρῶν δικαίων is not found elsewhere in Jewish or Christian texts. The Qumran scrolls have some remote parallels but they are too remote to allow the conclusion that this phrase comes from that source.[2] All this shows that the phrase is not a standing designation for the gathered congregation, but forged by the author for this particular situation.

These righteous men are further identified as ἐχόντων πίστιν θείου πνεύματος. This is rendered by Lake as: "who have the faith of the Divine Spirit"; apparently, he takes θείου πνεύματος as a subjective genitive. Most translators and commentators, however, understand it as an objective genitive and render 'faith in the divine Spirit'.[3] Syntactically, the latter is preferable in view of the repeated use of πίστις with objective genitive.[4] But there is more to this question than just the correct definition of the genitive. In 14 the same congregation is called πλήρης ἀνδρῶν δικαίων ἐχόντων πνεῦμα θεότητος, and in 15 it is called πνεύματα δικαίων! When it is also taken into account that faith itself is described in terms which apply also to the

---

[1] Vis. I 4, 2: τοῖς δικαίοις contrasts with τοῖς ἔθνεσιν καὶ τοῖς ἀποστάταις. II 2, 5: τοῖς δικαίοις together with τοῖς ἁγίοις contrasts with τοῖς ἔθνεσιν. Sim. III 2: οἱ δίκαιοι over against οἱ ἁμαρτωλοί. IV 2ff.: id. over against τὰ ἔθνη καὶ οἱ ἁμαρτωλοί. VIII 9, 1: the people who had been faithful but became rich and arrogant, οὐκ ἐκολλήθησαν τοῖς δικαίοις (cf. Vis. III 6, 2 and Sim. VIII 8, 1: μὴ κολλώμενοι τοῖς ἁγίοις). IX 17, 5: some people, after joining the church, ἐμίαναν ἑαυτοὺς καὶ ἐξεβλήθησαν ἐκ τοῦ γένους τῶν δικαίων. For a similar contrast between οἱ δίκαιοι and others cf. also Mt. 13:43; 25:37, 46. This takes up the Old Testament contrast between the righteous and the ungodly and sinners, cf. G. Schrenk, art. δίκαιος Th. W. N. T. II, p. 187, 192.

[2] Cf. e.g. C D 20, 2: 'the congregation of the men of perfect holiness'; 1 Q M 12, 7: 'the congregation of thy saints'; 4Q p Ps 37 II 5: 'the congregation of his elect'.

[3] Thus Harnack, Weinel, Dibelius, Snyder and Joly.

[4] Cf. Vis. IV 1, 8: τὴν πίστιν τοῦ κυρίου (also Mand. XI 4 and Sim. VI 1, 2); Sim. IX 16, 5: πίστει τοῦ υἱοῦ τοῦ θεοῦ.

Spirit,[1] then it is clear that 'faith in the divine Spirit' expresses the consciousness of the presence of the divine Spirit in the church.

The differentiation between the divine Spirit and the Holy Spirit discovered and discussed above[2], is also here relevant. In the light of that differentiation, we can define the idea of the presence of the Spirit in the church more precisely. In the case of the prophet, the endowment with the divine Spirit means that he is under the constant guidance and influence of the Spirit: the same is true of the other members of the church. The presence of the divine Spirit makes the prophet fit to speak as a prophet, and makes the congregation fit to pray for the Holy Spirit to come down and fill the prophet. For prayer is a gift of the Spirit and at the same time a means to stir the Spirit. In *Sim.* V 4, 4 the Shepherd says that Hermas is ἐνδεδυναμωμένος ὑπὸ τοῦ ἐνδόξου ἀγγέλου καὶ εἰληφὼς παρ' αὐτοῦ τοιαύτην ἔντευξιν, i.e. he has received the power of the Spirit and the gift of prayer. In another passage the gift of prayer seems to be the prerogative of the poor, but it is emphasised that he has received this richness from the Lord (ἔλαβεν παρὰ τοῦ κυρίου). At the same time the power of the Spirit is active in prayer, for δύναμιν μεγάλην ἔχει ... ἡ ἔντευξις αὐτοῦ (viz. of the poor man).[3] In *Mand.* X 3, 2 the sorrowful man is said to grieve the Spirit and is therefore unable to pray. The underlying idea is that it is the Spirit itself that prays.[4]

All this applies to the situation in the 11th Mandate. The endowment with the divine Spirit includes the gift of prayer. When this gift is used, it releases, in its turn, the power of the Holy Spirit; then the Spirit fills a member of the congregation and makes him speak as a prophet.

A member of the congregation, and not someone who bears the title 'prophet'! In this crucial passage the word προφήτης is conspicuously absent. Instead, the Shepherd refers to the prophet as ὁ ἄνθρωπος

---

[1] *Mand.* IX 11: ἡ πίστις ἄνωθέν ἐστι παρὰ τοῦ κυρίου καὶ ἔχει δύναμιν μεγάλην; cf. *Mand.* XI 21: τὸ πνεῦμα τὸ θεῖον ἄνωθεν ἐρχόμενον δυνατόν ἐστι and *ib.* 8.

[2] Cf. *supra*, p. 112ff.

[3] *Sim.* II 5-7.

[4] Ὁ δὲ λυπηρὸς ἀνὴρ ... λυπῶν τὸ πνεῦμα τὸ ἅγιον ἀνομίαν ἐργάζεται, μὴ ἐντυγχάνων μηδὲ ἐξομολογούμενος τῷ κυρίῳ (2). ἡ λύπη μεμιγμένη μετὰ τοῦ ἁγίου πνεύματος τὴν αὐτὴν ἔντευξιν οὐκ ἔχει (3). As Dibelius, p. 535 points out, not λύπη but τὸ ἅγιον πνεῦμα should be the subject of the clause. Hermas' idea of prayer is that of the *oratio infusa*, cf. Fr. Heiler, *Das Gebet*, p. 224ff.

ὁ ἔχων τὸ πνεῦμα τὸ θεῖον. His endowment with the Spirit is not different from that of his fellow believers with whom he is gathered in the congregation. He is not a πνευματικός over against a congregation which is endowed with the Spirit to a lesser degree. It is the false prophet who alleges that he is a πνευματοφόρος, and thereby discredits himself by this very allegation.[1] When, however, the congregation and the prophet have the same endowment with the divine Spirit, then it certainly follows that any member of the congregation can be chosen by the Spirit to be filled and to speak as the Lord wills. The church consists of potential prophets. There is no specific προφητικὴ τάξις within the church, but the church itself is a προφητικὴ τάξις.[2]

At this juncture we may recall Greeven's statement on the development of prophecy quoted above.[3] The 11th Mandate is unequivocal evidence that prophecy as a congregational *charisma* is found in the second century A.D. But more important than that is another set of questions: what was the nature of the endowment with the Spirit to which Hermas witnesses? Is it different from that of the primitive church? Are the dependence of the prophetic *charisma* upon the presence of the Spirit in the church, and the absence of πνευματικοί peculiar to Hermas? Or are they consistent with primitive Christian experience? Only when these questions have been answered, can Hermas' view of the relationship between prophecy and the church be seen in the perspective of the history of early Christianity.

Starting point for our enquiry is Opitz' interpretation of the 11th

---

[1] Cf. *supra*, p. 90, and Opitz, *op. cit.*, p. 111f.

[2] The phrase is found in an Oxyrhynchus papyrus (Grenfell and Hunt, *The Oxyrhynchus Papyri* I (London, 1898), nr 5, p. 8f). Following a quotation of *Mand.* XI 9-10a the text reads: τὸ γὰρ προφητικὸν πνεῦμα τὸ σωματεῖόν ἐστιν τῆς προφητικῆς τάξεως, ὅ ἐστιν τὸ σῶμα τῆς σαρκὸς Ἰησοῦ Χριστοῦ τὸ μιγὲν τῇ ἀνθρωπότητι διὰ Μαρίας. Harnack who was the first to point out the connection with Hermas (Über zwei von Grenfell und Hunt entdeckte und publicirte altchristliche Fragmente, *Sitzungsberichte der Akademie Berlin* 1898, p. 516-520), interpreted this to mean that within the church there was a body of prophets which claimed to be the body of Christ proper. This interpretation, however, makes the text say the opposite of the Hermas text which it quotes and purports to explain. Though the text is in need of a new treatment it may be posited here that the explanation that the body of Christ, the church, itself is τὸ σωματεῖον τῆς προφητικῆς τάξεως, and consists of prophets, is more obvious and more consistent with Hermas' view.

[3] Cf. *supra*, p. 8ff.

126   PROPHECY AND THE CHURCH

Mandate.[1] He assumes that, as a member of the Roman church, Hermas did not know pneumatic phenomena as described in 1 Cor. 12-14. Hermas, therefore, had no idea of the charismatic ministry of the primitive Christian prophet.[2] He does not call the prophet πνευμα-τοφόρος, nor does he make that claim for himself. His conception of his own ministry and of that of the prophet is non-charismatic. Charismata are for Hermas not extraordinary endowments, but moral qualities, virtues as the names of the virgins in *Sim.* IX 15, 1-2 betray.[3] Furthermore, Hermas does not differentiate between the gifts of the Spirit and the endowment with the Spirit, between "Geistesgaben" and "Geistbesitz". The motivation for charismatic action is not, as in the New Testament, the joy over the new life in the Spirit, but the expectation of future reward.[4] There is a prophetic Spirit which can enable any member of the church to speak as a prophet, but in the end the charismatic has completely become the instrument of the (local) church.

Finally, the *charisma* of prophetic speech and that of its interpretation which are kept apart in the New Testament, coincide in Hermas.[5] To conclude, the spiritual picture of the church and the prophet are fundamentally different from primitive Christianity. The church of Hermas is post-pneumatic, the prophet is post-charismatic. The former lacks a "Pentecostal experience", the latter an ecstatic experience.[6]

---

[1] *Op. cit.*, p. 111-115. To the present writer's knowledge this is the most extensive treatment of *Mand.* XI since Dibelius.

[2] Opitz even thinks that in *Mand.* VIII 10 ἐν γὰρ τῇ φιλοξενίᾳ εὑρίσκεται ἀγαθο-ποίησίς ποτε the last word ποτε (not found in Ath.[2] and L[2]) betrays a sceptical attitude towards the "übergemeindlichen Wandercharismatikertum" (p. 111, n. 138), but this stretches the evidence unreasonably.

[3] *Op. cit.*, p. 99f.

[4] *Op. cit.*, p. 106. For this remarkable statement Opitz does not refer to any text in Hermas.

[5] *Op. cit.*, p. 115: "für Hermas fallen die im Urchristentum getrennten Charismen des prophetischen Redens (in Extase) und der Hermeneutik dieses Redens zusammen. Dem letzeren legt er das entschieden gröszere Gewicht bei". In Opitz' view prophecy and glossolalia appear to be identical which is contrary to the unequivocal evidence of 1 Cor. 14. Also Hermas does not know any form of prophetic speech which is in need of ἑρμηνεία. Opitz' judgment is completely wrong and irrelevant.

[6] *Op. cit.*, p. 54f.: "Seine (i.e. des Geistes) Dynamis ... aüszert sich nicht in ausser-gewöhnlichen Taten, Erlebnissen oder Personen sondern in der aus der Kraft des Glaubens resultierenden sittlichen Grundhaltung des schlichten Gemeindechristen ... Das bedeutet ..., da das enthusiastische Moment grundsätzlich fehlt, einen entscheidenden Schritt

Opitz' interpretation rests on two assumptions concerning primitive Christianity: It is characterised: (a) by an 'enthusiastic' experience of the Holy Spirit; the absence of such an experience in Hermas implies that his pneumatology cannot be understood in terms of experience but only in terms of dogmatic, ecclesiastical and moral traditions; (b) by the differentiation between "Geistbesitz", the abiding endowment with the Spirit, and "Geistesgaben", charismatic and ecstatic gifts.[1] The former is something in which all believers share; the latter are the prerogative of the πνευματικοί who are independent from the congregation as far as their gifts are concerned; the absence of this differentiation in Hermas means that any church member may become a prophet, and this leads to a considerable loss of prophetic authority.

These assumptions bring us to the heart of the matter. In order to discuss them properly, we oppose to them two submissions of our own for which we will subsequently present the evidence. They are:

(a)   Hermas' idea of the presence of the Spirit in the church is not fundamentally different from that of the apostolic and early post-apostolic times;

(b)   Hermas' idea of the dependence of the prophet on the action of the Spirit in the gathered congregation represents primitive Christian experience and states explicitly what is implied in other and older evidence for prophetic activities.

THE PRESENCE OF THE SPIRIT

Before we turn to the experience of the Spirit in primitive Christianity, it is necessary to reconstruct Hermas' understanding of the presence of the Spirit. We have noted that the designation of the church members as those who have the divine Spirit in the 11th Mandate refers to this presence of the Spirit. This designation itself, however, does not betray how important the relationship between the Spirit

---

hinein in die frühkatholische Kirche". Elsewhere (p. 107), however, Opitz interprets the appearance of δύναμις among the charismata as a link between the moral 'virtue-spirits' and the power of ecstatic experience and as an enrichment of the idea of the Spirit in the Roman church from the part of the "Pentecostal experience", but he pays no further attention to this aspect.

[1] In the rest of this chapter we will use the terms 'endowment' and 'gifts' in this sense.

and the believer was to Hermas. This is what the present investigation attempts to discover.

Two preliminary remarks are to be made. In the first place, the following account is not a treatment of Hermas' doctrine of the Spirit. It touches upon this doctrine only in so far as it is necessary to understand the experience of the Spirit. In early Christianity the Spirit was a matter of experience before it became an object of reflection, even if the records of this experience already show the influence of such reflection.[1] Secondly, our aim is not to trace the "religionsgeschichtliche" background of the various materials which went into the making of Hermas' understanding of the Spirit. However necessary an investigation of these materials may be — and the preceding chapter has shown what interesting results such investigations may yield —, it is beyond the scope of the present study. We must confine ourselves to an account of the experiences to which these materials witness.

For Hermas the Christian experience of the Holy Spirit begins in baptism. In his explanation of why the faithful of the first and the second generation, and the prophets and servants of God (i.e. the believers of the old covenant) did come up out of the deep place, the Shepherd adds a general statement which expresses Hermas' view of baptism: πρὶν γάρ, φησί, φορέσαι τὸν ἄνθρωπον τὸ ὄνομα τοῦ υἱοῦ τοῦ θεοῦ, νεκρός ἐστιν· ὅταν δὲ λάβῃ τὴν σφραγῖδα, ἀποτίθεται τὴν νέκρωσιν καὶ ἀναλαμβάνει τὴν ζωήν. ἡ σφραγὶς οὖν τὸ ὕδωρ ἐστίν· εἰς τὸ ὕδωρ οὖν καταβαίνουσι νεκροὶ καὶ ἀναβαίνουσι ζῶντες.[2] Baptism is the act of rebirth as in Titus 3:5, where the Holy Spirit is mentioned explicitly.[3] This is not the case in Hermas; and yet it is hard to think of the Spirit as being absent in this act of renewal. A further study of the way in which Hermas uses the word σφραγίς elsewhere reveals that baptism and the receiving of the Spirit are closely connected. The word does not denote a well-defined concept, but is capable of various associations; each of which contributes to its full meaning. In the passage quoted above it is identified with baptism.[4] This identification however, is more in the nature of an asso-

---

[1] The absense of "das enthusiastische Moment" appears to justify a dogmatic treatment of the subject in the judgment of Opitz, cf. op. cit., p. 54f.; this justification presupposes his assumption (a).

[2] Sim. IX 16, 3f.

[3] Λουτρὸν παλιγγενεσίας καὶ ἀνακαινώσεως πνεύματος ἁγίου.

[4] Cf. G. H. W. Lampe, The Seal of the Spirit (London, 1951), p. 106, n. 1. Whether

ciation. With reference to *Sim.* VIII 6, 3: ἵνα ἀκούσαντες οἱ πιστεύσαντες καὶ εἰληφότες τὴν σφραγῖδα καὶ τεθλακότες αὐτὴν καὶ μὴ τηρήσαντες ὑγιῆ, ἐπιγνόντες τὰ ἑαυτῶν ἔργα μετανοήσωσιν, λαβόντες ὑπὸ σοῦ σφραγῖδα, καὶ δοξάσωσι τὸν κύριον, Pernveden rightly asserts that, if baptism and seal were synonymous, the renewed receiving of the seal by those who have repented would amount to anabaptism.[1] Yet the phrase λαμβάνειν τὴν σφραγῖδα, used twice and with different tenses of the verb, cannot but refer to two related events. As A. Benoit has pointed out, there exists a parallelism between baptism and the second μετάνοια; they have the same effects: forgiveness of sins, seal, gift of the Spirit.[2] This implies, however, that there exists a close association between the seal and the endowment with the Spirit. This association is found elsewhere in the book of Hermas. In the 17th chapter of the 9th Similitude, the Shepherd answers Hermas' question: Why were the stones that were placed in the tower, gleaming in one colour? This answer is an almost eschatological vision, because it says that all the nations that dwell under heaven hear and believe and are called by the name of the Son of God. Then the text continues: λαβόντες οὖν τὴν σφραγῖδα ... τὰ πνεύματα τῶν παρθένων μετὰ τοῦ ὀνόματος ἐφόρεσαν.[3] This does not mean that the seal and the endowment with the Spirit are identical, but that they are closely associated.

A similar association between the seal, the Spirit and baptism is found in Hermas' question which elicits the general statement on baptism quoted above:[4] διατί, φημί, κύριε, οἱ λίθοι ἐκ τοῦ βυθοῦ ἀνέβησαν καὶ εἰς τὴν οἰκοδομὴν τοῦ πύργου ἐτέθησαν, πεφορηκότες τὰ πνεύματα ταῦτα;[5] Here the perfect participle πεφορηκότες does not necessarily refer to an event which precedes that denoted by the main verb.[6] The line of thought is slightly inconsistent, because in the preceding section (15, 4-6) the representatives of the old coven-

---

this equation of σφραγίς with baptism was a common idea in the second century A. D. (cf. F. J. Dölger, *Sphragis* (Paderborn, 1911), p. 70) or an idea with which Hermas' milieu was not familiar (cf. J. Ysebaert, *Greek Baptismal Terminology, its Origin and Early Development* (Nijmegen, 1962), p. 391) is immaterial.

[1] *Op. cit.*, p. 169.
[2] A. Benoit, *Le baptême chrétien au second siècle* (Paris, 1953), p. 153.
[3] *Sim.* IX 17, 4; the text is quoted in full, *infra*, p. 132.
[4] Cf. *supra*, p. 128.
[5] *Ib.* 16, 1.
[6] For a different interpretation cf. Benoit, *op. cit.*, p. 131.

ant and the apostles and teachers of the proclamation of the Son of God are envisaged together, whereas 16, 1-7 clearly distinguishes between them. Hence the closing lines of 15, 6 which state that they all had the Spirits and that the Spirits did not leave them until they died, refer directly only to the apostles and teachers who died ἐν δυνάμει καὶ πίστει τοῦ υἱοῦ τοῦ θεοῦ (16, 5), and to the others only by implication. This means that for Hermas baptism, incorporation in the church, endowment with the Spirit and reception of the seal are closely connected.

Hermas' use of σφραγίς comprises yet another association which is relevant. The seal is also connected with the name of the Son of God. In the statement on baptism, quoted above, p. 128, this connection is explicitly made: before man bears the name of the Son of God, he is dead. When he receives the seal he puts aside deadness and receives life. To receive the seal is to receive the name of the Son of God. The believer is the bearer of the name.

Finally, there is the association of σφραγίς with ἱματισμός. In the 8th Similitude there are three groups of stick-bearers who are admitted to the tower without the intervention of the Angel of Repentance.[1] They represent the martyrs, the believers who were persecuted but did not suffer, and the reverent and righteous believers who walked with a very pure heart and kept the commandments of the Lord, i.e. those believers who did not need a second repentance. The martyrs receive crowns, the others a seal and white clothing, but presumably the martyrs also wear the same clothing. The scene has eschatological meaning and the seal is the seal of ownership which guarantees eschatological redemption.[2]

When we attempt to derive from all these associations one consistent concept of σφραγίς, we find, at best, various concepts. But what holds them together is not a conceptual unity but a unity of experience. Baptism, the name of the Son of God, the reception of the Spirit, the eschatological hope form together that which is commonly called Christian initiation.[3] There is no reason to assume that baptism conveys

---

[1] Sim. VIII 2, 1-4, esp. 4: δοὺς αὐτοῖς ἱματισμὸν λευκὸν καὶ σφραγῖδα.

[2] Cf. Lampe, op. cit., p. 105.

[3] Cf. A. Hamman, La signification de σφραγίς dans le Pasteur d'Hermas, Stud. Patr. IV (Berlin, 1961), p. 290: "La sphragis, chez Hermas, exprime ... la prise en charge paternelle et salvifique du chrétien par Dieu, et le baptême, par extension, en tant qu'il réalise cette prise de possession".

the Spirit. On the contrary, it is possible to bear the name of the Son of God without having the Spirit.[1] But in Christian initiation the reception of the Spirit goes together with baptism.

So much for the beginning of the Christian experience of the Spirit. This experience, however, remains fundamental in the life of the believers. "Πιστεύσαντες is the ever-returning description of those who belong to the church ... We can say ... that the concept of faith itself is of a double nature in so far as it is both to be understood as man's response to the invitation through the Son of God and also of something that comes to man and does not emanate from him".[2] This second aspect of faith is brought out in Mand. IX 11: ἡ πίστις ἄνωθέν ἐστι παρὰ τοῦ κυρίου καὶ ἔχει δύναμιν μεγάλην. Faith is born of the Spirit. Where believers meet the Spirit is present. This is one of the leading themes of the 9th Similitude. The twelve virgins who appear around the gate of the rock and carry through the gate the stones that find a place in the tower, are identified as ἅγια πνεύματα. No one can enter the kingdom of God unless the virgins clothe him with their clothes. It is not enough to bear the name of the Son of God, one needs also to receive clothes from them. But this is not an experience which has nothing to do with the Son of God, for the virgins are δυνάμεις τοῦ υἱοῦ τοῦ θεοῦ.[3] What this means with regard to the church appears from what follows: οἱ πιστεύσαντες τῷ κυρίῳ διὰ τοῦ υἱοῦ αὐτοῦ καὶ ἐνδιδυσκόμενοι τὰ πνεύματα ταῦτα, ἔσονται εἰς ἓν πνεῦμα, ἓν σῶμα καὶ μία χρόα ἱματίων αὐτῶν (13, 5). Of some who were later seduced by the counterpart of the virgins, the women dressed in black,[4] the Shepherd says: οὗτοι πάντες τὸ ὄνομα τοῦ υἱοῦ τοῦ θεοῦ ἔλαβον, ἔλαβον δὲ καὶ τὴν δύναμιν τῶν παρθένων τούτων. λαβόντες οὖν τὰ πνεύματα ταῦτα ἐνεδυναμώθησαν καὶ ἦσαν μετὰ τῶν δουλῶν τοῦ θεοῦ, καὶ ἦν αὐτῶν ἓν πνεῦμα καὶ ἓν σῶμα καὶ ἓν ἔνδυμα (13, 7). This shows that the formula ἓν πνεῦμα καὶ ἓν σῶμα refers to the spiritual unity of the gathered church here and now, rather than to the heavenly or the eschatological state of the universal church.[5] This is supported by 17, 4f.: (the people of the earth)

---

[1] Cf. Sim. IX 13, 1: ἐὰν γὰρ τὸ ὄνομα μόνον λάβῃς, τὸ δὲ ἔνδυμα παρὰ τούτων μὴ λάβῃς, οὐδὲν ὠφελήσῃ. For ἔνδυμα cf. infra, p. 133f.

[2] Pernveden, op. cit., p. 157.

[3] Sim. IX 13, 2.

[4] Cf. ib. 9, 5.

[5] Hermas does not use the formula consistently. The first time the believers will be (ἔσονται εἰς) one Spirit and one body, the second time they had (ἦν αὐτῶν) one

λαβόντες οὖν τὴν σφραγῖδα μίαν φρόνησιν ἔσχον καὶ ἕνα νοῦν, καὶ μία
πίστις αὐτῶν ἐγένετο καὶ μία ἀγάπη, καὶ τὰ πνεύματα τῶν παρθένων
μετὰ τοῦ ὀνόματος ἐφόρεσαν· διὰ τοῦτο ἡ οἰκοδομὴ τοῦ πύργου μιᾷ
χρόᾳ ἐγένετο λαμπρὰ ὡς ἥλιος. (5) μετὰ δὲ τὸ εἰσελθεῖν αὐτοὺς ἐπὶ
τὸ αὐτὸ καὶ γενέσθαι ἓν σῶμα, κτλ.

Here we meet another unity-formula which recurs in 18, 3,[1] and some
of the elements of 13, 5-7. But the parallel use of εἰσελθεῖν ἐπὶ τὸ
αὐτό and γενέσθαι ἓν σῶμα shows that the author has in mind the
gathered church.[2] Finally, there is 31,4 where the angel of repentance
summons people to repent and *in unum quoque spiritum fieri* (L[1]), or
γενέσθαι ἓν πνεῦμα.[3] These passages are of crucial importance to
understand Hermas' concept of the church. It functions as a spiritual
body in which the believers are gathered, and to which they must
cleave.[4] It hinges on the experience of the presence of the Spirit in
the church, the very experience which underlies the prophetic event
of the 11th Mandate.

Spirit and one body. The first time he adds μία χρόα which makes sense because it
refers to the unity of the believers (cf. 17, 3f.), the second time ἐν ἔνδυμα which is virtually equivalent to ἐν πνεῦμα. This suggests that the formula consisted of two members
ἐν πνεῦμα καὶ ἓν σῶμα to which Hermas added the third member. It recalls Eph. 4:4
ἓν σῶμα καὶ ἓν πνεῦμα where it appears as an exclamatory continuation of the preceding paraenesis.

[1] After the rejection of all sinners ἔσται ἡ ἐκκλησία τοῦ θεοῦ ἓν σῶμα, μία φρόνησις,
εἷς νοῦς, μία πίστις, μία ἀγάπη, i.e. the same four member formula preceded by ἐν σῶμα
(cf. καὶ ἔσται ἓν σῶμα τῶν κεκαθαρμένων in 3) which is, as it were, elaborated in the
formula. The formula consists of two typically Christian elements (μία πίστις, μία
ἀγάπη) and two more general elements, who do not appear in this combination in
earlier Christian texts (cf. Phil. 2:2: τὸ ἓν φρονοῦντες; Ign., *Magn.* 7, 1: ἐπὶ τὸ αὐτὸ μία
προσευχή, μία δέησις, εἷς νοῦς, μία ἐλπὶς ἐν ἀγάπῃ). φρόνησις and νοῦς occur in Hermas
usually together: *Sim.* IX 17, 2. 4; 18, 4.

[2] Ἐπὶ τὸ αὐτό (= ἐπὶ τὸν αὐτὸν τόπον, Hesychius, cf. e.g. Lk. 17:35, Bauer s.v.
αὐτός 4b) "means that the local separation is removed, the unity is restored" (W. C.
van Unnik, 1 Clement 34 and the "Sanctus", *Vig. Chr.* V (1951), 231); in Christian
texts it is a technical term for the meeting of the Christian congregation, cf. Acts 1:15;
2:1, 44; 1 Cor. 11:20; 14:23; *Barn.* 4, 10; 12, 7; Ign., *Eph.* 5, 3; 13, 1; *Magn.* 7, 1; *Philad.*
6, 2; 10, 1; *1 Clem.* 34, 7; Just., *Apol.* 67, 3, E. Schweizer, Gemeinde und Gemeindeordnung im Neuen Testament (Zürich, 1959), p. 201f.; it does not necessarily refer to the
Eucharist, cf. Van Unnik, art. cit., p. 229ff.

[3] Antiochus, *Hom.* 94, 1720 B, quoted by Whittaker ad loc. In the light of the other
places this appears to be what Hermas wrote. L[2] has *in uno spiritu efficiemini*; E is
rendered *estote in uno spiritu*.

[4] One of the reasons why believers are led astray is that they did not cleave to the
saints, cf. *Vis.* III 6, 2; *Sim.* VIII 8, 1; 9, 1; IX 20, 2; 26, 3.

The relevance of this idea of the spiritual church comes to light when Hermas' use of the imagery of clothing is considered further. To be clothed is, for Hermas, to be clothed with the Holy Spirit.¹ The Spirit, however, is diversified into ἅγια πνεύματα to which the names of the virgins refer: Πίστις, Ἐγκράτεια, Δύναμις, Μακροθυμία, Ἁπλότης, Ἀκακία, Ἁγνεία, Ἱλαρότης, Ἀλήθεια, Σύνεσις, Ὁμόνοια, Ἀγάπη.² Several of these occur elsewhere in connection with the image of clothing. When he meets the huge beast, Hermas, after some initial hesitation, proceeds towards the beast, ἐνδυσάμενος τὴν πίστιν τοῦ κυρίου.³ The charge to despise double-mindedness is motivated by the words ἐνδυσάμενος τὴν πίστιν τὴν ἰσχυρὰν καὶ δυνατήν, and the following words point unmistakably to the spiritual nature of faith.⁴ When Hermas is in doubt about the commandments which he had received, the Shepherd appears and tells him: ὅλως μηδὲν διψυχήσῃς, ἀλλ' ἔνδυσαι τὴν πίστιν τοῦ κυρίου.⁵ The same is said of μακροθυμία,⁶ of ἱλαρότης,⁷ and of ἀλήθεια.⁸ It is also applied to concepts which do not occur among the names of the virgins. The injunction to abstain from defamation is followed by the words: ἔνδυσαι δὲ τὴν σεμνότητα.⁹ A stronger emphasis on the moral aspect is also found.¹⁰ All in all, it is beyond doubt that the concept of clothing expresses the conviction that moral life is guided by the Spirit.¹¹

---

¹ Cf. Sim. IX 24, 2: ἐνδεδυμένοι τὸ πνεῦμα τὸ ἅγιον.

² Sim. IX 15, 2.

³ Vis. IV 1, 8.

⁴ Mand. IX 10f. (cf. supra, p. 131).

⁵ Sim. VI 1, 2.

⁶ Mand. V 2, 8: ἀπέχου ἀπὸ τῆς ὀξυχολίας, τοῦ πονηροτάτου πνεύματος· ἔνδυσαι δὲ τὴν μακροθυμίαν.

⁷ Mand. X 3, 1: ἔνδυσαι οὖν τὴν ἱλαρότητα τὴν πάντοτε ἔχουσαν χάριν παρὰ τῷ θεῷ, cf. also 4.

⁸ Mand. XI 4: ὅσοι οὖν ἰσχυροί εἰσιν ἐν τῇ πίστει τοῦ κυρίου, ἐνδεδυμένοι τὴν ἀλήθειαν ...

⁹ Mand. II 4. It is worth noting that σεμνότης occurs in the list Vis. III 8, 3-6, cf. Giet, op. cit., p. 149f.

¹⁰ Cf. Mand. I 2: ἐνδύσῃ πᾶσαν ἀρετὴν δικαιοσύνης; also Sim. VI 1, 4. Most of these concepts appear also within the framework of the Two Spirits doctrine and from the context it is clear that the underlying picture is that of a plurality of good spirits, cf. Dib., p. 518.

¹¹ The imagery of putting on, or being clothed with, is widespread, cf. A. Oepke, art. δύω, κτλ.. Th. W. N. T. II, p. 319f. That Hermas' use of it is influenced by Latin induere, as Bauer s. v. ἐνδύω 2 b suggests, is not probable and not supported by Wettstein's examples on Lk. 24:29. In the Septuagint a development can be traced from those places where the underlying picture is that of putting on special clothes for special occa-

Hermas' version of the Two Spirits' doctrine is another indication that the presence of the Spirit is a determining experience. What distinguishes this version from other presentations[1] is that it is connected with what may be called the "full-empty" conception: to be empty from the viewpoint of the Holy Spirit is tantamount to being full of an evil spirit.[2] This idea is not found outside the book of Hermas. Early Christian conviction is that a Christian has received, and is full of, the Spirit.[3] He may be exhorted to be filled with it.[4] He can grieve the Spirit,[5] he can even outrage it;[6] but all this is a far cry from Hermas' "full-empty" conception. Yet it is very probable that this conception was developed by Hermas himself in order to christianize the Two Spirits' doctrine by connecting it with the specific Christian conviction that a believer is full of the Holy Spirit. The "full-empty"

_____

sions, e.g. mourning (Baruch 5:1: τὴν στολὴν τοῦ πένθους), shame (Job. 8:22: ἐνδύσονται αἰσχύνην; Ps. 34 (35):26), royal robes of honour (Ps. 92 (93):1 εὐπρέπειαν ἐνεδύσατο), armour (Is. 59:17: ἐνεδύσατο δικαιοσύνην ὡς θώρακα, Sap. Sal. 5:18, cf. Rom. 13:12; Eph. 6:11), to others where the picture no longer plays a part and the idiom is more abstract than pictorial, as in Job 29:14: δικαιοσύνην ἐνεδεδύκειν, but the latter are very few. To Hermas' use of the picture they are not particularly relevant. More important are Col. 3:12 and 1 Clem. 30, 3 ἐνδυσάμεθα τὴν ὁμόνοιαν.With regard to Col. 3: 12 it appears probable that it is dependent upon v. 10 ἐνδυσάμενοι τὸν νέον (ἄνθρωπον) which is of a different pictorial nature. Perhaps we may posit that the image of putting on moral qualities has been enlivened, and at the same time transformed, by the image of putting on Christ (Gal. 3:27; Rom. 13:14) or the new man (Eph. 4:24; Col. 3:12). In view of the parallel between ἐνδύσασθαι τὸν καινὸν ἄνθρωπον and ἀνανεοῦσθαι τῷ πνεύματι τοῦ νοὸς ὑμῶν in Eph. 4:23f. it seems correct to assume that for Hermas to put on the Holy Spirit, or Spirits, corresponds to putting on the new man in Eph. and Col. Both are elaborated in a concrete sense by putting on qualities like faith, truth, gentleness, patience, cheerfulness, etc. Cf. also P.W. van der Horst, Observations on a Pauline Expression, N.T.S. 19 (1973), p. 181-187.

[1] The *Manual of Discipline* and the *Testaments of the Twelve Patriarchs*. The question of the origin of Hermas' doctrine of the two spirits has not been settled by the investigations of Audet (cf. *art. cit., supra,* p. 26, n. 1) and Lluis Font (cf. *art. cit., supra,* p. 26, n. 4) who pointed to Qumran, and to the *Man. of Disc.* in particular, and saw in Hermas a Christian of Essenian origin. Remarkably enough neither they nor Audet's critic, Joly (cf. *art. cit., supra,* p. 26, n. 5) refer to Dibelius' *Excursus* on the Pneumatology of the Mandates (p. 517ff.) or to the sources he mentions. The subject is in need of a fresh treatment.

[2] Cf. *supra,* p. 112.

[3] Cf. e.g. Acts 8:17; 10:47; 19:2; Rom. 8:15; 1 Cor. 2:12; 1 Jn 2:27; *Barn.* 1, 2 (to receive the Spirit); Acts 4:8; 6:3, 5; 7:55; 9:17; 11:24; 13:9, 52 (to be full of the Spirit).

[4] Eph. 5:18: πληροῦσθε ἐν πνεύματι.

[5] *Ib.* 4:30: μὴ λυπεῖτε τὸ πνεῦμα τὸ ἅγιον τοῦ θεοῦ.

[6] Hebr. 10:29: τὸ πνεῦμα τῆς χάριτος ἐνυβρίσας.

conception is a restatement of that conviction in terms of a dualistic pneumatology and, understood as such, another witness to the pre-eminence of the Spirit in Hermas' thinking and experience. In this experience, the Spirit is not neutral and does not behave passively and reflectively, as Opitz suggests.[1] The Shepherd tells Hermas repeatedly that the divine Spirit has δύναμις and the earthly spirit has not.[2] This is also true of faith, patience and cheerfulness and their counterparts, double-mindedness, ill temper and grief.[3]

This is the basic experience which pervades the whole book. To express this experience, Hermas uses a variety of conceptual and pictorial means which tend to involve students deeply in questions of origin and tradition. As a result Hermas may receive various labels, and the attention tends to focus on what distinguishes him from other Christian traditions. Unless, however, the fundamental understanding of the presence of the Spirit is taken into account, we fail to discern what is most dear to Hermas himself and to what purpose the various materials are used. This failure is the more obvious because the book is not an unequivocal witness to the predominance of this experience of the Spirit in the church. It is written out of a deep concern over the spiritual state of the believers. The Spirit is seriously affected, and at times even quenched, by various sins. Hence the book preaches a new μετάνοια, which is neither an ecclesiastical form of penance nor an emotional conversion experience, but a return to the first allegiance to the Lord which was sealed in baptism. This return, Hermas proclaims, will lead to an ἀνανέωσις τοῦ πνεύματος, a renewal of the spirit in a new experience of the Spirit.[4]

To sum up, in Hermas' understanding and experience, the Holy Spirit — which the believers received in their baptism and which changed their lives from death to life — forges them into the one body of the church. The Spirit is present and active in their daily life, and prepares them for the eschatological consummation. This daily life in the Spirit makes the believers fit to be filled with the Spirit when they meet and pray together. When this happens, one of them

---

[1] *Op. cit.*, p. 95: "Der Geist *wohnt*, ist hier *neutral* ... mit jener überwiegend passiven, reflektierenden Funktion die Sarx am Ende entweder zu rechtfertigen oder zu verklagen".

[2] *Mand.* XI, 2. 5. 6. 10. 11. 17. 21.

[3] *Mand.* IX, 11; V 2, 1-3; X 3, 2.

[4] *Vis.* III 13, 2. The new experience of the Spirit is a new reception of the seal, cf. *supra*, p. 129.

becomes a prophet and speaks to his fellow-believers as the Lord wants him to speak.

So much for the presence of the Spirit according to Hermas. Does it bear comparison with the experience of the Spirit in primitive Christianity ?

Since Gunkel's book on the working of the Holy Spirit, it has become fashionable to call the Spirit-experience of primitive Christianity 'enthusiastic'.[1] When this term is used, it appears to refer to Gunkel's discovery that for the Christians of the apostolic age the Spirit was: "Die übernatürliche Kraft Gottes welche im Menschen und durch den Menschen Wunder wirkt".[2] More specifically, it is connected with a differentiation to which Gunkel himself did not attach much weight: the distinction between the idea of the Spirit as "eine ruhende Kraft", and the opinion "dass jede besondere Geistestat Folge einer besonderen wiederholten Inspiration sei".[3] Thus Harnack, in a footnote referring to the term "Enthusiasmos", explains that the New Testament knows two concepts of the Spirit, and continues: "Nach der einen Auffassung kommt er stossweise auf die Gläubigen, äussert sich in sinnenfälligen Zeichen, benimmt den Menschen das Selbstbewusstsein und bringt sie ausser sich; nach der anderen ist der Geist ein stetiger Besitz des Christen, wirkt in ihm, indem er das Bewusstsein klärt und den Charakter festigt".[4] Though Harnack does not say so explicitly, it is the former concept to which the term "Enthusiasmos" refers. In terms of the preliminary classification which was presented in chapter I,[5] Harnack refers to a form of ecstasy which belongs to the first type. It remains to be seen whether such a degree of ecstasy and enthusiasm is characteristic of all phenomena of the Spirit which

---

[1] H. Gunkel, *Wirkungen* (cf. *supra*, p. 5, n. 5); Gunkel, however, does not use the term "Enthusiasmos".

[2] Gunkel, *op. cit.*, p. 23. Cf. Käsemann, art. Geist, *R. G. G.* II³, c. 1272: "Die Kraft des Wunders und der Ekstase".

[3] Gunkel, *op. cit.*, p. 29f.

[4] Harnack, *Dogmengeschichte* I⁴, p. 57, n. 1. Cf. also Bultmann, *Theologie des Neuen Testamentes* (Tübingen, 1958³), p. 165: "Aufs Ganze gesehen liegt eine doppelte Auffassung vom πνεῦμα vor. Es ist einerseits die in der Taufe verliehene Kraft, die den Christen zum Christen macht; die ihn schon jetzt aus der vergehenden Welt heraus nimmt und ihn für die kommende "versiegelt". Das πνεῦμα is andrerseits eine jeweils dem Christen geschenkte Kraft die ihn zu ausserordentlichen Leistungen befähigt". Bultmann does not appear to oppose the two ideas to one another to the same extent as Harnack.

[5] Cf. *supra*, p. 19.

appear suddenly.[1] But more important than that, if it is to such phenomena that the term enthusiasm refers, it is inadequate as a general
term covering all the workings of the Spirit. This applies in particular
to Opitz' characterisation of primitive Christianity as "enthusiastic".
It is, however, clear that the distinction between a permanent
presence of the Spirit and a momentary inspiration by the Spirit
in the New Testament is a real one. But are we to suppose that behind
this distinction are two different types of the experience of the Spirit,
as Harnack suggests?[2] And if so, which type must be considered
the more authentic of the two?

There is widespread agreement among scholars that the momentary
inspiration by the Spirit is, if not the most authentic, at least the
oldest Christian experience, and that the idea of the Spirit as the guid-
ing and determining force in daily life is a later development for which
Paul merits credit. Gunkel contended that the normal religious and
moral functions of the simple Christian were not experienced as gifts
of the Spirit.[3] Beversluis answered the question whether the earliest
Christians ascribed moral influence to the Spirit, in the negative.[4] For
both Gunkel and Beversluis, the book of Acts is the principal source.
More recent criticism takes a different view of Acts as a source of
knowledge of primitive, pre-pauline Christianity. When Käsemann
writes that "enthusiastische Anschauungen" prevented the earliest
Christians from understanding "dass der Geist das ganze Christen-
leben regiert",[5] he does not refer to any specific text. With regard
to Luke's idea of the Spirit, however, he contends: "Hier begründet
der Geist nicht mehr als Auferstehungsmacht den täglichen Wandel
des einzelnen Christen".[6] This would amount to a return to the earliest

---

[1] It is by no means certain that in all manifestations of the Spirit which occur *"stossweise"*, ecstasy and loss of consciousness happen, cf. also Harnack, *op. cit.*, p. 60 and
the list of Spirit-manifestations in his *Die Mission und Ausbreitung des Christentums
in den ersten drei Jahrhunderten* I[4], p. 221ff.

[2] Cf. the continuation *loc. cit., supra*, p. 136: "Paulus vor allem hat die Christen gelehrt
diese Früchte (i.e. the fruits of the Spirit as a permanent possession) höher zu schätzen
als alle andere Wirkungen des Geistes. Allein eine vollstandige Klärung hier hat er noch
keineswegs erreicht; denn er "redete selbst mehr mit Zungen als sie Alle". Noch lagen
"Geist" und "Geist" in einander."

[3] *Op. cit.*, p. 8, cf. also p. 71ff.

[4] M. Beversluis, *De Heilige Geest en zijne werkingen* (Utrecht, 1896), p. 249-257.

[5] *Art. cit.*, c. 1273.

[6] *Ib.*, c. 1277.

understanding. A slightly different view is taken by Eduard Schweizer, who thinks that Luke's judaistic concept of the Spirit as essentially the Spirit of prophecy prevented him from regarding the Spirit as the direct source of the gifts of healing on the one hand, and on the other hand of more distinctly ethical phenomena such as the community life of the early church.[1] Basically, Luke cannot get away from understanding the Spirit only as merely an exceptional power which makes possible unusual feats of strength.[2] Again, the experience of the earliest Christians and the view of their historian appear to converge.

This is not the place to enter into a discussion on the value and meaning of Acts as a source for the history of primitive Christianity. But the fact remains that, on this point, we have access to primitive Christianity, its beliefs and experiences, mostly only through the intermediary of Luke. On the other hand, Luke did not intend to write the history of the primitive church. The book of Acts is a missionary book. In the programmatic verse 1:8 the Spirit is presented as the force that will enable the apostles to carry their witness to Christ to the end of the earth.[3] This purpose did not prevent Luke from understanding the Spirit as the source of other than missionary phenomena; but at the same time ensured that he had little reason to point to them. Furthermore, we forget easily that for the early Christians the presence of the Holy Spirit was a reality. They did not feel the need to ascribe all their experiences and doings to the Spirit in so many words. It is, for instance, true that in Acts 2:42-47 the community life of the church is not actually described as being due to the Spirit.[4] It is also not very probable that κοινωνία in v. 42 explicitly denotes the common partaking of the Spirit as in 2 Cor. 13:13 and Phil. 2:1.[5] But at the same time the absolute use of κοινωνία makes any definite interpretation less than adequate.[6] It carries overtones of the corporate life of the church, and the fact that the passage is the immediate sequel of the account

---

[1] *Th. W. N. T.* VI, p. 407.

[2] *Ib.*, p. 409.

[3] Cf. Haenchen, *Apostelgeschichte* (Göttingen, 1961[13]), p. 112f., *ad loc.*

[4] Schweizer, *art. cit.*, ,p. 407, n. 500.

[5] Thus L. S. Thornton, *The common Life in the Body of Christ* (London, 1963), p. 70-76.

[6] E.g. "Gütergemeinschaft" (Conzelmann *ad loc.*, Haenchen *ad loc.*), "Tischgemeinschaft" (J. Jeremias, *Die Abendmahlsworte Jesu* (Göttingen, 1960[3]), p. 111ff., Bauernfeind *ad loc.*).

of the descent of the Spirit suggests that this corporate life was the result of the gift of the Spirit. "For this special type of social unity (viz. the corporate life of the church) Paul found the fitting expression: "the communion of the Holy Spirit" (2 Cor. xiii 13, Phil. ii 1). The phrase is his; the thing was there from the outset".[1]

There is, therefore, no reason to assume that the momentary inspiration by the Spirit is the most authentic and original experience of the Spirit in primitive Christianity. Both forms are there from the beginning. It is not a matter of choice, but of emphasis. There can be little doubt that the emphasis was on the permanent endowment of all believers with the Spirit. This is the distinctive mark of the Christian understanding. In contrast to the Old Testament, the Spirit is permanently present and active in the members of the church, and not only on special occasions; in contrast to hellenistic conceptions the abiding endowment with the Spirit is not the privilege of a happy few θεῖοι ἄνδρες, but of all believers.[2]

The presence of the Spirit was thus an all-pervading experience in the primitive church, and remained so for a long time. There is ample evidence that its constitutive elements were a reality in the apostolic and the post-apostolic age — elements which we noticed already when we investigated the book of Hermas on this point —, and that these elements fundamentally remained the same. They are the following: (1) the Holy Spirit is the eschatological gift; the Christian church lives in the last days; (2) the Holy Spirit is given to the church; life in the Spirit is corporate life; (3) the Holy Spirit relates to the moral life of the Christians.

(1) The Holy Spirit means the dawn of the New Age. In his account of Pentecost Luke inserts the words ἐν ταῖς ἐσχάταις ἡμέραις in the opening sentence of the quotation from Joel.[3] This expresses the general conviction of early Christians. The Spirit is the first fruit[4] or the first instalment of what is to come,[5] or the seal which guarantees

---

[1] C. H. Dodd, *The Apostolic Preaching and its Development* (London, 1944), p. 58f.
[2] Cf. Bultmann, *op. cit.*, p. 159.
[3] Acts 2:17. The change from μετὰ ταῦτα in Joël 3:1 to ἐν ταῖς ἐσχάταις ἡμέραις is intentional and emphatic (against Conzelmann). Haenchen's preference for B which follows the Septuagint is arbitrary.
[4] Ἀπαρχή (Rom. 8:23).
[5] Ἀρραβών (2 Cor. 1:22; Eph. 1:14).

redemption.[1] To receive the Spirit is to taste the powers of the age to come.[2] The early Christians, therefore, looked forward to the coming consummation with great joy and exultation.[3] This same understanding prevails in the post-apostolic age. A witness to this is Barnabas 1, 7: "For the Master has made known to us through the prophets what has already come to pass and what is now occurring, and he has given us a foretaste of what is about to happen".[4] Instead of simply writing τὰ μέλλοντα, the writer changes the sentence pattern considerably in order to bring out the experience that τὰ μέλλοντα are already beginning to happen. This experience he has observed among those to whom he writes, when he saw that they had implanted in them the gift of the Spirit and that the Spirit had been poured out on them from the abundance of the fountain of the Lord.[5] Hence he exhorts his readers to a richer and fuller life.[6] Elsewhere the author refers to the new creation which the believers experience and of which God's dwelling in them is a sign.[7]

The same connection between the outpouring of the Spirit and the the coming of the last days is found in Irenaeus. The promise of the Spirit is described in a quotation from Joel 3:1f., but in the form in which it is found in Acts 2:17.[8] He warns against those who reject the Spirit which has been poured out according to the good pleasure

---

[1] Eph. 1:13; 4:30: τὸ πνεῦμα τὸ ἅγιον τοῦ θεοῦ ἐν ᾧ ἐσφραγίσθητε εἰς ἡμέραν ἀπολυτρώσεως.

[2] Hebr. 6:4: μετόχους γενηθέντας πνεύματος ἁγίου καὶ ... γευσαμένους ... δυνάμεις τε μέλλοντος. αἰῶνος.

[3] Cf. 1 Pet. 1:7f. where the Spirit is not mentioned explicitly, but in 4:13f. the sharing in Christ's sufferings, the joy over the revelation of his glory and the presence of the Spirit in the believers are mentioned together.

[4] Ἐγνώρισεν γὰρ ἡμῖν ὁ δεσπότης διὰ τῶν προφητῶν τὰ παρεληλυθότα καὶ τὰ ἐνεστῶτα, καὶ τῶν μελλόντων δοὺς ἀπαρχὰς ἡμῖν γεύσεως. For this form of the so called tripartite formula cf. supra, p. 77ff. The clause clearly recalls Rom. 8:23 and Hebr. 6:4.

[5] Οὕτως ἔμφυτον τῆς δωρεᾶς πνευματικῆς χάριν εἰλήφατε (1,2) ... ἀληθῶς βλέπω ἐν ὑμῖν ἐκκεχυμένον ἀπὸ τοῦ πλουσίου τῆς πηγῆς κυρίου πνεῦμα ἐφ' ὑμᾶς. (1,3).

[6] 1,7: ὧν τὰ καθ' ἕκαστα βλέποντες ἐνεργούμενα, καθὼς ἐλάλησεν, ὀφείλομεν πλουσιώτερον καὶ ὑψηλότερον προσάγειν τῷ φόβῳ αὐτοῦ. Kraft translates: "we ought all the more abundantly and enthusiastically draw near in fear of him".

[7] 16, 8: ... ἐγενόμεθα καινοί, πάλιν ἐξ ἀρχῆς κτιζόμενοι· διὸ ἐν τῷ κατοικητηρίῳ ἡμῶν ἀληθῶς ὁ θεὸς κατοικεῖ ἐν ἡμῖν. The underlying metaphor is that of the church as the temple in which God or the Spirit dwells, cf. infra, p. 141f.

[8] A. H., III 17, 1: Hunc enim promisit per prophetas effundere se in novissimis temporibus super servos et ancillas ut prophetent.

of God in the last days because they are opposed to the false prophets.[1] Furthermore, he maintains that the truly spiritual man has always known the same God and the same Word of God and the same Spirit of God, even if it had been poured out anew in the last days.[2] This attempt to reconcile the unchangeability of the Triune God with the eschatological conception of the Spirit shows how dear the idea of the last days in which the church lives was to him.

(2) The Holy Spirit is the origin and the source of the corporate life of the church. It is a gift in which all believers share as members of the church. The classic expression for this is 1 Cor. 12:13: ἐν ἑνὶ πνεύματι ἡμεῖς πάντες εἰς ἓν σῶμα ἐβαπτίσθημεν.[3] To receive the Spirit is to be incorporated into Christ and his body, the church. The Spirit dwells in the believers because it dwells in the church. Yet the image of the body is not the most suitable to express the Spirit as the source of the corporate life of the church. When πνεῦμα and σῶμα occur together, the emphasis is usually on the unity of the church.[4] For the indwelling of the Spirit the image of the temple is more appropriate and this is best represented in the sources. Paul warns the Corinthians that they are a temple of God in which the Spirit of God dwells.[5] The church grows into a holy temple in the Lord, and into a dwelling place of God in the Spirit.[6] This experience of God's indwelling in the Spirit appears also as a ground for an appeal to the church to live up to it. Ignatius exhorts the Ephesians to act ὡς αὐτοῦ ἐν ἡμῖν κατοικοῦντος, ἵνα ὦμεν αὐτοῦ ναοὶ καὶ αὐτὸς ἐν

---

[1] Ib., III 11, 9: Alii vero ut donum Spiritus frustrentur quod in novissimis temporibus secundum placitum Patris effusum est in humanum genus, illam speciem non admittunt (i.e. the Johannine teaching on the Paraclete), etc.

[2] Ib., IV 33, 15: Semper eundem Deum sciens, et semper eundem Verbum Dei cognoscens ... et semper eundem Spiritum Dei cognoscens etiamsi in novissimis temporibus nove effusus est in nos. That the phrase 'in the last days' has its full eschatological meaning is shown by W. C. van Unnik, Der Ausdruck "In den letzten Zeiten" bei Irenaeus, Neotestamentica et Patristica, Freundesgabe Oscar Cullmann (Leiden, 1962), p. 293-304.

[3] For this combination of baptism and the Spirit cf. present writer, The Holy Spirit in Baptism, The Baptist Quarterly XIX (1961-1962), p. 339-351; J. D. G. Dunn, Baptism in the Holy Spirit (London, 1970), p. 129-131.

[4] Cf. Eph. 4:4; Hermas, Sim. IX 13, 5; cf. supra, p. 131f.

[5] 1 Cor. 3:16. The introductory οὐκ οἴδατε intimates that what follows is not new but generally known, cf. O. Michel, art. ναός, Th. W. N. T. IV, p. 890f.

[6] Eph. 2:21: εἰς ναὸν ἅγιον ἐν κυρίῳ ... εἰς κατοικητήριον τοῦ θεοῦ ἐν πνεύματι. Cf. 1 Peter 2:5: ὡς λίθοι ζῶντες οἰκοδομεῖσθε οἶκος πνευματικός.

ἡμῖν θεὸς ἡμῶν.[1] This passage shows at the same time that the image of the temple is apt to develop and to come to refer to the body of the individual believer. His body is a temple of the Holy Spirit which he has from God.[2] A further development is that the image refers to the heart of the believers.[3] Such ideas are more than images or theological concepts. They spring from a living experience. There is often a note of abundance in the sayings on the Spirit. It is not by measure that God gives the Spirit.[4] The experience of the Spirit is like rivers of living water flowing out from within.[5] The Spirit comes from the richness of the fountain of the Lord.[6] The believers are exhorted to be full of the Spirit,[7] or to be rich in the Spirit.[8] 1 Clement describes the life of the church in Corinth before the strife as a profound and rich peace and an insatiable desire to do good;[9] then he adds καὶ πλήρης πνεύματος ἁγίου ἔκχυσις ἐπὶ πάντας ἐγίνετο. This does not mean that the Spirit is a reward for moral conduct, as a kind of conscientia bona consequens.[10] It denotes the inner force that is behind the peace and the desire to do good.[11] This power was not a conclusion of reflection, but of experience; and it assured the believers that they might hope for even greater things. This assurance has found its classic expression in Ephesians 3:20f.: "To him who by the power at work within us is

---

[1] Eph. 15, 3. Cf. also the impressive picture of the church as a temple in Barn. 16, 8 quoted infra, p. 150.

[2] Cf. 1 Cor. 6:19; again the introduction is ἢ οὐκ οἴδατε. 2 Clem. 9, 3: δεῖ οὖν ἡμᾶς ὡς ναὸν θεοῦ φυλάσσειν τὴν σάρκα.

[3] Barn. 6, 15: ναὸς γὰρ ἅγιος, ἀδελφοί μου, τῷ κυρίῳ τὸ κατοικητήριον τῆς καρδίας. Cf. also the remarkable argument in Tatian, Oratio ad Graecos 15, 2: in a passage on the recovery of the συζυγία of the soul and the spirit he argues that the union of the soul with the body prevents this recovery: τὸ δὲ τοιοῦτον τῆς συστάσεως εἶδος εἰ μὲν ὡς ναὸς εἴη, κατοικεῖν ἐν αὐτῷ θεὸς βούλεται διὰ τοῦ πρεσβεύοντος πνεύματος.

[4] Jn 3: 34: οὐ γὰρ ἐκ μέτρου δίδωσιν τὸ πνεῦμα.

[5] Jn 7:38f.

[6] Barn. 1, 3 quoted supra, p. 140, n. 5.

[7] Eph. 5:18.

[8] Barn. 19, 2: ἔσῃ ἁπλοῦς τῇ καρδίᾳ καὶ πλούσιος τῷ πνεύματι.

[9] 1 Clem. 2, 2: εἰρήνη βαθεῖα καὶ λιπαρά ... καὶ ἀκόρεστος πόθος εἰς ἀγαθοποιίαν, cf. W. C. van Unnik, "Tiefer Friede" (1. Klemens 2, 2), Vig. Christ. 24 (1970), p. 261-279.

[10] Thus Knopf, H. N. T. ad loc., p. 46; Opitz, op. cit., 25f.

[11] The imperfect ἐγίνετο indicates, not that "Clemens sich das Ereignis einer Geistausgiessung auf die ganze Gemeinde als wiederholbar vorstellt" (Opitz, loc. cit.), but rather that the working of the Spirit is continuous. In 46, 6 the aorist ἐκχυθέν refers to the "heilsgeschichtliche" fact of Pentecost.

able to do far more abundantly than all that we ask or think, to Him be glory in the church and in Christ Jesus to all generations, for ever and ever. Amen".

(3) Several of the passages on the corporate and personal life in the Spirit, quoted in the preceding section, clearly show the connection between the Spirit and the moral life of the believers. It is indeed impossible to separate the corporate and the moral life. Again, the fitting expression is from Paul: καρπὸς τοῦ πνεύματος (Gal. 5:22). But the truth of this was recognised from the outset, and has found various expressions. To quote one example, Ignatius writes at the end of a passage dealing with the contrast between flesh and Spirit: ἃ δὲ καὶ κατὰ σάρκα πράσσετε, ταῦτα πνευματικά ἐστιν· ἐν Ἰησοῦ γὰρ Χριστῷ πάντα πράσσετε.[1] This account of the various ways in which the presence of the Spirit was experienced in the early church intends to be representative, rather than exhaustive; it is sufficient evidence to show that, apart from differences in imagery and concepts, the experience of the Spirit was fundamentally the same. As far as this experience is concerned, Hermas is in the main stream of first and second century Christianity.

THE PROPHET, THE CHURCH AND THE SPIRIT

In the view of Hermas, a Christian prophet depends upon the church for his inspiration by the Spirit. Apart from that specific inspiration he has the Spirit to the same degree as his fellow believers. When we submit that this view makes explicit what is implied in other evidence the question is raised: what is the relationship in early Christianity between prophecy and the church vis à vis the Spirit ?

Before entering upon a discussion of this question, we must take into account the two forms of prophecy mentioned by Greeven.[2] Both in Acts and 1 Corinthians we find alongside persons who are called prophets, and a prophetic ministry exercised by ordinary church members.[3] Traces of the same situation are found in the Apocalypse.[4]

---

[1] *Eph.* 8, 2.

[2] Cf. *supra*, p. 8f.

[3] Prophets are mentioned 1 Cor. 12:28f.: 14:29, 32, 37, but it is hard to distinguish them from prophesying church members; Eph. 2:20; 3:5; 4:11; Acts 11:27; 13:1; 15:32; 21:10. Prophecy as a ministry of all members: 1 Thess. 5:19f; 1 Cor. 11:4f.; 12:10; 13:2, 9; 14:1, 24, 31, 39; Rom. 12:6.

[4] Christian prophets are mentioned in 11:18; 16:6; 18:20, 24; 22:9, sometimes distin-

As far as the prophetic ministry of the ordinary church member is concerned, there need be no doubt that the picture of the 11th Mandate applies to it. But the other prophets may be a different matter. Long ago, H. B. Swete suggested that "only a relatively small number of believers were 'established to be prophets', forming a charismatic order in the Church".[1] Recently, J. Lindblom wrote: "Es gab in den ersten Gemeinden Propheten, die das prophetische Charisma als einen dauernden Besitz hatten, die sozusagen berufsmässige Propheten waren".[2] These statements distinguish the prophets as a group from their fellow believers. In this light, our question must be reformulated as follows; what is the relationship between these prophets and the church *vis à vis* the Spirit?

This question brings us back to the twofold conception of the Spirit in the primitive church as described by Harnack and Bultmann.[3] According to the latter, the general endowment with the Spirit is ignored when there are in the church people who rate in a special way as πνευματικοί.[4] But did the primitive church distinguish in its ranks a special group of πνευματικοί?

The use of πνευματικός as a substantive in early Christianity is restricted to Paul and to one place in Barnabas. In 1 Cor. 2:14ff. Paul contrasts the 'unspiritual man' (ψυχικὸς ἄνθρωπος) and the 'spiritual man' (πνευματικός). Conzelmann thinks that this refers to two distinct groups in the church: a group of πνευματικοί, to which Paul himself claims to belong because of v. 16b: ἡμεῖς δὲ νοῦν Χριστοῦ ἔχομεν; and the rest of the believers addressed in 3:1 as ὑμῖν ... σαρκί-νοις.[5] This, however, is improbable. It is conceivable that in Corinth

---

guished explicitly from the church members who are called ἅγιοι. But since the believers are addressed as οἱ ἔχοντες τὴν μαρτυρίαν Ἰησοῦ (12:17), and ἡ μαρτυρία Ἰησοῦ ἐστιν τὸ πνεῦμα τῆς προφητείας (19:10), they also share in the prophetic Spirit. Satake, *Die Gemeindeordnung in der Johannesapokalyps*, p. 71f. accepts this interpretation and then rejects the clause as a gloss. This is not necessary, cf. D. Hill, Prophecy and Prophets in the Revelation of St John, *N. T. S.* 18 (1972), p. 401-418, esp. 413.

[1] *The Holy Spirit in the New Testament* (London, 1910, repr. Grand Rapids, 1964), p. 377.

[2] *Gesichte und Offenbarungen* 179f. Cf. also E. Earle Ellis, The Role of the Christian Prophet in Acts, *Apostolic History and the Gospel, Biblical and Historical Essays presented to F.F. Bruce.* ed. by W. Ward Gasque and R. P. Martin (London, 1970), p. 56-67, esp. p. 62f.

[3] Cf. *supra*, p. 136, n. 4.

[4] *Op. cit.*, p. 160.

[5] *Der erste Brief an die Korinther*, p. 87f., *ad loc.*

there were individual members who called themselves πνευματικοί,[1] but Paul does not distinguish himself from other Christians as a πνευματικός. In his pneumatology there is no place for πνευματικοί as a distinct group.[2] The ironical tone of the passage suggests that Paul takes up the vocabulary of the Corinthians, turns it against them and then drops it.[3] Yet in 3:16 he reminds them that the Spirit of God dwells in them! In any case, the passage 2:6-3:3 does not suggest the existence of a group of πνευματικοί in the church. In Galatians 6:1: οἱ πνευματικοί is addressed to the whole church and not to a group within it.[4] This is also the case in Barnabas 4:11: γενώμεθα πνευματικοί, γενώμεθα ναὸς τέλειος τῷ θεῷ.[5]

It is, however, conceivable that in the primitive church there were special Spirit-bearers, "Pneumatiker", but that the word πνευματικοί was not applied to them.[6] There are, for instance, the seven men who were to serve the church in Jerusalem at the tables: they had to be πλήρεις πνεύματος καὶ σοφίας and one of them, Stephen, is called rather emphatically πλήρης πίστεως καὶ πνεύματος ἁγίου and πλήρης χάριτος καὶ δυνάμεως.[7] But this does not mark them as standing

---

[1] Cf. 14: 37: εἰ τις δοκεῖ προφήτης εἶναι ἢ πνευματικός. This may refer to the presumption of individuals to be πνευματικοί or be understood in the light of vv. 14ff., where the repeated use of ἐν πνεύματι refers to glossolaly.

[2] Cf. H. D. Wendland, Das Wirken des Heiligen Geistes in den Gläubigen nach Paulus, Th. L. Z. 77 (1952), c. 457-470, esp. 460: "der Gerechtfertigte is der Pneumatiker"

[3] In 2:16 ἡμεῖς refers to all Christians as contrasted to people who did not receive the Spirit of God, i.e. the non-Christians; in 3:1ff. Paul returns to his admonition of the Corinthians.

[4] Whether it means 'you, who are spiritual' or 'you who presume to be spiritual' (Lietzmann, H. N. T. ad loc.) is immaterial. W. Schmithals, Paulus und die Gnostikei (Hamburg, 1965), p. 32, thinks that the phrase refers to a Gnostic group within the churcl but there is no evidence that the referent of ὑμεῖς is different from e.g. ὑμῖν, ἀδελφο· in 1:11, ὑμεῖς in 3:28, or ὑμεῖς ..., ἀδελφοί in 4:28.

[5] Also Ign., Eph. 8, 2 οἱ πνευματικοί denotes the Christians in general. Polyc. 2, 2 σαρκικὸς εἰ καὶ πνευματικός is not relevant. Οἱ πνευματικοί as a group-indication is noi used in Christian literature before the Gnostics, cf. e.g. Iren. A. H. I 6, 4: αὐτοῖς (i.e. the Valentinians) πνευματικοῖς τε καὶ τελείοις καλουμένοις. In contrast to all who presume to be πνευματικοί Irenaeus describes in A. H. IV 33, 1-8 the true spiritual man, cf. supra, p. 62.

[6] Cf. Käsemann, art. cit., c. 1273: "So treten von Anfang an besondere Pneumatikei aus der übrigen Gemeinde heraus". Käsemann mentions "Wundertäter, Propheten, Bekenner".

[7] Acts 6:3, 5, 8. He performed signs and miracles. In 7:55 ὑπάρχων πλήρης πνεύματος ἁγίου is inserted with regard to the subsequent vision, cf. Haenchen ad. loc.

apart from the rest of the community as special Spirit-bearers. When Luke can say that Peter was filled with the Holy Spirit when he began to speak to the Sanhedrin (Acts 4:8), it is clear that he does not consider the apostle as a "Pneumatiker" who is in the abiding possession of the Spirit in a measure beyond that of the other members of the church.[1] What distinguishes the apostle from the others was not his endowment with the Spirit but his apostolic commission. The same applies to Paul: he does not claim apostolic authority by pointing to his Spirit-endowment but by referring to the grace that was given to him.[2] This χάρις does not set him apart from the church since the commission of the believers is also κατὰ τὴν χάριν.[3] Hence Käsemann comments: "Apostolat und Gemeinde sind pneumatische Realitäten. Darum erhält jedes nur im Zusammenhang mit dem andern Sinn und Gewicht, wie beides im Geber des Geistes begründet ruht".[4] This is true not only of the apostleship but of all gifts of the Spirit. In the last analysis there is no primitive Christian "Pneumatikertum" in the sense of a group or a person with a greater and higher endowment with the Spirit than the rest of the church.[5] The church itself is a corporate "Pneumatikertum", consisting of πνευματικοί even if the Spirit may manifest itself in its members in different ways and to different degrees. Far from ignoring the general endowment with the Spirit, it rather confirms it, because the endowment with the Spirit is a dynamic experience which is subject to change and may rise and fall. The gifts of the Spirit are a part of this endowment with the Spirit. They are given to the body and not to the members individually.

Here a discussion of 1 Corinthians 12:31 and 14:1.39 is relevant. According to Bultmann, the striving for the gifts of the Spirit is another example of how the general endowment with the Spirit is ignored in primitive Christianity from time to time.[6] He does not translate the word ζηλοῦν, apparently assuming that its meaning is unambiguous; and indeed most translators and commentators do take it to mean

---

[1] To be filled with the Spirit was the experience of the whole church (2:4; 4:31).

[2] Cf. Rom. 1:5; 12:3; 15:15; 1 Cor. 3:10; Gal. 2:9. 2 Cor. 10:13: κατὰ τὸ μέτρον τοῦ κανόνος οὗ ἐμέρισεν ἡμῖν ὁ θεός, may also be understood along the same lines, cf. H. W. Beyer, art. κανών, Th. W. N. T. III, p. 603f. Käsemann, Die Legitimität des Apostels, Z. N. W., XLI (1942), p. 58f.

[3] Cf. Rom. 12:6; 1 Cor. 1:4.

[4] Käsemann, Die Legitimität, p. 60.

[5] The term is, therefore, inappropriate, and it is advisable not to use it at all.

[6] Op. cit., p. 160.

'to strive to obtain' or a similar phrase.[1] But a closer inspection of the places in question[2] shows that this interpretation is not satisfactory. It implies that the object (τὰ χαρίσματα τὰ μείζονα, τὰ πνευματικά, τὸ προφητεύειν) is something which the Corinthians do not as yet have. Hence some commentators understand ζηλοῦν as 'to pray for',[3] but this is not what it can mean. Furthermore, to suggest that the church members did not have gifts and should do their best to obtain one or more of them, is not consistent with 1:4-7, 12:4-11 and 14:26. Yet ζηλοῦν undoubtedly denotes a human activity. But how can human activity go together with a gift from God?

W. C. van Unnik has argued for another meaning of ζηλοῦν, namely 'to practice zealously'.[4] He adduces a number of places where the word has this meaning. A few of them may be quoted here. In Josephus, *Ant.* XX 41 it is said of king Izates that he κέκρικε ζηλοῦν τὰ πάτρια τῶν 'Ιουδαίων. After he had been circumcised his own people considered him a τῶν παρ' ἑτέροις ζηλωτὴν ἐθῶν (ib. 47).[5] Philo calls the pagan seers: "those who practice zealously the counterfeit and ribald divination".[6] In the context of 1 Corinthians 12-14, this means that the gifts are not things to be striven after. They were present in the church and the members were ζηλωταὶ πνευμάτων: zealous practicians of the spiritual gifts. The Spirit-endowment of the church comprises also the gifts that serve for the upbuilding of the church. They come to life in the gathering of the church, because the Spirit is present there.

On this point, the 11th Mandate of the Shepherd states explicitly

---

[1] This interpretation is found already in Johann. Chrysost., *Homil. in 1 Cor.* 32, 9 (289 A) who renders μένετε ἐπιθυμοῦντες χαρισμάτων, and Theodorus (ὅλως γὰρ ἐφίεσθε τῶν μειζόνων χαρισμάτων, Cramer, *Catenae* V, 246). Of modern commentators Robertson-Plummer, Findlay, Weiss, Bachmann, Schmiedel, Lietzmann, Conzelmann, Héring, Heinrici.

[2] 1 Cor. 12:31: ζηλοῦτε δὲ τὰ χαρίσματα τὰ μείζονα. 14:1: ζηλοῦτε δὲ τὰ πνευματικά 12: ἐπεὶ ζηλωταί ἐστε πνευμάτων, 39: ζηλοῦτε τὸ προφητεύειν.

[3] Thus e.g. Heinrici, Robertson-Plummer, Grosheide, Barrett.

[4] The meaning of 1 Corinthians 12:31 (as yet unpublished).

[5] Cf. also Philo, *Spec. Leg.* II 253: he who swears vainly will not escape the revenge of men: μυρίοι γὰρ ἔφοροι, ζηλωταὶ νόμων, φύλακες τῶν πατρίων ἀκριβέστατοι.

[6] *Spec. Leg.* IV 50: τῶν τὴν παράσημον καὶ βωμολόχον μαντικὴν ζηλούντων. Cf. also ib., 199: τοῖς δὲ τοιούτων ἐργάταις τε καὶ ζηλωταῖς ἐπανατείνεται θεοῦ φόβον ὁ νόμος, referring to people who insult the dumb and hinder the blind. Other places quoted by Van Unnik are Jos., *Ant.* VI 343, Philo, *De Virt.* 194, Diod. Sic. I 81, 4; IV 71, Plut., *Vita Alex.* 2, Euseb., *Praep. Evang.* IV 16, 20.

that which is implied and presupposed in 1 Corinthians 14. The two documents are otherwise vastly different and represent two different worlds. There is on the one hand the greatest apostle of the primitive church and a young church where the Spirit abounds and shows forth manifold gifts. It is Paul's task, not to quench the fire, but to channel the stream of the Spirit. There is on the other hand Hermas, a simple Christian, representing "das Alltagschristentum der kleinen Leute",[1] and there is a church which is spiritually threatened and in need of a new conversion. The spirit is not lacking, but its fire is not bursting forth in the way in which it happened in Corinth. The spiritual atmosphere is completely different. Yet in both documents prophecy functions fundamentally in the same way. Both testify that the functional structure of Christian prophecy is congregational. The Spirit which is in the church becomes active when the church gathers in worship and fellowship, and breaks forth in the words of the prophet. The prophet needs the church, for it is through her that he is filled with the Spirit. The church needs the prophet, for it is through him that she hears what the Spirit says to the church.

There are no other documents from the same period which state the interdependence of the church and its prophets, and their common dependence on the Spirit with the same clarity. Yet there are here and there scraps of evidence which may betray the same fundamental understanding. It is generally known that the community gathering for worship and fellowship, is, as it were, a magnetic field of the Holy Spirit. The relevant material has been collected and discussed by W. C. van Unnik.[2] The classic formulation is found in the *Apostolic Tradition* of Hippolytus: *Unusquisque sollicitus sit ire ad ecclesiam, locum ubi spiritus sanctus floret.*[3] Now we read in the *Didache*: τοῖς δὲ προφήταις

---

[1] Dib., p. 425.

[2] Dominus Vobiscum, *New Testament Essays, Studies in Memory of T. W. Manson* (Manchester, 1959), p. 270-305, esp. p. 294ff. Another aspect of the presence of the Spirit in worship is that it destroys the power of the devil, cf. Ign., *Eph.* 13, 1: σπουδάζετε οὖν πυκνότερον συνέρχεσθαι εἰς εὐχαριστίαν θεοῦ καὶ εἰς δόξαν· ὅταν γὰρ πυκνῶς ἐπὶ τὸ αὐτὸ γίνεσθε, καθαιροῦνται αἱ δυνάμεις τοῦ σατανᾶ. Though the Spirit is not mentioned, the underlying thought obviously is that the gathering of the church is, as it were, a concentration of the power of the Spirit.

[3] Ed. B. Botte (*Sources Chrétiennes*; Paris, 1968), 41, p. 124f. (cf. also *ib.* 35, p. 118f.). This is said in the context of an injunction to go to the church for instruction. The church is also a *locus ubi docetur.* When all are there, *Tunc dabitur ei qui loquitur ut dicat ea quae utilia sunt unicuique, et audies quae non cogitas, et proficies in iis quae spiritus*

ἐπιτρέπετε εὐχαριστεῖν, ὅσα θέλουσιν.[1] This freedom of prayer is granted to the prophets as prophets speaking ἐν πνεύματι. But they are ἐν πνεύματι because the church is gathered for the purpose of the εὐχαριστία which is also an event in the Spirit. This finds its liturgical expression in the salutation which in the *Apostolic Tradition* of Hippolytus precedes the great eucharistic prayer.[2] This dialogical salutation probably dates from the middle of the second century A.D., but the reality which it expresses is, of course, as old as the Lord's Supper itself. Luke writes that the community in Jerusalem used to break the bread and to share their meals ἐν ἀγαλλιάσει which is almost the fixed term for the joy of expectation in the Spirit.[3] This sphere of joy is the sphere in which the Spirit might fill the prophet and inspire him to lead the church in thanksgiving. Thus the freedom of the prophets in the thanksgiving prayer appears to rest on the same basis as found in 1 Corinthians 14 and the 11th Mandate, though it is not a case of prophetic speech proper.

A vestige of the same conception is found also in the famous prophetic outburst of Ignatius in the church of Philadelphia: ἐκραύγασα, μεταξὺ ὤν, ἐλάλουν μεγάλῃ φωνῇ, θεοῦ φωνῇ· Τῷ ἐπισκόπῳ προσέχετε καὶ τῷ πρεσβυτερίῳ καὶ διακόνοις. Some people suspected that he had been informed beforehand about the division of some but he assures them that he had no human knowledge of it: τὸ δὲ πνεῦμα ἐκήρυσσεν λέγον τάδε.[4] This happened when he was in their midst (μεταξὺ ὤν). It is well possible that this phrase means more than just his physical presence and that it is a veiled, or perhaps even an unconscious intimation that the gathering of the church was the right place for this to happen. *Ephesians* 5, 2 and 13, 1 show that the meeting of the church

---

sanctus tibi dabit per eum qui instruit (*ib.* 41). Here the teacher has taken the place of the prophet but otherwise the similarities with 1 Cor. 14 and *Mand.* XI are striking. For the place of the teachers in the church of Hippolytus cf. A. Hamel, *Kirche bei Hippolyt von Rom* (Gütersloh, 1951), p. 159ff.

[1] 10, 7.

[2] 4, p. 46f.: *Dominus vobiscum*; *Et cum spiritu tuo.*

[3] Acts 2:46; cf. 1 Pet. 1:6-8; 4:13; Lk. 10:21; E. Schweizer, art. Abendmahl I, *R.G.G.* I[3], c. 11. Bultmann, art. ἀγαλλιάομαι, *Th. W. N. T.* I, p. 20, thinks that possibly in 1 Cor. 11:26: τὸν θάνατον τοῦ κυρίου καταγγέλλετε, ἄχρι οὗ ἔλθῃ, might be similar to an act of ἀγαλλίασις.

[4] *Philad.* 7, 1-2; cf. the same introductory formula in Agabus' prophecy in Acts 21: 11.

is a center of spiritual power.[1] Behind all this is the same conception of the Spirit, the church and the prophet.[2]

Finally, there is the enigmatic passage in Barnabas 16, 8-10 which speaks of the church as the new temple: ἐν τῷ κατοικητηρίῳ ἡμῶν ἀληθῶς ὁ θεὸς κατοικεῖ ἐν ἡμῖν.[3] How? His word of faith, his invitation of promise, the wisdom of his ordinances, the commandment of his teaching, αὐτὸς ἐν ἡμῖν προφητεύων, αὐτὸς ἐν ἡμῖν κατοικῶν. These are the signs of God's indwelling and among them is prophecy through which God speaks in the church. The line of thought is not very consistent, for the sentence ends: εἰσάγει εἰς τὸν ἄφθαρτον ναόν, shifting from being in the temple to entering the temple. What follows seems to reflect the impression which the prophetic speech in the church makes upon an outsider who is attracted to the message: ὁ γὰρ ποθῶν σωθῆναι βλέπει οὐκ εἰς τὸν ἄνθρωπον, ἀλλ' εἰς τὸν ἐν αὐτῷ κατοικοῦντα καὶ λαλοῦντα, ἐπ' αὐτῷ ἐκπλησσόμενος, ἐπὶ τῷ μηδέποτε μήτε τοῦ λέγοντος τὰ ῥήματα ἀκηκοέναι ἐκ τοῦ στόματος μήτε αὐτός ποτε ἐπιτεθυμηκέναι ἀκούειν. τοῦτό ἐστιν πνευματικὸς ναὸς οἰκοδομούμενος τῷ κυρίῳ. This is "a syntactical nightmare",[4] but in the "blurred picture" there are some points fairly clear: the outsider to his amazement hears someone he knows suddenly speak out as a prophet. This sudden and unexpected event is a specimen of αὐτὸς ἐν ἡμῖν προφητεύων, which, in its turn, is a result of αὐτὸς ἐν ἡμῖν κατοικῶν. Here the same pattern emerges: the indwelling of God through the Spirit in the church; prophetic speaking as a result and a sign of this; a member of the church unexpectedly beginning to speak as a prophet.

Though the evidence is indirect and, as it were, under the surface, the basic triangular structure of the Spirit, the church and the prophet

---

[1] 5, 2: εἰ γὰρ ἑνὸς καὶ δευτέρου προσευχὴ τοσαύτην ἰσχὺν ἔχει, πόσῳ μᾶλλον ἥ τε τοῦ ἐπισκόπου καὶ πάσης τῆς ἐκκλησίας; this power has been defined previously as πνευματική. For 13, 1 cf. supra, p. 148, n. 2.

[2] Though Ignatius is not called a prophet but a bishop, and emphasizes the episcopal ministry strongly he is not set apart from the church as a special Spirit-bearer. If his second name Θεοφόρος is to be understood as related to πνευματοφόρος, this does not set him apart from his readers to whom he writes: θεοῦ γέμετε (Magn. 14, cf. W. Bauer, H. N. T. ad loc., p. 190). What happened in Philadelphia is a prophetic event in any case.

[3] Κατοικητήριον refers here to the church, in 6, 15 to the individual believer, like ναός in 1 Cor. 3:16 and 6:19.

[4] R. A. Kraft, Barnabas and the Didache, p. 132 ad loc.

appears to underly the three situations with which we have dealt. We may therefore assume that this structure underlies all Christian prophecy in the first two centuries A.D.

THE PROPHET AND THE MINISTRY

So far no mention has been made of the ecclesiastical structure of the church, and indeed the absence of any reference to church officers in the 11th Mandate is, at first sight, striking. Also, it is striking that the prophets are nowhere else mentioned together with the officers of the church.[1] The question of church and ministry in Hermas is difficult because of the nature of the material. Hermas' primary interest is not the proper structure and functioning of the church. What concerns him can be seen clearly in *Sim.* VIII 6, 4 - 10, 4 the allegory of the stick-bearers. It is the conduct and the faithfulness of the believers and the repentance of those among them who had gone astray. This may include members of the leadership of the church, as those who brought in διδαχὰς ἑτέρας (6, 5), and those who were jealous περὶ πρωτείων καὶ περὶ δόξης τινός (7, 4), but they are not identified as officers of the church. In the related allegorical interpretation of the twelve mountains in *Sim.* IX 19-29, the people of the fifth mountain are identified as those who θέλουσιν ἐθελοδιδάσκαλοι εἶναι, but it is hardly possible that this refers to teachers of the church.[2] In the same context 26, 2 mentions διάκονοι who stole the livelihood of the widows and the orphans, and in 27, 2 ἐπίσκοποι are mentioned who have entertained the servants of God in their homes and ἐν τῇ διακονίᾳ ἑαυτῶν have sheltered the widows and the destitute. Only in the last two places do we find a mention of church officers; and then not as such but with regard to the way in which they have acquitted themselves of their ministry. They have this in common with all the other believers who have been mentioned.

---

[1] Cf. *Sim.* IX 15, 4: οἱ λε' προφῆται τοῦ θεοῦ καὶ διάκονοι αὐτοῦ. They appear to belong to the (third) generation which precedes that of the ἀπόστολοι καὶ διδάσκαλοι τοῦ κηρύγματος τοῦ υἱοῦ τοῦ θεοῦ and hence to refer to the Old Testament prophets. Pernveden, *op. cit.*, p. 146, does not seem to make this distinction.

[2] 22, 2. It is probably Gnostic teachers that are envisaged, cf. *supra*, p. 66. Whether the church of Hermas had teachers among its ministers is doubtful because they are always mentioned together with the apostles in a context that seems to refer to the past, cf. *Sim.* IX 15, 4-6 (μέχρι τῆς κοιμήσεως αὐτῶν.); 16, 5 (κοιμηθέντες.); 25, 2. For a different view cf. Pernveden, *op. cit.*, p. 147f.

152   PROPHECY AND THE CHURCH

All this has little relevance to the position of the prophet in the
church and his relationship with the ministry .Two other passages,
however, are important because they reveal something about the relationship of Hermas as the receiver of divine revelations, and the pres-
byters.¹ The first is *Vis.* III 1, 8. When Hermas is invited by the Elderly
Lady to sit down on the couch which has been brought by the young
men, he replies: κυρία, ἄφες τοὺς πρεσβυτέρους πρῶτον καθίσαι.
This is interpreted in various ways. Pernveden thinks that it is a
recognition of the precedence of the church leaders over himself,² but
he does not take into account the fact that the Elderly Lady curtly
tells Hermas to sit down nonetheless.³ Weinel finds here an indication
of a competition between the ordained ministry and the charismatics
and martyrs.⁴ This is denied by Dibelius who compares *Vis.* I 2, 2,⁵
and thinks that this time Hermas is allowed to sit down because he
has repented since his first meeting with the Elderly Lady.⁶ According to Dibelius, this repentance is alluded to in *Vis.* II 3, 2, but this
connection seems a little far-fetched. The little scene in *Vis* III 1, 8f.
serves a twofold purpose. Its most obvious function is to mark a
new stage in the revelatory process.⁷ To that is added the question
of rank and precedence in the church. Hermas is prepared to let the

---

¹ For the church order according to Hermas cf. *Dibelius*, p. 634f., Pernveden, *op. cit.*,
p. 144-155, Schweizer, *Gemeinde und Gemeindeordnung*, p. 141-145, H. von Campenhausen
Kirchliches Amt, p. 103ff. Though much is uncertain we may assume that the church
is led by a group of πρεσβύτεροι and that the ἐπίσκοποι and διάκονοι are probably
members of this group with a special function. Whether the former had the presidency
in worship (cf. *Sim.* IX 27, 3 λειτουργοῦντες κυρίῳ and Dibelius *ad. loc.*) is uncertain
but not relevant to our investigation.

² *Op. cit.*, p. 150, 152. The same view in R. Seeberg, *Lehrbuch der Dogmengeschichte* I⁴
(repr. Basel, 1953), p. 241f.

³ Ὅ σοι λέγω, φησίν, κάθισον.

⁴ Weinel, *ad loc.*, p. 297, and cf. also Schweizer, *Gemeinde und Gemeindeordnung*,
p. 143. Harnack, *ad loc.*, p. 31f. thinks of a conflict between presbyters and laymen.

⁵ Ἦλθεν γυνὴ πρεσβῦτις ... καὶ ἐκάθισεν μόνη.

⁶ P. 456f. He is followed in this by Peterson, *Frühkirche*, p. 267.

⁷ After the discussion Hermas asks again to be shown the vision: ἡ δὲ πάλιν
ἐπελάβετό μου τῆς χειρὸς καὶ ἐγείρει με καὶ καθίζει με ἐπὶ τὸ συμψέλιον ἐξ εὐωνύμων·
ἐκαθέζετο δὲ καὶ αὐτὴ ἐκ δεξιῶν (III 2, 4), and then the revelation commences (cf. *P. G.
M.* VII 744ff., Preis. II, p. 33, quoted by Peterson: χρηματίσατέ μοι περὶ τοῦ δεῖνα
πράγματος ... πάντως δέομαι, ἱκετεύω, δοῦλος ὑμέτερος καὶ τεθρονισμένος ὑμῖν). The first
revelation concerned Hermas himself and was addressed to him. In *Vis.* III Hermas
receives a revelation which he had to transmit. From a recipient of revelation he
becomes an agent and transmittor.

elders sit down first, but the Elderly Lady rebukes him and bids him
to sit down. This means clearly that between Hermas and the presbyters there can be no question of rank. They are in the same group.
The only difference in position which is recognised is that between
the martyrs and the other believers.¹
The second place is *Vis.* II 4, 3: σὺ δὲ ἀναγνώσῃ εἰς ταύτην
τὴν πόλιν μετὰ τῶν πρεσβυτέρων τῶν προϊσταμένων τῆς ἐκκλησίας.
The situation is that, after having received the first written revelation
(II 1, 3f.), Hermas has another vision in which the Elderly Lady tells
him that she wants to add to the preceding revelation. What these
additional words refer to is not clear from the context, but, conceivably, it is the content of *Vis.* III which is envisaged. Leaving out of
account the other details of *Vis.* II 4, we may conclude that Hermas
is ordered to present his prophetic message in the church with the
consent and the cooperation of the leaders of the church.
This means that there are no traces of a conflict between the prophets
and the ordained ministry.² The latter is accepted as an existing institution, but the prophet is not dependent on, or subordinate to it. His
functioning is dependent only on the presence and the action of the
gathered community and the divine Spirit prevailing there. On the
other hand, a church prophet, like the one of the 11th Mandate
will not have held a position of leadership in the church because of
his occasional prophesying. The πρωτοκαθεδρία is not something which
he seeks to obtain.
In view of this situation there is no need here to investigate at length
the intricate problems of the position of the prophets in the church
of the first and second century A.D.³ This position is tangible only

¹ Cf. III 2, 1: because of what they have suffered ἐκείνων ἐστὶν τὰ δεξιὰ μέρη τοῦ
ἁγιάσματος, καὶ ὃς ἐὰν πάθῃ διὰ τὸ ὄνομα. The picture of the couch is momentarily
suspended and replaced by that of the heavenly sanctuary. The couch is not "das
Abbild des Heiligtums" (Dibelius) nor "Abbild des Altars" (Peterson); for the former
there is no evidence, the latter is inappropriate. The distinction between right and left
does not refer to the last judgment as in Mt. 25:33, but to rank and dignity in the church.
In Clem. Alex., *Strom.* IV 15, 6 and 30, 1 τὰ δεξιὰ τοῦ ἁγιάσματος refers to eternal
salvation, but there is no reference to the left side. For the place of the martyrs in the
church in Hermas cf. 5, 2; *Sim.* VIII 3, 6; IX 28, 2f. Cf. also *Traditio Apostolica* 9, ed.
Botte p. 64: *Confessor ... habet honorem presbyteratus per suam confessionem.*
² Thus also von Campenhausen, *op. cit.*, p. 103: "Zwischen Geistesmännern und Amts-
trägern scheint danach das beste Einvernehmen zu bestehen". He sees in Hermas' conception of the ministry a sign that the influence of 1 Clement should not be overrated.
³ For a brief survey cf. *supra*, p. 7ff.

in the case of the people who bear the title 'prophet' as a permanent designation. In the case of the church members who were occasionally called to prophesy, the situation will, as a rule, have been similar to that which the 11th Mandate describes.

This concludes the picture of the Christian prophet as portrayed by Hermas. There remains one important question to be answered: is this portrait relevant to the portrait of its author, or is it merely an isolated picture in his work ? In the last part of this chapter we have already used materials which concerned Hermas personally to clarify the position of the prophet in the church, thereby tacitly assuming that these materials were relevant to the interpretation of the 11th Mandate. Our last task is to test this assumption by investigating the relevance of the 11th Mandate to Hermas' understanding of his own ministry.

CHAPTER SEVEN

HERMAS AND THE PROPHET

So far the eleventh Mandate has yielded a rich harvest of information about the true and the false prophets and their connection with the church. It is, however, silent on one very important aspect of prophecy, namely the prophetic message. The prophet speaks καθὼς ὁ κύριος βούλεται, but this short statement is not elaborated. This silence, however, is determined by the context and the purpose of the Mandate. Its aim is to provide guidance for distinguishing true and false prophecy. The most important criterion which distinguishes the true prophet is that he is filled with the Holy Spirit through the prayer of the gathered community. When this happens, the prophet cannot but speak καθὼς ὁ κύριος βούλεται. The content and the form of his message are not relevant to the purpose of the Mandate. This is regrettable because our knowledge of the speech forms which pre-Montanist Christian prophets used is extremely limited. Conceivably, there are among the synoptic sayings of Jesus some that stem originally from Christian prophets and were later considered to be authentic sayings of Jesus.[1] But Paul's explicit distinction between words of the Lord and his own pronouncements as one who has the Spirit does not support this possibility.[2] Since the prophetic ministry is primarily a ministry of the spoken word, it is no wonder that relatively few prophetic words have come down to us.[3] Most Christian prophetic utterances will have been spoken in specific situations, and heeded but not recorded. Agabus' prophecy concerning Paul is a good example of a recorded prophetic utterance, and probably in its authentic form.[4] But the

---

[1] Cf. Bultmann, *Geschichte der synopt. Tradition* (Göttingen, 1958⁴), p. 132-138; Vielhauer, in Hennecke-Schneemelcher II³, p. 426.

[2] 1 Cor. 7:10-40; cf. F. Neugebauer, Geistsprüche und Jesuslogien, *Z. N. W.* 53 (1962), p. 218-228, and K. Berger, Zu den sogenannten Sätzen Heiligen Rechts, *N. T. S.* 17 (1970), p. 10-40, who shows convincingly that Käsemann's attribution of these sentences to Christian prophets exercising the *ius talionis*, is not correct.

[3] This statement applies to Christian, not to Hebrew prophecy; for the latter, cf. Lindblom, *Prophecy*, p. 220ff.

[4] Acts 21:11: τάδε λέγει τὸ πνεῦμα τὸ ἅγιον· τὸν ἄνδρα οὗ ἐστιν ἡ ζώνη αὕτη οὕτως δήσουσιν ἐν Ἰερουσαλὴμ οἱ Ἰουδαῖοι καὶ παραδώσουσιν εἰς χεῖρας ἐθνῶν.

156   HERMAS AND THE PROPHET

letters to the seven churches in the Apocalypse of John which have a
similar introductory formula already show traces of a process of gener-
alization to which all recorded prophecy is subjected.[1] A good specimen
of a prophetic utterance which is probably recorded in an authentic
form, is to be found in Ignatius, *Philadelphians* 7: τῷ ἐπισκόπῳ
προσέχετε καὶ τῷ πρεσβυτερίῳ καὶ διακόνοις ... χωρὶς τοῦ ἐπισκόπου
μηδὲν ποιεῖτε. τὴν σάρκα ὑμῶν ὡς ναὸν θεοῦ τηρεῖτε, τὴν ἔνωσιν
ἀγαπᾶτε, τοὺς μερισμοὺς φεύγετε, μιμηταὶ γίνεσθε Ἰησοῦ Χριστοῦ.[2]
This form of direct prophetic speech is a terse sequence of asyndetic
imperatives.[3]

Either of the two forms of prophetic speech quoted above would
fit the situation in the 11th Mandate perfectly. There is no hint of a
vision or an audition. When the prophet is filled with the Holy Spirit
he immediately begins to speak to the congregation. Direct speech
appears to be the characteristic result of being filled with the Spirit.
Luke relates that Elisabeth was filled with the Holy Spirit and immediately cried out aloud.[4] In the same way Zechariah was filled with
the Holy Spirit and started to prophesy.[5] The same happens to the
church of Jerusalem on the day of Pentecost.[6] Peter is filled with the
Holy Spirit when he begins to speak to the rulers of the people and the
elders.[7] A corporate experience of being filled with the Spirit results
in a speaking of the word of God with boldness.[8] When Paul perceives
the attempts of Elymas to oppose him, he is filled with the Holy
Spirit and starts to speak against him.[9]

In Philo the concept of being filled with the Spirit appears to have

---

[1] Cf. Lohmeyer, *Die Offenbarung des Johannes*, H. N. T. 16, p. 40 *ad loc.*

[2] Cf. Grant, *Ignatius of Antioch, The Apostolic Fathers*, vol. 4 (London, 1966), p. 104f.
ad loc. The fact that Ignatius does not present himself as a prophet shows that it is not
the title claimed, but the function performed which counts. Cf. also *supra*, p. 149.

[3] "Wirkliche pneumatische Worte sind abgerissene, knappe Sätze, oft in poetischer
oder ihr nahestehender Form" (Weinel, *Wirkungen* p. 89). His conclusion that the prophetic utterances in the 11th Mandate will have been those in which "der Geist in der ersten
Person aus dem Pneumatiker spricht", because the prophet and the Spirit are speaking
alternately (p. 88), overlooks that in the decisive part, the inspiration event, it is the
prophet who speaks and not the Spirit.

[4] Lk. 1:41.

[5] Lk. 1:67.

[6] Acts 2:4.

[7] Acts 4:8.

[8] Acts 4:31.

[9] Acts 13:9.

a similar connotation. Moses is said to have been inspired by the Spirit and to have prophesied.[1] In the curious story of Bileam the seer is reported to have been inspired by the prophetic Spirit which drove the technical divination from his soul and made him speak in favour of the people of Israel.[2]

As in the 11th Mandate we find that this concept may be applied to genuine prophets,[3] and to false prophets.[4] But in all evidence, being filled with the Spirit results in direct prophetic speech. This applies also to the prophet of the 11th Mandate.[5]

At this point there is a great difference between Hermas himself and the man whom he describes as the true prophet. It is worthwhile to describe and assess this difference because it has a bearing upon the question how Hermas understood his own ministry. To this end we will briefly review the accounts of Hermas' own revelation experiences.

His first experience is an *Entrückungsvision*: while walking on the road to Cumae Hermas gets into a state of somnambulism,[6] and is carried away by a Spirit through a pathless region to a level ground; here Hermas begins to pray and to confess his sins. While he is praying heaven opens and he sees his former mistress. Then the dialogue on Hermas' personal sins begins and after a while the heavens are closed

---

1 *Vita Mosis* I 175: ἔνθους γίνεται καταπνευσθεὶς ὑπὸ τοῦ εἰωθότος ἐπιφοιτᾶν αὐτῷ πνεύματος καὶ θεσπίζει προφητεύων τάδε.

2 *Ib.* I 277: ἔνθους αὐτίκα γίνεται, προφητικοῦ πνεύματος ἐπιφοιτήσαντος, ὃ πᾶσαν αὐτοῦ τὴν ἔντεχνον μαντικὴν ὑπερόριον τῆς ψυχῆς ἤλασε ... ὥσπερ ἑρμηνεὺς ὑποβάλλοντος ἑτέρου θεσπίζει τάδε.

3 Cf. e.g. Epiphan., *Panar.* 48, 3: ὅτε γὰρ ἦν χρεία ἐν προφήταις ... οἱ αὐτοὶ ἅγιοι τὰ πάντα ἐπροφήτευον, ἐμπιμπλώμενοι πνεύματος ἁγίου.

4 Cf. e.g. Euseb., *H. E.* V 16, 9: (of the Montanist prophetesses) νόθου πνεύματος πληρῶσαι, ὡς καὶ λαλεῖν ἐκφρόνως, κτλ.

5 It is worth noting that the concept of being filled with the Spirit (and its counterpart) occurs also in the *Epistula Jacobi Apocrypha* 4, 18f., ed. Malinine, Puech, Quispel, Till and Kasser (Zürich, 1968), p. 8f. (English transl. p. 118): "[Become (?)] therefore filled with the Spirit" (cf. also 3, 8.35f., p. 6f., where the Spirit is not mentioned), but the context shows no connection with prophetic inspiration; it may even contain a note of criticism of prophecy, since in the curious passage 6, 21-36 it is said that "they have hewn off the head of prophecy with John" (English transl. p. 120), which is interpreted by Puech and Quispel as supposing "une réaction ou une critique à l'endroit de la "prophétie", telle qu'elle était en usage dans les anciennes communautés chrétiennes". This use of the concept of being filled deserves a treatment of its own.

6 Ἀφύπνωσα refers to an experience which occurs to Hermas while he is walking, cf. Dib. 431f.

and Hermas remains alone, shuddering and distressed.[1] This vision is immediately followed by another: Hermas sees before him a great white chair. An elderly woman appears with a book in her hand, sits down on the chair and greets Hermas. This is the beginning of a conversation between her and Hermas on the sins of Hermas and those of his family, after which she reads from the book to Hermas, When she has finished reading she rises from the chair and the chair is taken away by four young men. The woman speaks again to Hermas but is carried away by two men toward the east.[2]

According to the 2nd Vision, the rapture experience is repeated a year after the first and again while Hermas is on his way to Cumae. He is carried to the same place of the previous vision. After his prayer he sees the Elderly Lady before him, this time walking about and reading from a little book which she gives to Hermas in order to copy it. After he has done this the book is snatched from his hand but he does not see by whom. The departure of the Elderly Lady is not related.[3]

Since Hermas did not understand the content of the book he had copied, he fasts and prays earnestly to the Lord for two weeks and then the meaning of the writing is revealed to him.[4] Then follows the text of the writing. Where and how this revelation takes place is not indicated.

The next experience is when in a dream a handsome young man appears to Hermas and tells him that the Elderly Lady is the Church.[5] This is followed by a vision in his house: the Elderly Lady comes because she has to make additions to the book which Hermas was to give to the elders of the church.[6] No further details of the appearance of the Elderly Lady are given.

The 3rd Vision begins with a nightly appearance of the Elderly Lady after Hermas had fasted a long time and prayed the Lord to grant him the promised revelation. She tells Hermas to go to the field where he raises groats; at the fifth hour she will appear there and show

---

[1] *Vis.* I 1, 3-2, 1.
[2] I 2, 2-4, 3.
[3] II 1, 1-4.
[4] II 2, 1: ἀπεκαλύφθη μοι ἡ γνῶσις τῆς γραφῆς.
[5] II 4, 1: ἀπεκαλύφθη δέ μοι ... κοιμωμένῳ.
[6] II 4, 2: ὅρασιν εἶδον ἐν τῷ οἴκῳ μου.

him what he should see.[1] This is merely an introductory vision which prepares for the vision of the tower.

The next day Hermas sees in the arranged part of the field an ivory couch with a linen cushion and a linen cloth spread over it. After an initial reaction of fear and shudder Hermas offers a prayer of confession and then the Elderly Lady appears with the six young men which Hermas had seen in her company previously. Then follows the discussion on the right and the left place on the couch which has already been investigated in chapter VI.[2] At the end Hermas is given the place on the left.[3] Then the vision of the tower and the stones is told in a few lines.[4] It is followed by a long and detailed explanation of the vision, after which the six young men appear and carry her and the couch into the tower.[5]

As she is going away Hermas asks him to give him a revelation about the three forms in which she had appeared to him, but she tells him to ask someone else to give that revelation,[6] and in a vision of the night she appears again, tells Hermas to fast and promises him that he will receive the revelation. One day afterwards in the night a young man appears who warns Hermas to be careful about asking for revelations lest he injures his body but Hermas insists on obtaining the revelation.[7] Then follows the explanation of the three forms.

The 4th Vision relates two appearances. When Hermas is walking

---

[1] III 1, 1- 2.

[2] Cf. *supra*, p. 152ff.

[3] III 1, 4 - 2, 4. It is interesting that after giving her explanation of the right and the left place, the Elderly Lady intends to depart but at Hermas' earnest request she stays and leads Hermas to the couch.

[4] III 2, 5-9.

[5] III 10, 1.

[6] III 10, 2. The description of the three forms (10, 3-5) in which she had appeared which follows is not quite consistent with the accounts of the three appearances: the γυνὴ πρεσβῦτις (I 2, 2) is now λίαν πρεσβυτέρα; the second appearance (II 1, 3) does not mention any change in countenance or outlook; the third appearance (III 1, 6) does not refer to them at all. Also the fact that the Lady is old is explained differently in II 4, 1 (ὅτι πάντων πρώτη ἐκτίσθη) and in III 11, 1f. (ὅτι τὸ πνεῦμα ὑμῶν πρεσβύτερον κτλ.). This shows that the three forms and their interpretation are an additional item which is not related to the other revelations.

[7] III 10, 6-10. The warning to beware of injuring the body may refer to the consequences of fasting (Weinel, *Wirkungen* p. 225f.), or to the psycho-somatic effects of the visions (cf. the question of the young man whether Hermas can stand ἰσχυροτέρας ἀποκαλύψεις than those already received, in 8), probably to both.

on the Via Campana[1] and prays for the completion of the revelation
and the visions he hears something like the sound of a voice (ὡς ἦχος
φωνῆς) saying to him not to be double-minded. This injunction anti-
cipates the appearance of a huge beast which has all the marks of an
apocalyptic monster.[2] When Hermas approaches the beast stretches
itself out on the ground and Hermas passes by unharmed.[3]

After going on about thirty feet he sees a young lady coming to him,
adorned as if coming from a bridal chamber. From the previous visions
Hermas recognises her as the Church. The young lady begins the conversation and explains to him the meaning of the huge beast and, at
Hermas' request, adds an explanation of the four colours which
the beast had on its head.[4]

So much for the revelations by the Elderly Lady or the Church
and those by the young man who provides information about her.
They are described in more detail than those by the Shepherd to which
we now turn.

The appearance of the Shepherd in the 5th Vision marks the beginning of a new part of the book of Hermas, possibly even the beginning
of a separate book of the same author.[5] The picture of the Shepherd
is composite. He is guardian angel, angel of repentance and revealer
at the same time.[6] He enters Hermas' house where Hermas was praying
and sitting on a bed. He looks like a shepherd but presently his appearance is changed and Hermas recognises him as his guardian angel.
In the closing sentence of the Vision the Shepherd is further identified
as the angel of repentance. What concerns us in the present investigation is the transmission of the revelation. The Shepherd says to Hermas
that he is sent to him to show him again what he had seen before,
and orders him to write down the commandments and the parables.
The former refers, strictly speaking, only to *Sim.* IX and indeed at
the beginning of that writing explicit reference is made to the vision

---

[1] For the Via Campana cf. Dib., p. 482, *ad loc.*

[2] Cf. Dib., p. 483ff., and Peterson's searching analysis in *Frühkirche*, p. 285-309.
His interpretation of the monster as Gehinnom is rejected by Snyder, p. 56f., who understands it to refer to the threat of a persecution by the state, presumably the threat
of Trajan. This is not quite convincing.

[3] IV 1, 1-10.

[4] IV 2, 1-3,7.

[5] Cf. the readings of L¹ (*Initium pastoris*) and L² (*Incipiunt pastoris mandata duo-
decim*) in *Vis.* V 1.

[6] Cf. Dibelius' analysis referred to *supra*, p. 20, n. 9.

of the tower which the Church has shown to Hermas.¹ The latter refers to the Mandates and the first eight Similitudes.² The emphasis on writing down is remarkable, as it is repeated four times in the last paragraphs of the 5th Vision.³ Not that any reference to writing had been lacking in the preceding Visions.⁴ This time, however, the order to write down what will be shown is so explicitly made that it almost seems as if a new stage in the revelatory process has begun. At the same time the manner of communication changes. The Mandates do not relate any coming or appearance of the Shepherd. He is there and gives his commandments and explanations, interrupted only by reactions and questions of Hermas. This element of dialogue, however, is, on the whole, minimal.⁵ Yet it is indispensable because it witnesses to the revelation process and serves to authenticate Hermas' message.⁶ Only in the closing part of the 12th Mandate the dialogue increases but this is due to a personal factor as it portrays Hermas' own inner struggle to accept the twofold ministry of living by the message of the second repentance himself and of communicating it to his fellow believers.⁷

The Similitudes show more traces of revelations. The second Simili-

---

¹ *Vis.* V 5: ἵνα ἃ εἶδες πρότερον πάντα σοι πάλιν δείξω, and cf. *Sim.* IX 1, 1, quoted *infra*, p. 162f.

² Cf. *Sim.* IX 1, 1: μετὰ τὸ γράψαι με τὰς ἐντολὰς καὶ παραβολὰς τοῦ ποιμένος, τοῦ ἀγγέλου τῆς μετανοίας, κτλ.

³ *Vis.* V 5-7: σὺ οὖν πρῶτον πάντων τὰς ἐντολάς μου γράψον καὶ τὰς παραβολάς ... ἐντέλλομαί σοι πρῶτον γράψαι, κτλ. ... ἔγραψα οὖν κτλ. ... ταῦτά μοι πάντα οὕτως γράψαι ὁ ποιμὴν ἐνετείλατο.

⁴ Cf. *Vis.* II 1, 4: Hermas copies the booklet which the Elderly Lady had given to him; 4, 3: γράψεις οὖν δύο βιβλαρίδια, κτλ.

⁵ There is no dialogue in *Mand.* I and II; III 3-5 brings some real dialogue; in IV Hermas puts in a number of questions which serve to change the subject; in V occurs only one question which serves the same purpose (1, 7); VI begins with a reference to I by the Shepherd which Hermas acknowledges (1, 1); in 1, 5 Hermas affirms his willingness to travel on the road which the Shepherd had described; in 2, 2 and 5 Hermas asks questions which the Shepherd answers; in VII there is only one question (5); in VIII four questions (2; 3; 5; 8) and twice Hermas answers to a question by the Shepherd 6; 11); in IX there is no dialogue at all; in X there is some dialogue at the beginning (1, 1-3), and a question of Hermas in 3, 3; in XI Hermas speaks three times (1; 7; 19).

⁶ Such revelatory dialogue is not only characteristic of Jewish-Christian apocalyptic, but also well represented in hellenistic revelation literature, cf. the classification of the various types in A. J. Festugière, *La Révélation d'Hermès Trismégiste* I (Paris, 1944), p. 309-354.

⁷ Cf. *infra*, p. 168f.

tude presents Hermas as walking to his field and observing an elm
and a vine; then the Shepherd appears and begins to talk to him about
the elm and the vine and explains their relationship allegorically.[1]
The 3rd and 4th have the same opening formula ἔδειξέ μοι as the
11th Mandate[2]. The 5th Similitude shows Hermas fasting and sitting
on a mountain, thanking the Lord, when he suddenly sees the Shepherd
sitting beside him.[3] Then follows a discussion on fasting and the
parable of the faithful servant and its application.

The 6th Similitude relates an appearance in Hermas' house: he is
sitting there and praising the Lord for all that he has seen, and talks
to himself; then he suddenly sees the Shepherd sitting beside him,
and the usual dialogue begins.[4] Presently, the Shepherd suggests
to Hermas to go to the country where he will show him the Shepherd
of the sheep. Then follows the vision of the sheep and the angel-
shepherds with ensuing explanations.[5] The 7th Similitude relates an
encounter between Hermas and the Shepherd in the same plain where
he had seen the shepherds,[6] and the Shepherd tells Hermas why the
punishing shepherd must still stay in Hermas' house.

The 8th Similitude is more in the nature of a parable, like the 3rd
and the 4th, and like them begins with ἔδειξέ μοι. This introduces
the parable of the willow tree and the sticks. A new element, however,
is that the Shepherd and Hermas themselves play a part in the story,[7]
but otherwise the revelatory structure is the same: the Shepherd
explains and Hermas assents or asks for further explanations. An
order to call the believers to repentance concludes the writing.

The 9th Similitude begins with a reference to the 3rd Vision which
is very important as far as Hermas' understanding of the origin of
his revelations is concerned. The Shepherd says to him: θέλω σοι δεῖξαι
ὅσα σοι ἔδειξε τὸ πνεῦμα τὸ ἅγιον τὸ λαλῆσαν μετὰ σοῦ ἐν μορφῇ
τῆς Ἐκκλησίας ... νῦν δὲ ὑπὸ ἀγγέλου βλέπεις, διὰ τοῦ αὐτοῦ μὲν

---

[1] Sim. II 1: φανεροῦταί μοι ὁ ποιμήν.
[2] Cf. supra, p. 28, n. 2.
[3] Sim. V 1, 1: βλέπω τὸν ποιμένα παρακαθήμενόν μοι.
[4] VI 1, 2: βλέπω αὐτὸν ἐξαίφνης παρακαθήμενόν μοι.
[5] VI 1, 5 - 5, 7.
[6] VII 1: εἶδον αὐτὸν εἰς τὸ πεδίον τὸ αὐτό.
[7] The Shepherd is ordered by the angel of the Lord to examine the sticks and send
their bearers inside the walls accordingly and orders Hermas to assist him (VIII 2, 5f.;
also in 4, 1ff.).

πνεύματος.¹ Dibelius is right when he says that this is "nur eine literarische Verklammerung".² But this is only possible because of the underlying conviction of Hermas that his visions are from the Holy Spirit. At the same time this text reveals that in Hermas' own revelation idiom δεικνύναι is the general term for revealing and βλέπειν for receiving a revelation. The vision of this Similitude happens in Arcadia where Hermas is lead by the Shepherd.³

The last Similitude is a kind of a postscript to the whole book. Here suddenly appears *nuntius ille qui me tradiderat huic pastori*.⁴ His words are little more than a repetition of themes which have already appeared. The texts do not add to the evidence on Hermas' revelations.

This account of Hermas' revelation-experiences concerns only the structure of the events, not the religio-historical background of the materials which the author used,⁵ nor the question of their genuineness.⁶ At this juncture we must compare the structure of these revelation events with that of the inspiration of the prophet as told in the 11th Mandate. This comparison yields the following picture:

(1) The inspiration of the prophet takes place when he comes into the congregation of believers who have the Spirit .We have noticed the crucial importance of this triangular structure of the Spirit, the church and the prophet in chapter VI.⁷ The prophet needs the action of the church in order to be filled with the Holy Spirit. His inspiration is congregationally determined; it is a personal and a corporate event at the same time.

Hermas, however, receives his revelations when he is alone. He may be walking along the road or sitting in his home, he may be awake or asleep, his experiences are strictly individual. He does not depend on his fellow believers to receive the revelations. Rather, his accounts suggest that he must be removed from the company of others, if he is to receive them. The prophetic situation in the 11th Mandate is the opposite of Hermas' own revelation situation.

---

¹ *Sim.* IX 1, 1f.
² P. 602.
³ *Sim.* IX 1, 4: ἀπήγαγέ με εἰς τὴν Ἀρκαδίαν.
⁴ X 1, 1. referring back to *Vis.* V 2, cf. Dib., p. 491.
⁵ For this, cf. Peterson, *Frühkirche*, p. 254-270, and *supra*, p. 21f.
⁶ For this, cf. *infra*, p. 170.
⁷ Cf. *supra*, p. 122ff.

(2)   As pointed out above, the prophet of the 11th Mandate begins to speak immediately. There is no sign of an intermediate stage in which his message is shown or spoken to him. The verb λαλεῖν is the operative word as far as the prophet's action is concerned.[1] He does not relate or repeat a message given to him previously but is the immediate speech-instrument which the Lord uses. He is a word-prophet.

Hermas, however, characterises his revelations as visions shown to him and seen by him.[2] Also that which comes to him in word-form, namely the explanations of the visions and the ensuing expositions and admonitions, comes to him in the framework of an apparition of either the Elderly Lady or the Shepherd. He is a visionary, not a word-prophet.

(3)   At first sight it appears as if the presence of an angel is a common feature of Hermas and the prophet of the 11th Mandate. But a closer search reveals that exactly at this point the difference is fundamental. Both Hermas and the prophet have a guardian angel, the Shepherd,[3] and the angel of the prophetic Spirit,[4] but here the similarity ends. When the moment of revelation comes, the angel of the prophetic Spirit fills the prophet with the Holy Spirit and disappears from the picture. He plays no further part in the revelation process. His only task appears to be to establish a link between the prophet and the Lord by filling the former with the Spirit. He is not a bearer of revelation. It is the prophet, not the angel who speaks.

In the case of Hermas himself, however, the situation is completely reverse. As we have seen,[5] both the Elderly Lady and the Shepherd represent the Holy Spirit. Yet the Spirit is never named as the agent of the revelations but remains, so to speak, hidden behind the Elderly Lady and the Shepherd. Hermas pictures them as the revealers and himself as the recipient of their revelations. Only in a secondary sense he is also the transmitter of the revelations.

The tension between reception and transmission is a very significant feature in Hermas' self-portrait and the subject deserves to be treated

---

[1] It occurs 10 times in the 11th Mandate and refers either to the prophet or the false prophet.

[2] Cf. the use of the technical terms δεικνύαι and βλέπειν, supra, p. 163.

[3] Cf. supra, p. 160, n. 6.

[4] Cf. supra, p. 104ff.

[5] Cf. supra, p. 162f.

at some length. At several occasions the revealers point out to Hermas that, though he is the first to benefit from the revelations, they are not merely for his own personal good. They mean more. The Elderly Lady says to Hermas: ἀλλ' οὐ σοὶ μόνῳ ἀπεκαλύφθη, ἀλλ' ἵνα πᾶσιν δηλώσεις αὐτά ... ἐντέλλομαι δέ σοι πρῶτον, 'Ερμᾶ, τὰ ῥήματα ταῦτα ἅ σοι μέλλω λέγειν, λαλῆσαι αὐτὰ πάντα εἰς τὰ ὦτα τῶν ἁγίων.¹ When she has explained to him the meaning of the huge monster she says: ὕπαγε οὖν καὶ ἐξήγησαι τοῖς ἐκλεκτοῖς τοῦ κυρίου τὰ μεγαλεῖα αὐτοῦ καὶ εἰπὲ αὐτοῖς ὅτι τὸ θηρίον τοῦτο τύπος ἐστὶν θλίψεως τῆς μελλούσης τῆς μεγάλης.²

In the 5th Vision the Shepherd makes his entrance and orders Hermas to write down the Mandates and the Similitudes so that he may read them constantly and be able to keep them.³ Then he continues: ἐὰν οὖν ἀκούσαντες αὐτὰς φυλάξητε ..., and this shows that Hermas must not only read them and keep them for his own benefit but pass them on to the believers.⁴ A similar situation is found in Sim. VIII 11, 1 where the Shepherd, after giving his explanations of the sticks, says to Hermas: ὕπαγε καὶ πᾶσι λέγε ἵνα μετανοήσωσι καὶ ζήσωσι τῷ θεῷ. This certainly has little resemblance to the calling of the great prophets of the Old Testament, or of a man like Paul. But those men should not set the standards by which the average prophets are to be measured. Hermas is not one of the greatest and for him these almost overexposed scenes are meaningful because they prove that he is a man with a message for the church.⁵ This message is that the Lord has granted a second μετάνοια and that all Christians who have sinned should turn to Him and repent, the more so because the great tribulation is coming.⁶

These commission-scenes (to which Vis. II 2, 6 may be added) implicitly suggest that at some time after the reception of the revela-

---

¹ Vis. III 8, 10f.

² Vis. IV 2, 5.

³ V 5; ὑπὸ χεῖρα, 'constantly', is sometimes rendered 'at once', but cf. Dibelius, p. 478, on Vis. III 10, 7, and Bauer s. v. χείρ 2c.

⁴ Vis. V 5-7: whether ταῦτα πάντα in the closing sentence also includes the preceding passage which addresses the future hearers, is irrelevant.

⁵ This is what Hermas has in common with the prophet of the 11th Mandate and justifies the use of materials concerning Hermas personally to clarify the position of the prophet in the church vis à vis the ministry, cf. supra, p. 151-154.

⁶ Cf. Dib., p. 420: "Die Gewissheit dass auch der Christ Busse brauche ... ist dem Hermas als entscheidende Offenbarung zuteil geworden".

tions Hermas was to speak to the church in order to transmit the
messages which they contained. Since the revelations themselves
were also recorded after their reception, it is conceivable that the
work of Hermas contains traces of the transmission, reminiscenses
of the words spoken to the church. In some of the commission-scenes
the commission to speak to the believers is immediately followed by
an unexpected address in the second person plural, as if the believers
were actually present. It is tempting to see in those passages reflections
of Hermas' address to the church. But a closer investigation shows
that Hermas does not attempt to convey to his readers the idea that
this was the way in which he addressed the church. Quite on the
contrary, he is at pains to emphasize that it is not he who addresses
them but the Elderly Lady or the Shepherd. A brief review of the
passages concerned will make this clear.

In *Vis.* IV 2,5-6 Hermas is ordered to go and tell the elect of the
Lord about the coming great tribulation.[1] Then follows an address
which runs as follows:

ἐὰν οὖν προετοιμάσησθε καὶ μετανοήσητε ἐξ ὅλης καρδίας
ὑμῶν πρὸς τὸν κύριον,
    δυνήσεσθε ἐκφυγεῖν αὐτήν,
ἐὰν ἡ καρδία ὑμῶν γένηται καθαρὰ καὶ ἄμωμος
καὶ τὰς λοιπὰς τῆς ζωῆς ἡμέρας ὑμῶν δουλεύσητε τῷ κυρίῳ ἀμέμπτως.
ἐπιρίψατε τὰς μερίμνας ὑμῶν ἐπὶ τὸν κύριον,
    καὶ αὐτὸς κατορθώσει αὐτάς.
πιστεύσατε τῷ κυρίῳ, οἱ δίψυχοι,
    ὅτι πάντα δύναται καὶ ἀποστρέφει τὴν ὀργὴν αὐτοῦ ἀφ᾽ ὑμῶν
    καὶ ἐξαποστέλλει μάστιγας ὑμῖν τοῖς διψύχοις.
οὐαὶ τοῖς ἀκούσασιν τὰ ῥήματα ταῦτα καὶ παρακούσασιν·
    αἱρετώτερον ἦν αὐτοῖς τὸ μὴ γεννηθῆναι.

However unexpected, this address fits its context, with which it
is connected by οὖν, well. The first sentence contains several references
to the message of the coming great tribulation. The vocabulary is
that of Hermas. It is, therefore, not an insertion; it is Hermas' own.
It lends great emphasis and force to the message of the coming tribulation. Yet it is not a terse sequence of imperatives like other prophetic

---

[1] Cf. *supra*, p. 165.

utterances,[1] but shows more elaborate literary forms, including two nearquotations from Scripture.[2]

In *Vis.* II 2, 7 after the announcement of the second repentance for the believers Hermas is ordered to tell the leaders of the church to set straight their way in righteousness that they may receive in full the promises with great glory.[3] Then follows:

ἐμμείνατε οὖν οἱ ἐργαζόμενοι τὴν δικαιοσύνην καὶ μὴ διψυχήσητε,
    ἵνα γένηται ὑμῶν ἡ πάροδος μετὰ τῶν ἀγγέλων τῶν ἁγίων.
μακάριοι ὑμεῖς ὅσοι ὑπομένετε τὴν θλῖψιν τὴν ἐρχομένην τὴν μεγάλην,
καὶ ὅσοι οὐκ ἀρνήσονται τὴν ζωὴν αὐτῶν.

This is followed by a denouncement of those who will deny the Lord in the coming tribulation. Then Hermas is again addressed personally (7). The passage is connected with what precedes by οὖν, but it is more than a message for the leaders of the church. It concerns all members.

In *Vis.* V 5-7 the situation is different.[4] The Shepherd orders Hermas to write down the mandates and the similitudes, and Hermas does as he is told. Then the text continues:

ἐὰν οὖν ἀκούσαντες αὐτὰς φυλάξητε
καὶ ἐν αὐταῖς πορευθῆτε
καὶ ἐργάσησθε αὐτὰς ἐν καθαρᾷ καρδίᾳ,
    ἀπολήμψεσθε ἀπὸ τοῦ κυρίου ὅσα ἐπηγγείλατο ὑμῖν·
ἐὰν δὲ ἀκούσαντες μὴ μετανοήσητε,
ἀλλ' ἔτι προσθῆτε ταῖς ἁμαρτίαις ὑμῶν.
    ἀπολήμψεσθε παρὰ τοῦ κυρίου τὰ ἐναντία.

The Vision is concluded as follows: ταῦτά μοι πάντα οὕτως γράψαι ὁ ποιμὴν ἐνετείλατο, ὁ ἄγγελος τῆς μετανοίας. Here the address to the believers interrupts, not the Revealer when he speaks to Hermas, but Hermas himself when he tells how he copied down the mandates and

---

[1] Cf. *supra*, p. 155f.
[2] Ps. 54(55):23; Mt. 26:24; in the latter case it is not sure that the Gospel-text was in Hermas' mind, since the saying occurs in various forms in many other texts, cf. Strack-Billerbeck I, p. 989f.
[3] Cf. *supra*, p. 165.
[4] Cf. *supra*, p. 160f.

the similitudes. This interruption serves as an anticipating admonition to heed that which follows.[1]

The Mandates which this Vision introduces are full of exhortatory materials some of which are only marginally connected with the theme of the second repentance. The basic literary pattern is the same of that of the Visions and the Similitudes, namely that of the revelatory dialogue. At the end an address to the hearers occurs which has the form of a final appeal (*Mand.* XII 4, 5 - 6, 3). It interrupts a dialogue between the Shepherd and Hermas, after the completion of the mandates.[2] The Shepherd urges Hermas to walk in them and to exhort those who listen to him to repent: this is to be Hermas' διακονία. Then follows a discussion in which Hermas expresses his doubts whether a man will be able to keep the commandments, and the Shepherd angrily rebukes him and says that the mandates are hard and difficult to heed only for those who have the Lord on their lips but whose heart is hardened and who are far from God. At this point, the Shepherd begins to address them personally. He exhorts them to place the Lord in their hearts; then they will know that nothing is easier or sweeter than the commandments. He calls on them to be converted and not to fear the devil because there is no power in him.[3] He himself, the angel of repentance, is with them.

Here Hermas ventures to interrupt the Shepherd, and says that however anxious man might be to walk in the commandments, yet the devil is hard to overcome. This triggers off a new speech of the Shepherd which runs till 6, 3. In this he repeats that the devil has no power.[4] Suddenly the address in the plural reappears and in 6, 1 the speech again develops into a forceful appeal not to fear the devil, but to fear and believe and serve God. It closes with the promise καὶ ζήσεσθε τῷ θεῷ. As in the first appeal the Shepherd points to his own mission: he was sent to be with those who repent and to strengthen them in the faith.

After this appeal Hermas says that he is now strengthened in all the commandments and that he expects to be able to keep them.

---

[1] This admonition has a conditional form as often found in the O.T., cf. e.g. Lev. 26:3-45; Deut. 21:1-68; 30:15-18.

[2] XII 3, 2: συνετέλεσεν οὖν τὰς ἐντολὰς τὰς δώδεκα καὶ λέγει μοι, κτλ.

[3] For this point cf. *supra*, p. 45f.

[4] This is illustrated by means of a parable on full and empty jars, comparable to that in XI 15, cf. *supra*, p. 39.

The Shepherd assures him that he will keep them if, his heart is pure toward the Lord. The address in the plural is, as it were, embedded in the dialogue between the Shepherd and Hermas.

Another example of a sudden shift from the dialogue to the address in the plural is found in *Sim.* VI 1, 1-4. This passage serves more or less as an introduction to the Similitudes VI-IX which deal with the accomplishing of the second repentance.[1] Hermas is in doubt whether he will be able to walk in the commandments; then the angel of repentance suddenly appears and takes him to task about his doubts: Hermas must put on faith in the Lord and walk in the commandments. The commandments are beneficial for those who are going to repent. If they do not walk in them their μετάνοια will be in vain. Then those who repent are addressed directly.

These four passages, dealt with somewhat extensively, are the most impressive forms of personal address in the plural which are found in Hermas. They are not the only ones but the other passages add little to the picture and may be left undiscussed.[2] All these passages have in common that in them the church is indeed addressed, but not by Hermas. Though from the literary point of view, the addresses are his own, Hermas is anxious to make them appear as the words of the revealers. Their words, directed to the believers, are, so to speak passing right through Hermas without becoming his words. In addressing the church in this way the revealers themselves assume the role of the prophet and speak to the church καθὼς ὁ κύριος βούλεται. Hermas himself does not even dare to act as their mouth-piece but restricts his role to that of a reporter.

In the light of this self-appreciation of Hermas it is understandable that he never calls himself a prophet. What he has in common with the Christian prophet whom he describes in the 11th Mandate is that both have a message for the church. Both are used by the Lord, but in an opposite way: the prophet is used as a direct spokesman of the divine message, Hermas as a reporter of what the divine speakers have to say.

Hermas' understanding of his own role is confirmed by the use which Clement of Alexandria makes of his work. Clement holds it in high regard and quotes from it several times in his *Stromata*. But apart

---

[1] Cf. Dib., p. 577f.

[2] They are *Vis.* III 9; 11-13; IV 3, 1-6; *Sim.* I; V 1, 2-3; IX 23, 5; 24, 4; 28, 5; 29, 3; 31, 3-33, 1; X 4, 4.

from the first line of this work,¹ the quotations are always explicitly identified as words of the revealers to Hermas. The name of Hermas occurs only in the dative in clauses in which either the Church or the Shepherd are the subject.² This means that he does not consider Hermas as a prophet but assigns authority to the book as a divine revelation because of the divine revealers.³

This concludes the self-portrait of Hermas as it is brought into relief by a comparison with his picture of the prophet. It leaves us with the question of the religio-historical and phenomenological identification of Hermas. If he is not a prophet, what is he? An apocalyptic in the Jewish-Christian tradition? This question cannot be dealt with in the context of the present study. It requires an opinion on the ticklish question whether Hermas' records rest on genuine experiences or are literary fictions.⁴ Furthermore, it is part of the larger problems of the relationship between prophecy and apocalyptic. That problem, however, is itself part of a larger complex, namely that of revelation in general. Hence a careful investigation of the manyfold forms of revelation in the first centuries A.D. is necessary. If anything, our study of the 11th Mandate has shown that in such an investigation not only Jewish or Christian evidence must be taken into account but also evidence from the non-Christian surroundings.

---

¹ *Strom.* I 1, 1: ... ἵνα ὑπὸ χεῖρα ἀναγινώσκῃς αὐτὰς καὶ δυνηθῇς φυλάξαι αὐτάς, quoting *Vis.* V 5. Since the preceding page of the manuscript is lost it is impossible to decide whether the introductory formula was used; in the light of the other quotations it is highly improbable that the formula was lacking.

² Cf. *Strom.* VI 131, 2: ἣ γὰρ οὐχὶ καὶ ἐν τῇ ὁράσει τῷ ʽΕρμᾷ ἡ δύναμις ἐν τῷ τύπῳ τῆς ἐκκλησίας φανεῖσα ἔδωκεν τὸ βιβλίον εἰς μεταγραφὴν, κτλ. I 181, 1: θείως τοίνυν ἡ δύναμις ἡ τῷ ʽΕρμᾷ κατὰ ἀποκάλυψιν λαλοῦσα ... φησίν, κτλ. II 3, 5: φησὶ γὰρ ἐν τῷ ὁράματι τῷ ʽΕρμᾷ ἡ δύναμις ἡ φανεῖσα, κτλ. I 85, 4: λέγει δὲ καὶ ὁ ποιμήν, ὁ ἄγγελος τῆς μετανοίας, τῷ ʽΕρμᾷ περὶ τοῦ ψευδοπροφήτου, κτλ. Cf. also II 43, 5; 55, 3.6; IV 74, 4; VI 46, 5, where words of the Shepherd are quoted as such but Hermas is not mentioned.

³ This does not, however, mean that Clement considered the Shepherd to be canonical. The same is true with regard to the often quoted passage Irenaeus, *A. H.* IV 20, 1: *bene igitur scriptura quae dicit*, introducing a quotation from *Mand.* I; *scriptura* is to be understood here as 'writing', cf. A. Rousseau, *Irénée de Lyon, Contre les Hérésies Livre IV* (Paris, 1965), I, p. 248ff., II, p. 629, and H. von Campenhausen, *Die Entstehung der christlichen Bibel* (Tübingen, 1968), p. 255, n. 52. Eusebius, *H. E.* V 8, 7 (ἀποδέχεται τὴν τοῦ Ποιμένος γραφήν) was the first to misinterpret Irenaeus. It is not until the Ethiopian version of the Shepherd that Hermas is called a prophet, cf. George H. Schodde *Hêrmâ Nabî, the Ethiopic Version of Pastor Hermae examined* (Leipzig, 1876), p. 13.

⁴ For these terms and their implications, cf. Festugière, *op. cit.*, p. 309ff., and: L'Expérience du médecin Thessalos, *R. B.* 48 (1939), p. 45ff., repr. in *Hermétisme et Mystique païenne* (Paris, 1967), p. 141ff., esp. p. 150f. For Hermas cf. *supra*, p. 163.

CHAPTER EIGHT

CONCLUSIONS

The 11th Mandate has proved to be a rich source of information in several ways. We will try here to bring together the conclusions suggested by this investigation, and to formulate a number of points which will have to be taken into account in future research.

CHRISTIANITY AND ANTIQUITY

To the study of the relationship between Christianity and Antiquity the 11th Mandate has an important contribution to make. It shows that one of the areas in which pagan influences are present is that of prophecy and divination. There is, on the one hand, the shift of emphasis towards the predictive in the concept of prophecy, even to the extent that orthodox writers like Irenaeus and Hippolytus define prophecy in the selfsame terms which pagan writers use to define divination. We can hardly suppose that they were not aware of what they were doing. There is, on the other hand, the intrusion of pagan divination in the church and its competition with prophecy as it existed in the church. Though the 11th Mandate is the only unequivocal witness to this intrusion, there is no reason to assume that it depicts a situation which was found only in the church to which Hermas belonged. On this point the 11th Mandate may represent a struggle which was found in more churches in a pagan milieu.

The type of divination which we find in our source is one of the 'lower' types. The materials which we used to make it come to life are drawn from sources in which Chaldaeans, magicians and even outright swindlers like Alexander of Abonuteichos are depicted. But 'lower' should not be understood in a sociological sense, because this form of divination was definitely not restricted to the lower strata of society. It is lower because it is divination only. Different from the prophecy which uses the Tripartite formula, it does not go beyond "the merely temporal aspect" and it does not touch upon "the mystery of existence".[1] This lower form is, as it were, neutral because it simply

---

[1] W. C. van Unnik, A Formula describing Prophecy, p. 93.

and only responds to a basic need of human beings who are unsure of their personal future. This neutral character made it easy for Christians to take over divinatory practices from their pagan environment.

At the same time, the 11th Mandate shows beyond doubt that this intrusion of divination did not go uncontested. The Christian μάντις and his followers are denounced in no uncertain terms, several of which derived their incisiveness from overtones which are heard only when these terms are placed against their pagan background. Yet the terms and concepts which are used to complete the unmasking of divination by a contrastive description of the true prophet and his inspiration, cannot, in their turn, be understood unless they also are placed against a pagan background! This really adds a new dimension to the problem of Christianity and Antiquity. It is inconceivable that Hermas consciously borrowed the δαίμων πάρεδρος conception, or the idea of the 'potential spirit'. He must have shared them with his environment, and he must have used them without for one moment considering their hellenistic origin. He needed them because they enabled him to bring out points for which the Jewish-Christian tradition did not offer the necessary materials. He used them because they belonged to his own mental property. On this point, Hermas represents a 'frontier-situation', the frontier between Christianity and hellenistic religion. On both sides of the frontier the inhabitants are conscious of what distinguishes from the other side and are apt to signalize what is coming in from the other side. But at the same time they have more in common with one another than people which live at a greater distance from the dividing line. Hermas is an example of the way in which Christians who lived close to the frontier used materials which were then common property in order to express what divided them from those with whom the common property was shared. This has a bearing on the hermeneutics of early Christian history. Since the rise of form criticism and, in its wake, of tradition criticism, it has been fashionable to trace traditions of thought within the early church. Usually, the traditions traced and described in this way were seen as more or less intra-Christian, with due recognition of Jewish and hellenistic influences. The finds of Qumran and Nag Hammadi have shown that the frame within which tradition criticism operated was much too narrow. It is sufficient to point to the discovery of heterodox Judaism and its influence upon early Christianity, which has so decisively broadened the perspective within which we must view the developments of early Christianity. It would seem that our study of the 11th Mandate has added something to this broadened perspective because it brings in the Christians of the 'frontier-situation' and the way they used to express their beliefs and experiences. In this case it is not only commendable to look for hellenistic parallels, but even necessary. Unless we are prepared to take into account the meaning of those parallels, and to interpret them in terms of their function in the thought of the writer which we study, we shall be unable to penetrate the deepest level of his thoughts.

HERMAS

From our study of the 11th Mandate, there emerges a picture of Hermas as a Christian who is deeply familiar with hellenistic traditions and ideas. It is difficult to conceive of him as a man who learned these traditions and ideas as an outsider, and subsequently started to use them deliberately in order to explain his beliefs. Rather, his picture is that of a hellenistic Christian who was so imbued with hellenistic thought and pictures that he put them to Christian use without hesitation. Such a picture, however, differs greatly from that which is current nowadays. Audet, Lluis-Font and Daniélou depict him as a man of Qumran converted to the Christian faith.[1] Pernveden assumes a double background to the Shepherd, formed on the one hand by late Jewish sapiential tradition, and on the other hand by late Jewish apocalyptic.[2] Obviously, these questions cannot be decided merely on the basis of a study of the 11th Mandate, but this study has shown that the concept of prophecy in the Shepherd is neither that of Qumran nor that of Jewish apocalyptic. It is a Christian concept expressed in the language and the pictures of the author's milieu. This milieu is predominantly hellenistic, though elements from sapiential and apocalyptic traditions are also present; but in the 11th Mandate they are definitely subordinate to the hellenistic elements.

The Christian nature of Hermas' concept of prophecy raises yet another point regarding the various traditions which are found in his book. Jewish traditions were current in the Christian church from the beginning and any converted gentile came under their influence. It is highly improbable that Hermas had access to those Jewish traditions bypassing the Christian community. Dibelius'

---

[1] Cf. *supra*, p. 25f.
[2] *Op. cit.*, p. 289.

judgment that the contacts with Jewish traditions found in Hermas
are no reason to conclude that the author was of Jewish-Christian
origin, still stands.[1] It has been confirmed in our analysis of one particular concept.

If the conclusions drawn above are correct, there is reason to revise
Peterson's judgment on the hellenistic elements in the Visions.[2]
They are not just "Einkleidung", wording, which can, as it were,
be detached without altering the portrait of the author's work and
message, but there is good reason to see them as part of Hermas'
work. This applies not only to the revelatory apparatus which so closely
resembles that of hellenistic divination, but is valid for the whole
work. Admittedly, our study has dealt with an object in which hellenistic influence may more readily be expected than in others. But
perhaps future research into Hermas should reckon more seriously
than up to now with the probability that the hellenistic elements
in the Shepherd belong to the author's original world.

Pernveden's remark "that Hermas concentrates his conceptual
world and choice of images with reference to a particular object",[3]
is, when understood in a less specific way than Pernveden does, a
sound hermeneutical principle. It is important not only to trace the
origin and transmission of the various traditions in The Shepherd,
but also to interpret them with regard to their function in Hermas'
message. In the 11th Mandate, hellenistic traditions serve to bring
out genuinely Christian points. But it remains to be seen whether
Hermas uses these and other traditions with reference to one single
particular object, as is implied in Pernveden's thesis that Hermas'
primary theme was the church. The world of Hermas is a complex one,
too complex to need only one key to understand it. Furthermore,
Pernveden "attributes to Hermas ... a degree of theological precision
and reflection which the text of the *Shepherd* hardly supports".[4]
But our study of the 11th Mandate has shown that the church is,
if not the main theological theme, yet a primary concern of the author
In this context at least, his aim is pastoral rather than theological.
It may prove to be worth while to bear in mind this pastoral concern
in future study of Hermas.

---

[1] P. 423.

[2] Cf. *supra*, p. 21f.

[3] *Op. cit.*, p. 291.

[4] L. W. Barnard, The Shepherd of Hermas in Recent Study, p. 34.

Christian Prophecy

The clear witness of the 11th Mandate to the correlation between prophecy and the church in (the context of) a common partaking in the Spirit, is its most important feature with regard to Christian prophecy. Once detected here, this correlation appeared, in the course of our investigation, to be present also in other situations relating to prophecy; both in those where the title 'prophet' is used, and in those where the gift of prophecy is given to various church members. It is beyond doubt that the prophet of the 11th Mandate represents this latter situation, and this proves that the process which Greeven supposed to have taken place, from an original common sharing in the gift of prophecy to the emergence of a limited group of prophets, distinguished from the other church members by their prophetic *charisma*,[1] had not yet been completed by the time of Hermas! There is more evidence of the living anonymous prophecy in the second century.[2] It is more adequate to view the development of Christian prophecy in a different way and to assume that both types existed alongside each other till the Montanist crisis jeopardized the ministry of those who bore the title 'prophet', to the extent that in the 3rd century A.D. the prophets, either Old Testament or Christian, are seen as belonging to the past.

Not less important is that prophets of both types are not "Pneumatiker" in the sense that they possess the Spirit to a higher degree than the ordinary members of the church. The Christian religion is a religion of the Spirit in which all members partake, not a religion of special Spirit-bearers. In a time in which it has become fashion to speak about Christian 'enthusiasts', 'ecstatics', 'pneumatics', etc., the clear evidence of an abundant life in the Spirit as a common characteristic of early Christianity should make us somewhat more careful in the use of these and similar terms.

The picture of the church which plays such an active role in the prophetic event, is that of a gathered community. This idea also appeared to be present elsewhere in Hermas and we may safely assume that this was the church as Hermas experienced it and in which he lived. As such, it may supplement the theological concept of the church

---

[1] Cf. *supra*, p. 9.
[2] Cf. *supra*, p. 10.

CONCLUSIONS

to which Dr. Pernveden's penetrating study is devoted.[1] Yet in whatever way Hermas' ecclesiology is to be understood, it is clear that the
church as a gathered community is indispensable if prophecy is to
function properly. This we also found to be true elsewhere in early
Christianity. Is it possible that here our study has touched upon an
issue which is vital to the Christian church in general? The church
of Christ cannot function properly unless it functions as a gathered
community in which all share in the gift of the Spirit. When it functions
in this way, it may fulfill Paul's exhortation: ζηλοῦτε ἵνα προφη-
τεύητε.

---

[1] Cf. also C. Andresen, *Die Kirchen der alten Christenheit, Die Religionen der Mensch-
heit, herausgeg. v. C. M. Schröder*, Band 29, 1-2 (Stuttgart, 1971), p. 31-35.

APPENDIX

THE TEXT OF THE ELEVENTH MANDATE

Ἐντολὴ ια′

1 Ἔδειξέ μοι ἐπὶ συμψελλίου καθημένους ἀνθρώπους, καὶ ἕτερον ἄνθρωπον καθήμενον ἐπὶ καθέδραν. καὶ λέγει μοι· Βλέπεις τοὺς ἐπὶ τοῦ συμψελλίου καθημένους; Βλέπω, φημί, κύριε. Οὗτοι, φησί, πιστοί εἰσι, καὶ ὁ καθήμενος ἐπὶ τὴν καθέδραν ψευδοπροφήτης ἐστὶν ἀπολλύων τὴν διάνοιαν τῶν δούλων τοῦ θεοῦ· τῶν διψύχων δὲ ἀπόλλυσιν, οὐ τῶν πιστῶν. 2 οὗτοι οὖν οἱ δίψυχοι ὡς ἐπὶ μάντιν ἔρχονται καὶ ἐπερωτῶσιν αὐτόν, τί ἄρα ἔσται αὐτοῖς· κἀκεῖνος ὁ ψευδοπροφήτης, μηδεμίαν ἔχων ἐν ἑαυτῷ δύναμιν πνεύματος θείου, λαλεῖ μετ᾽ αὐτῶν κατὰ τὰ ἐπερωτήματα αὐτῶν καὶ κατὰ τὰς ἐπιθυμίας τῆς πονηρίας αὐτῶν, καὶ πληροῖ τὰς ψυχὰς αὐτῶν καθὼς αὐτοὶ βούλονται. 3 αὐτὸς γὰρ κενὸς ὢν κενὰ καὶ ἀποκρίνεται κενοῖς· ὃ γὰρ ἐὰν ἐπερωτηθῇ, πρὸς τὸ κένωμα τοῦ ἀνθρώπου ἀποκρίνεται. τινὰ δὲ καὶ ῥήματα ἀληθῆ λαλεῖ· ὁ γὰρ διάβολος πληροῖ αὐτὸν τῷ αὐτοῦ πνεύματι, εἴ τινα δυνήσεται ῥῆξαι τῶν δικαίων. 4 ὅσοι οὖν ἰσχυροί εἰσιν ἐν τῇ πίστει τοῦ κυρίου, ἐνδεδυμένοι τὴν ἀλήθειαν, τοῖς τοιούτοις πνεύμασιν οὐ κολλῶνται, ἀλλ᾽ ἀπέχονται ἀπ᾽ αὐτῶν. ὅσοι δὲ δίψυχοί εἰσι καὶ πυκνῶς μετανοοῦσι, μαντεύονται ὡς καὶ τὰ ἔθνη, καὶ ἑαυτοῖς μείζονα ἁμαρτίαν ἐπιφέρουσιν εἰδωλολατροῦντες· ὁ γὰρ ἐπερωτῶν ψευδοπροφήτην περὶ πράξεώς τινος εἰδωλολάτρης ἐστὶ καὶ κενὸς ἀπὸ τῆς ἀληθείας καὶ ἄφρων. 5 πᾶν γὰρ πνεῦμα ἀπὸ θεοῦ δοθὲν οὐκ ἐπερωτᾶται, ἀλλὰ ἔχον τὴν δύναμιν τῆς θεότητος ἀφ᾽ ἑαυτοῦ λαλεῖ πάντα, ὅτι ἄνωθέν ἐστιν ἀπὸ τῆς δυνάμεως τοῦ θείου πνεύματος. 6 τὸ δὲ πνεῦμα τὸ ἐπερωτώμενον καὶ λαλοῦν κατὰ τὰς ἐπιθυμίας τῶν ἀνθρώπων ἐπίγειόν ἐστι καὶ ἐλαφρόν, δύναμιν μὴ ἔχον. καὶ ὅλως οὐ λαλεῖ ἐὰν μὴ ἐπερωτηθῇ. 7 Πῶς οὖν, φημί, κύριε, ἄνθρωπος γνώσεται τίς αὐτῶν προφήτης καὶ τίς ψευδοπροφήτης ἐστίν; Ἄκουε, φησί, περὶ ἀμφοτέρων τῶν προφητῶν· καὶ ὥς σοι μέλλω λέγειν, οὕτω δοκιμάσεις τὸν προφήτην καὶ τὸν ψευδοπροφήτην. ἀπὸ τῆς ζωῆς δοκίμαζε τὸν ἄνθρωπον τὸν ἔχοντα τὸ πνεῦμα τὸ θεῖον. 8 πρῶτον μὲν ὁ ἔχων τὸ πνεῦμα τὸ ἄνωθεν πραΰς ἐστι καὶ ἡσύχιος καὶ ταπεινόφρων καὶ ἀπεχόμενος ἀπὸ πάσης πονηρίας καὶ ἐπιθυμίας ματαίας τοῦ αἰῶνος

178 THE TEXT OF THE ELEVENTH MANDATE

τούτου καὶ ἑαυτὸν ἐνδεέστερον ποιεῖ πάντων τῶν ἀνθρώπων, καὶ οὐδενὶ
οὐδὲν· ἀποκρίνεται ἐπερωτώμενος, οὐδὲ καταμόνας λαλεῖ, οὐδὲ ὅταν
θέλῃ ἄνθρωπος λαλεῖν, λαλεῖ τὸ πνεῦμα <τὸ> ἅγιον, ἀλλὰ τότε λαλεῖ
ὅταν θελήσῃ αὐτὸν ὁ θεὸς λαλῆσαι. **9** ὅταν οὖν ἔλθῃ ὁ ἄνθρωπος
ὁ ἔχων τὸ πνεῦμα τὸ θεῖον εἰς συναγωγὴν ἀνδρῶν δικαίων τῶν ἐχόντων
πίστιν θείου πνεύματος, καὶ ἔντευξις γένηται πρὸς τὸν θεὸν τῆς συναγωγῆς τῶν ἀνδρῶν ἐκείνων, τότε ὁ ἄγγελος τοῦ πνεύματος τοῦ προφητικοῦ ὁ κείμενος ἐπ᾽ αὐτῷ πληροῖ τὸν ἄνθρωπον καὶ πλησθεὶς ὁ ἄνθρωπος
ἐκεῖνος τῷ πνεύματι τῷ ἁγίῳ λαλεῖ εἰς τὸ πλῆθος καθὼς ὁ κύριος βούλεται.
10 οὕτως οὖν φανερὸν ἔσται τὸ πνεῦμα τῆς θεότητος. ὅση οὖν περὶ τοῦ
πνεύματος τῆς θεότητος τοῦ κυρίου ἡ δύναμις, αὕτη. **11** ἄκουε νῦν,
φησί, περὶ τοῦ πνεύματος τοῦ ἐπιγείου καὶ κενοῦ καὶ δύναμιν μὴ
ἔχοντος, ἀλλὰ ὄντος μωροῦ. **12** πρῶτον μὲν ὁ ἄνθρωπος ἐκεῖνος ὁ
δοκῶν πνεῦμα ἔχειν ὑψοῖ ἑαυτὸν καὶ θέλει πρωτοκαθεδρίαν ἔχειν, καὶ
εὐθὺς ἰταμός ἐστι καὶ ἀναιδὴς καὶ πολύλαλος καὶ ἐν τρυφαῖς πολλαῖς
ἀναστρεφόμενος καὶ ἐν ἑτέραις πολλαῖς ἀπάταις, καὶ μισθοὺς λαμβάνων
τῆς προφητείας αὐτοῦ· ἐὰν δὲ μὴ λάβῃ, οὐ προφητεύει. δύναται οὖν
πνεῦμα θεῖον μισθοὺς λαμβάνειν καὶ προφητεύειν; οὐκ ἐνδέχεται τοῦτο
ποιεῖν θεοῦ προφήτην, ἀλλὰ τῶν τοιούτων προφητῶν ἐπίγειόν ἐστι
τὸ πνεῦμα. **13** εἶτα ὅλως εἰς συναγωγὴν ἀνδρῶν δικαίων οὐκ ἐγγίζει,
ἀλλ᾽ ἀποφεύγει αὐτούς. κολλᾶται δὲ τοῖς διψύχοις καὶ κενοῖς, καὶ κατὰ
γωνίαν αὐτοῖς προφητεύει, καὶ ἀπατᾷ αὐτοὺς λαλῶν κατὰ τὰς ἐπιθυμίας αὐτῶν πάντα κενῶς· κενοῖς γὰρ καὶ ἀποκρίνεται. τὸ γὰρ κενὸν
σκεῦος μετὰ τῶν κενῶν συντιθέμενον οὐ θραύεται, ἀλλὰ συμφωνοῦσιν
ἀλλήλοις. **14** ὅταν δὲ ἔλθῃ εἰς συναγωγὴν πλήρη ἀνδρῶν δικαίων
ἐχόντων πνεῦμα θεότητος, καὶ ἔντευξις ἀπ᾽ αὐτῶν γένηται, κενοῦται
ὁ ἄνθρωπος ἐκεῖνος, καὶ τὸ πνεῦμα τὸ ἐπίγειον ἀπὸ τοῦ φόβου φεύγει
ἀπ᾽ αὐτοῦ, καὶ κωφοῦται ὁ ἄνθρωπος ἐκεῖνος καὶ ὅλως συνθραύεται,
μηδὲν δυνάμενος λαλῆσαι. **15** ἐὰν γὰρ εἰς ἀποθήκην στιβάσῃς οἶνον
ἢ ἔλαιον καὶ ἐν αὐτοῖς θῇς κεράμιον κενόν, καὶ πάλιν ἀποστιβάσαι
θελήσῃς τὴν ἀποθήκην, τὸ κεράμιον ἐκεῖνο ὃ ἔθηκας κενόν, κενὸν καὶ
εὑρήσεις· οὕτω καὶ οἱ προφῆται οἱ κενοὶ ὅταν ἔλθωσιν εἰς πνεύματα
δικαίων, ὁποῖοι ἦλθον, τοιοῦτοι καὶ εὑρίσκονται. **16** ἔχεις ἀμφοτέρων
τῶν προφητῶν τὴν ζωήν. δοκίμαζε οὖν ἀπὸ τῶν ἔργων καὶ τῆς ζωῆς
τὸν ἄνθρωπον τὸν λέγοντα ἑαυτὸν πνευματοφόρον εἶναι. **17** σὺ δὲ
πίστευε τῷ πνεύματι τῷ ἐρχομένῳ ἀπὸ τοῦ θεοῦ καὶ ἔχοντι
δύναμιν· τῷ δὲ πνεύματι τῷ ἐπιγείῳ καὶ κενῷ μηδὲν πίστευε, ὅτι
ἐν αὐτῷ δύναμις οὐκ ἔστιν· ἀπὸ τοῦ διαβόλου γὰρ ἔρχεται. **18** ἄκου-
σον <οὖν> τὴν παραβολὴν ἣν μέλλω σοι λέγειν. λάβε λίθον καὶ
βάλε εἰς τὸν οὐρανόν, ἴδε εἰ δύνασαι ἅψασθαι αὐτοῦ· ἢ πάλιν λάβε

σίφωνα ὕδατος καὶ σιφώνισον εἰς τὸν οὐρανόν, ἴδε εἰ δύνασαι τρυπῆσαι τὸν οὐρανόν. **19** Πῶς, φημί, κύριε, δύναται ταῦτα γενέσθαι ; ἀδύνατα γὰρ ἀμφότερα ταῦτα εἴρηκας. Ὡς ταῦτα οὖν, φησίν, ἀδύνατά ἐστιν, οὕτω καὶ τὰ πνεύματα τὰ ἐπίγεια ἀδύνατά ἐστι καὶ ἀδρανῆ. **20** λάβε νῦν τὴν δύναμιν τὴν ἄνωθεν ἐρχομένην. ἡ χάλαζα ἐλάχιστόν ἐστι κοκκάριον, καὶ ὅταν ἐπιπέσῃ ἐπὶ κεφαλὴν ἀνθρώπου, πῶς πόνον παρέχει· ἢ πάλιν [λάβε τὴν] σταγόνα ἢ ἀπὸ τοῦ κεράμου πίπτει χαμαὶ καὶ τρυπᾷ τὸν λίθον. **21** βλέπεις οὖν ὅτι τὰ ἄνωθεν ἐλάχιστα πίπτοντα ἐπὶ τὴν γῆν μεγάλην δύναμιν [ἔχουσιν·] οὕτω καὶ τὸ πνεῦμα τὸ θεῖον ἄνωθεν ἐρχόμενον δυνατόν ἐστι· τούτῳ οὖν τῷ πνεύματι πίστευε, ἀπὸ δὲ τοῦ ἑτέρου ἀπέχου.

INDEX OF AUTHORS

INDEX OF SOURCE REFERENCES